Property of Wayne Helms

An

AUTOBIOGRAPHY

of

JOHN MUIR

An

AUTOBIOGRAPHY

of

JOHN MUIR

Edited and Introduced by
Stephen Brennan

SKYHORSE PUBLISHING

Skyhorse Publishing books may be purchased in bulk at special discounts for sales promotion, corporate gifts, fund-raising, or educational purposes. Special editions can also be created to specifications. For details, contact the Special Sales Department, Skyhorse Publishing, 307 West 36th Street, 11th Floor, New York, NY 10018 or info@skyhorsepublishing.com.

Skyhorse® and Skyhorse Publishing® are registered trademarks of Skyhorse Publishing, Inc.®, a Delaware corporation.

Visit our website at www.skyhorsepublishing.com.

10 9 8 7 6 5 4 3 2 1

Library of Congress Cataloging-in-Publication Data is available on file.

Cover design by: Jane Sheppard

ISBN: 978-1-62873-767-7
E-book ISBN: 978-1-62914-136-7

Printed in the United States of America

Contents

∽

Introduction

"Strange friend," I said, "here is no cause to mourn."
"None," said the other, "save the undone years,
The hopelessness. Whatever hope is yours
Was my life also; I went hunting wild
After the wildest beauty in the world."

—Wilfred Owen
STRANGE MEETING

"I only went out for a walk, but finally concluded
to stay out 'til sundown, for going out, I found,
was really going in!"

—John Muir

∽

John Muir was born on April 21, 1838, in the seaport town of Dunbar, East Lothian, Scotland, to Daniel Muir and Ann Gilrye. The third of eight children, young John spent his early boyhood rough-housing with his friends in the wild places, the broken heathery fields and sea-cliffs that surrounded the town. His family practiced a strict Presbyterianism and they (especially his father) tended to regard any occupation other than schoolwork and Bible-study as frivolous activity and a waste of time. Thus little John, who gloried in the rowdy, unchecked out-of-doors adventures with his friends was often punished; "subject to lashings," as he was later to recall it. Still, by his eleventh year, Muir was later to claim, he had memorized all of the New Testament and much of the Old Testament. Already we can see evident, even at this tender age, several facets of his character that were to make the man; a love of a life out-of-doors—the adventure of it—a budding spiritualism and the sense of the importance of faith in a person's life—the struggle of it—and a personal integrity, and a quiet discipline, which were to prove hallmarks of his life and work.

In 1849 the Muirs emigrated to the United States—first the father and sons, John and elder brother Dan—the rest of the family was to follow. In America they joined the church of the *Disciples of Christ*. Daniel Muir considered the Presbyterian Church in America insufficiently rigorous. They established a farm near Portage, Wisconsin; clearing the land, building a house, planting and getting in the first crops. The work was hard, backbreaking and seemingly unending; but still, the brothers Muir were sometimes able to escape the severe and judgmental eye of their father to roam the woods, the lakesides and the rich green dells. They were high-spirited, were these boys, and they seemed to take the inevitable corporal punishments meted out by their father in their stride, if not quite, as in justice, their due. Apart from his school-work, his farm-work, Bible-study and church, John found time to undertake a his own study of "higher arithmetic," and to fashion various inventions of his own devising.

In 1860 John Muir (aged 22) matriculated at the University of Wisconsin, in Madison. He supported himself by taking all manner of odd jobs. His family might well have assisted him, their homestead, *Fountain Lake Farm,* was prosperous, but

> "When I told father that I was about to leave home, and inquired whether, if I should happen to be in need of money, he would send me a little, he said, 'No; depend entirely on yourself.' Good advice, I suppose, but surely needlessly severe for a bashful, home-loving boy who had worked so hard."

Initially, Muir's plan was to study the practical sciences, with the aim perhaps of making himself an engineer, and to thereby further his already considerable prowess as an inventor. But he soon found himself captivated by the study of the natural world—"God's inventions" he called them—and switched the focus of his inquiries to the life sciences, to biology and to chemistry and geology. Whenever he could manage it, he would flee to the backwoods, the wild places and there undertake his own separate course of study—in the "book of nature."

In 1864, with the Civil War well into its fourth bloody year, *flight* took on another meaning altogether, as John downed his books and followed his brother Dan to Canada. There is some dispute as to whether the brothers Muir can be fairly tagged as draft dodgers. Neither young man was actually a citizen (John was to be naturalized years later) and their names did not appear on the draft rolls, but there can be little doubt that their intention was to avoid the whole awful man-killing mess. John spent the warm months tramping the forests around Lake Huron and studying the wetland flora. Eventually the brothers joined up and found work together at a sawmill in Ontario.

Nearly a year after the War's end, in March of 1866, John returned to the United States, taking a job in a wheel factory in Indianapolis. There he suffered an accident that was to nearly cost him his sight. A tool slipped, hit his eye, and he was struck blind. For six weeks he lay healing in a darkened room. The example of the story of the blinding of Saint Paul on the road to Damascus and of the saint's subsequent conversion and radical change of outlook could not have been lost on the heavily bearded young nomad and Bible scholar.

His recovery complete, Muir decided to "be true to myself" and to dedicate himself to the things—and to a life—he best loved: exploration and the study of the natural world. The next year he began his now famous hike from Indiana to Florida (chronicled in his 1916 book *A Thousand-mile Walk to the Gulf*). In Florida he caught a boat to Cuba, and for a time delighted himself investigating the diverse and myriad tropical flora. But a bout of malaria put paid to this idyll, and he soon sailed for New York City. From there he took passage to San Francisco, thence to Yosemite in the Sierra Nevada, there to begin the real work of his life.

The number of autobiographical works—memoirs, reminiscences and journals—by Muir is considerable and well beyond the scope of any single volume, but even so, this version of *An Autobiography of John Muir* offers a sampling of some of his more telling publications, articles and essays. It is composed of a slightly edited rendering of Muir's 1913 book *The Story of My Boyhood and Youth*, selections from *My First Summer in the Sierra,* and *Stickeen;*

the aim being, as T.E. Shaw put it, to "deduce the author from the self-betrayal in his work." The illustrations have been chosen from contemporaneous photos, as well as plans, sketches and drawings, many of them by Muir himself.

Stephen Vincent Brennan
West Cornwall, CT

John Muir

Keynote

◡◠◡

Moral improvers have calls to preach. I have a friend who has a call to plough, and woe to the daisy sod or azalea thicket that falls under the savage redemption of his keen steel shares. Not content with the so-called subjugation of every terrestrial bog, rock, and moorland, he would fain discover some method of reclamation applicable to the ocean and the sky, that in due calendar time they might be brought to bud and blossom as the rose. Our efforts are of no avail when we seek to turn his attention to wild roses, or to the fact that both ocean and sky are already about as rosy as possible—the one with stars, the other with dulse, and foam, and wild light. The practical developments of his culture are orchards and clover-fields wearing a smiling, benevolent aspect, truly excellent in their way, though a near view discloses something barbarous in them all. Wildness charms not my friend, charm it never so wisely: and whatsoever may be the character of his heaven, his earth seems only a chaos of agricultural possibilities calling for grubbing-hoes and manures.

Sometimes I venture to approach him with a plea for wildness, when he good-naturedly shakes a big mellow apple in my face, reiterating his favorite aphorism, "Culture is an orchard apple; Nature is a crab." Not all culture, however, is equally destructive and inappreciative. Azure skies and crystal waters find loving recognition, and few there be who would welcome the axe among mountain pines, or would care to apply any correction to the tones and costumes of mountain waterfalls. Nevertheless, the barbarous notion is almost universally entertained by civilized man, that there is in all the manufactures of Nature something essentially coarse which can and must be eradicated by human culture. I was, therefore, delighted in finding that the wild wool growing upon mountain sheep in the neighborhood of Mount Shasta was much finer than the average grades of cultivated wool. This FINE discovery was made some three months ago, while hunting among the Shasta sheep between Shasta and Lower Klamath Lake. Three fleeces were obtained—one that belonged to a large ram about four years old, another to a ewe about the same age, and another to a yearling lamb. After parting their beautiful wool on the side and many places along the back, shoulders, and hips, and examining it closely with my lens, I shouted: "Well done for wildness! Wild wool is finer than tame!"

My companions stooped down and examined the fleeces for themselves, pulling out tufts and ringlets, spinning them between their fingers, and measuring the length of the staple, each in turn paying tribute to wildness. It WAS finer, and no mistake; finer than Spanish Merino. Wild wool IS finer than tame.

"Here," said I, "is an argument for fine wildness that needs no explanation. Not that such arguments are by any means rare, for all wildness is finer than tameness, but because fine wool is appreciable by everybody alike—from the most speculative president of national wool-growers' associations all the way down to the gudewife spinning by her ingleside."

Nature is a good mother, and sees well to the clothing of her many bairns—birds with smoothly imbricated feathers, beetles with shining jackets, and bears with shaggy furs. In the tropical south, where the sun warms like a fire, they are allowed to go thinly clad; but in the snowy northland she takes care to clothe warmly. The squirrel has socks and mittens, and a tail broad enough for a blanket; the grouse is densely feathered down to the ends of his toes; and the wild sheep, besides his undergarment of fine wool, has a thick overcoat of hair that sheds off both the snow and the rain. Other provisions and adaptations in the dresses of animals, relating less to climate than to the more mechanical circumstances of life, are made with the same consummate skill that characterizes all the love work of Nature. Land, water, and air, jagged rocks, muddy ground, sand beds, forests, underbrush, grassy plains, etc., are considered in all their possible combinations while the clothing of her beautiful wildlings is preparing. No matter what the circumstances of their lives may be, she never allows them to go dirty or ragged. The mole, living always in the dark and in the dirt, is yet as clean as the otter or the wave-washed seal; and our wild sheep, wading in snow, roaming through bushes, and leaping among jagged storm-beaten cliffs, wears a dress so exquisitely adapted to its mountain life that it is always found as unruffled and stainless as a bird.

No dogma taught by the present civilization seems to form so insuperable an obstacle in the way of a right understanding of the relations which culture sustains to wildness as that which regards the world as made especially for the uses of man. Every animal, plant, and crystal controverts it in the plainest terms. Yet it is taught from century to century as something ever new and precious, and in the resulting darkness the enormous conceit is allowed to go unchallenged.

I have never yet happened upon a trace of evidence that seemed to show that any one animal was ever made for another as much as it was made for itself. Not that Nature manifests any such thing as selfish isolation. In the making of every animal the presence of every other animal has been recognized. Indeed, every atom in creation may be said to be acquainted with and married to every other, but with universal union there is a division sufficient in degree for the purposes of the most intense individuality; no matter, therefore, what may be the note which any creature forms in the song of existence, it is made first for itself, then more and more remotely for all the world and worlds.

Were it not for the exercise of individualizing cares on the part of Nature, the universe would be felted together like a fleece of tame wool. But we are governed more than we know, and most when we are wildest. Plants, animals, and stars are all kept in place, bridled along appointed ways, WITH one another, and THROUGH THE MIDST of one another—killing and being killed, eating and being eaten, in harmonious proportions and quantities. And it is right that we should thus reciprocally make use of one another, rob, cook, and consume, to the utmost of our healthy abilities and desires. Stars attract one another as they are able, and harmony results. Wild lambs eat as many wild flowers as they can find or desire, and men and wolves eat the lambs to just the same extent.

It is now some thirty-six hundred years since Jacob kissed his mother and set out across the plains of Padan-aram to begin his experiments upon the flocks of his uncle, Laban; and, notwithstanding the high degree of excellence he attained as a wool-grower, and the innumerable painstaking efforts subsequently made by individuals and associations in all kinds of pastures and climates, we still seem to be as far from definite and satisfactory results as we ever were. In one breed the wool is apt to wither and crinkle like hay on a sun-beaten hillside. In another, it is lodged and matted together like the lush tangled grass of a manured meadow. In one the staple is deficient in length, in another in fineness; while in all there is a constant tendency toward disease, rendering various washings and dippings indispensable to prevent its falling out. The problem of the quality and quantity of the carcass seems to be as doubtful and as far removed from a satisfactory solution as that of the wool. Desirable breeds blundered upon by long series of groping experiments are often found to be unstable and subject to disease—bots, foot rot, blind staggers, etc.—causing infinite trouble, both among breeders and manufacturers. Would it not be well, therefore, for some one to go back as far as possible and take a fresh start?

PART ONE

From *The Story of My Boyhood and Youth*

A Boyhood In Scotland

∾

When I was a boy in Scotland I was fond of everything that was wild, and all my life I've been growing fonder and fonder of wild places and wild creatures. Fortunately around my native town of Dunbar, by the stormy North Sea, there was no lack of wildness, though most of the land lay in smooth cultivation. With red-blooded playmates, wild as myself, I loved to wander in the fields to hear the birds sing, and along the seashore to gaze and wonder at the shells and seaweeds, eels and crabs in the pools among the rocks when the tide was low; and best of all to watch the waves in awful storms thundering on the black headlands and craggy ruins of the old Dunbar Castle when the sea and the sky, the waves and the clouds, were mingled together as one. We never thought of playing truant, but after I was five or six years old I ran away to the seashore or the fields almost every Saturday, and every day in the school vacations except Sundays, though solemnly warned that I must play at home in the garden and back yard, lest I should learn to think bad thoughts and say bad words. All in vain. In spite of the sure sore punishments that followed like shadows, the natural inherited wildness in our blood ran true on its glorious course as invincible and unstoppable as stars.

My earliest recollections of the country were gained on short walks with my grandfather when I was perhaps not over three years old. On one of these walks grandfather took me to Lord Lauderdale's gardens, where I saw figs growing against a sunny wall and tasted some of them, and got as many apples to eat as I wished. On another memorable walk in a hay-field, when we sat down to rest on one of the haycocks I heard a sharp, prickly, stinging cry, and, jumping up eagerly, called grandfather's attention to it. He said he heard only the wind, but I insisted on digging into the hay and turning it over until we discovered the source of the strange exciting sound,—a mother field mouse with half a dozen naked young hanging to her teats. This to me was a wonderful discovery. No hunter could have been more excited on discovering a bear and her cubs in a wilderness den.

I was sent to school before I had completed my third year. The first school day was doubtless full of wonders, but I am not able to recall any of them. I remember the servant washing my face and getting soap in my eyes, and mother hanging a little green bag with my first book in it around my neck so I would not lose it, and its blowing back in the sea-wind like a flag. But before I was sent to school my grandfather, as I was told, had taught me my letters from shop signs across the street. I can remember distinctly how proud I was when I had spelled my way through the little first book into the second, which seemed large and important, and so on to the third. Going from one book to another formed a grand triumphal advancement, the memories of which still stand out in clear relief.

The third book contained interesting stories as well as plain reading-and spelling-lessons. To me the best story of all was "Llewellyn's Dog," the first animal that comes to mind after the needle-voiced field mouse. It so deeply interested and touched me and some of my classmates that we read it over and over with aching hearts, both in and out of school and shed bitter tears over the brave faithful dog, Gelert, slain by his own master, who imagined that he had devoured his son because he came to him all bloody when the boy was lost, though he had saved the child's life by killing a big wolf. We have to look far back to learn how great may be the capacity of a child's heart for sorrow and sympathy with animals as well as with human friends and neighbors. This auld-lang-syne story stands out in the throng of old school day memories as clearly as if I had myself been one of that Welsh hunting-party—heard the bugles blowing, seen Gelert slain, joined in the search for the lost child, discovered it at last happy and smiling among the grass and bushes beside the dead, mangled wolf, and wept with Llewellyn over the sad fate of his noble, faithful dog friend.

Another favorite in this book was Southey's poem "The Inchcape Bell," a story of a priest and a pirate. A good priest in order to warn seamen in dark stormy weather hung a big bell on the dangerous Inchcape Rock. The greater the storm and higher the waves, the louder rang the warning bell, until it was cut off and sunk by wicked Ralph the Rover. One fine day, as the story goes, when the bell was ringing gently, the pirate put out to the rock, saying, "I'll sink that bell and plague the Abbot of Aberbrothok." So he cut the rope, and down went the bell "with a gurgling sound; the bubbles rose and burst around," etc. Then "Ralph the Rover sailed away; he scoured the seas for many a day; and now, grown rich with plundered store, he steers his course for Scotland's shore." Then came a terrible storm with cloud darkness and night darkness and high roaring waves, "Now where we are," cried the pirate, "I cannot tell, but I wish I could hear the Inchcape bell." And the story goes on to tell how the wretched rover "tore his hair," and "curst himself in his despair," when "with a shivering shock" the stout ship struck on the Inchcape Rock, and went down with Ralph and his plunder beside the good priest's bell. The story appealed to our love of kind deeds and of wildness and fair play.

A lot of terrifying experiences connected with these first school-days grew out of crimes committed by the keeper of a low lodging-house in Edinburgh, who allowed poor homeless wretches to sleep on benches or the floor for a penny or so a night, and, when kind Death came to their relief, sold the bodies for dissection to Dr. Hare of the medical school. None of us children ever heard anything like the original story. The servant girls told us that "Dandy Doctors," clad in long black cloaks and supplied with a store of sticking-plaster of wondrous adhesiveness, prowled at night about the country lanes and even the town streets, watching for children to choke and sell. The Dandy Doctor's business method, as the servants explained it, was with lightning quickness to clap a sticking-plaster on the face of a scholar, covering mouth and nose, preventing breathing or crying for help, then pop us under his long black cloak and carry us to Edinburgh to be sold and sliced into small pieces for folk to learn how we were made. We always mentioned the name "Dandy Doctor" in a fearful whisper, and never dared venture out of doors after dark. In the short winter days it got dark before school closed, and in cloudy weather we sometimes had difficulty in finding our way home unless a servant with a lantern was sent for us; but during the Dandy Doctor period the school was closed earlier, for if detained until the usual hour the teacher could not get us to leave the schoolroom. We would rather stay all night supperless than dare the mysterious doctors supposed to be lying in wait for us. We had to go up a hill called the Davel Brae that lay between the schoolhouse and the main street. One evening just before dark, as we were running up the hill, one of the boys shouted, "A Dandy Doctor! A Dandy Doctor!" and we all fled pell-mell back into the schoolhouse to the astonishment of Mungo Siddons, the teacher. I can remember to this day the amused look on the good dominie's face as he stared and tried to guess what had got into us, until one of the older boys breathlessly explained that there was an awful big Dandy Doctor on the Brae and we couldna gang hame. Others corroborated the dreadful news. "Yes! We saw him, plain as onything, with his lang black cloak to hide us in, and some of us thought we saw a sticken-plaister ready in his hand." We were in such a state of fear and trembling that the teacher saw he wasn't going to get rid of us without going himself as leader. He went only a short distance, however, and turned us over to the care of the two biggest scholars, who led us to the top of the Brae and then left us to scurry home and dash into the door like pursued squirrels diving into their holes.

Just before school skaled (closed), we all arose and sang the fine hymn "Lord, dismiss us with Thy blessing." In the spring when the swallows were coming back from their winter homes we sang—

> *"Welcome, welcome, little stranger,*
> *Welcome from a foreign shore;*
> *Safe escaped from many a danger ..."*

and while singing we all swayed in rhythm with the music. "The Cuckoo," that always told his name in the spring of the year, was another favorite song, and when there was nothing in particular to call to mind any special bird or animal, the songs we sang were widely varied, such as

> "The whale, the whale is the beast for me,
> Plunging along through the deep, deep sea."

But the best of all was "Lord, dismiss us with Thy blessing," though at that time the most significant part I fear was the first three words.

With my school lessons father made me learn hymns and Bible verses. For learning "Rock of Ages" he gave me a penny, and I thus became suddenly rich. Scotch boys are seldom spoiled with money. We thought more of a penny those economical days than the poorest American schoolboy thinks of a dollar. To decide what to do with that first penny was an extravagantly serious affair. I ran in great excitement up and down the street, examining the tempting goodies in the shop windows before venturing on so important an investment. My playmates also became excited when the wonderful news got abroad that Johnnie Muir had a penny, hoping to obtain a taste of the orange, apple, or candy it was likely to bring forth.

At this time infants were baptized and vaccinated a few days after birth. I remember very well a fight with the doctor when my brother David was vaccinated. This happened, I think, before I was sent to school. I couldn't imagine what the doctor, a tall, severe-looking man in black, was doing to my brother, but as mother, who was holding him in her arms, offered no objection, I looked on quietly while he scratched the arm until I saw blood. Then, unable to trust even my mother, I managed to spring up high enough to grab and bite the doctor's arm, yelling that I wasna gan to let him hurt my bonnie brither, while to my utter astonishment mother and the doctor only laughed at me. So far from complete at times is sympathy between parents and children, and so much like wild beasts are baby boys, little fighting, biting, climbing pagans.

Father was proud of his garden and seemed always to be trying to make it as much like Eden as possible, and in a corner of it he gave each of us a little bit of ground for our very own in which we planted what we best liked, wondering how the hard dry seeds could change into soft leaves and flowers and find their way out to the light; and, to see how they were coming on, we used to dig up the larger ones, such as peas and beans, every day. My aunt had a corner assigned to her in our garden which she filled with lilies, and we all looked with the utmost respect and admiration at that precious lily-bed and wondered whether when we grew up we should ever be rich enough to own one anything like so grand. We imagined that each lily was worth an enormous sum of money and never dared to touch a single leaf or petal of them. We really stood in awe of them. Far, far was I then from the wild lily gardens of California that I was destined to see in their glory.

When I was a little boy at Mungo Siddons's school a flower-show was held in Dunbar, and I saw a number of the exhibitors carrying large handfuls of dahlias, the first I had ever seen. I thought them marvelous in size and beauty and, as in the case of my aunt's lilies, wondered if I should ever be rich enough to own some of them.

Although I never dared to touch my aunt's sacred lilies, I have good cause to remember stealing some common flowers from an apothecary, Peter Lawson, who also answered the purpose of a regular physician to most of the poor people of the town and adjacent country. He had a pony which was considered very wild and dangerous, and when he was called out of town he mounted this wonderful beast, which, after standing long in the stable, was frisky and boisterous, and often to our delight reared and jumped and danced about from side to side of the street before he could be persuaded to go ahead. We boys gazed in awful admiration and wondered how the druggist could be so brave and able as to get on and stay on that wild beast's back. This famous Peter loved flowers and had a fine garden surrounded by an iron fence, through the bars of which, when I thought no one saw me, I oftentimes snatched a flower and took to my heels. One day Peter discovered me in this mischief, dashed out into the street and caught me. I screamed that I wouldna steal any more if he would let me go. He didn't say anything but just dragged me along to the stable where he kept the wild pony, pushed me in right back of its heels, and shut the door. I was screaming, of course, but as soon as I was imprisoned the fear of being kicked quenched all noise. I hardly dared breathe. My only hope was in motionless silence. Imagine the agony I endured! I did not steal any more of his flowers. He was a good hard judge of boy nature.

I was in Peter's hands some time before this, when I was about two and a half years old. The servant girl bathed us small folk before putting us to bed. The smarting soapy scrubbings of the Saturday nights in preparation for the Sabbath were particularly severe, and we all dreaded them. My sister Sarah, the next older than me, wanted the long-legged stool I was sitting on awaiting my turn, so she just tipped me off. My chin struck on the edge of the bath-tub, and, as I was talking at the time, my tongue happened to be in the way of my teeth when they were closed by the blow, and a deep gash was cut on the side of it, which bled profusely. Mother came running at the noise I made, wrapped me up, put me in the servant girl's arms and told her to run with me through the garden and out by a back way to Peter Lawson to have something done to stop the bleeding. He simply pushed a wad of cotton into my mouth after soaking it in some brown astringent stuff, and told me to be sure to keep my mouth shut and all would soon be well. Mother put me to bed, calmed my fears, and told me to lie still and sleep like a gude bairn. But just as I was dropping off to sleep I swallowed the bulky wad of medicated cotton and with it, as I imagined, my tongue also. My screams over so great a loss brought mother, and when she anxiously took me in her arms and inquired what was the matter, I told her that I had swallowed my tongue. She only laughed at me, much to my astonishment, when I expected that she would bewail the awful loss her boy had sustained. My sisters, who were older than I, oftentimes said when I happened to be talking too much, "It's a pity you hadn't swallowed at least half of that long tongue of yours when you were little."

It appears natural for children to be fond of water, although the Scotch method of making every duty dismal contrived to make necessary bathing for health terrible to us. I well remember among the awful experiences of childhood being taken by the servant to the seashore when I was between two and three years old, stripped at the side of a deep pool in the rocks, plunged into it among crawling crawfish and slippery wriggling snake-like eels, and drawn up gasping and shrieking only to be plunged down again and again. As the time approached for this terrible bathing, I used to hide in the darkest corners of the house, and oftentimes a long search was required to find me. But after we were a few years older, we enjoyed bathing with other boys as we wandered along the shore, careful, however, not to get into a pool that had an invisible boy-devouring monster at the bottom of it. Such pools, miniature maelstroms, were called "sookin-in-goats" and were well known to most of us. Nevertheless we never ventured into any pool on strange parts of the coast before we had thrust a stick into it. If the stick were not pulled out of our hands, we boldly entered and enjoyed plashing and ducking long ere we had learned to swim.

One of our best playgrounds was the famous old Dunbar Castle, to which King Edward fled after his defeat at Bannockburn. It was built more than a thousand years ago, and though we knew little of its history, we had heard many mysterious stories of the battles fought about its walls, and firmly believed that every bone we found in the ruins belonged to an ancient warrior. We tried to see who could climb highest on the crumbling peaks and crags, and took chances that no cautious mountaineer would try. That I did not fall and finish my rock-scrambling in those adventurous boyhood days seems now a reasonable wonder.

Among our best games were running, jumping, wrestling, and scrambling. I was so proud of my skill as a climber that when I first heard of hell from a servant girl who loved to tell its horrors and warn us that if we did anything wrong we would be cast into it, I always insisted that I could climb out of it. I imagined it was only a sooty pit with stone walls like those of the castle, and I felt sure there must be chinks and cracks in the masonry for fingers and toes. Anyhow the terrors of the horrible place seldom lasted long beyond the telling; for natural faith casts out fear.

Most of the Scotch children believe in ghosts, and some under peculiar conditions continue to believe in them all through life. Grave ghosts are deemed particularly dangerous, and many of the most credulous will go far out of their way to avoid passing through or near a graveyard in the dark. After being instructed by the servants in the nature, looks, and habits of the various black and white ghosts, boowuzzies, and witches we often speculated as to whether they could run fast, and tried to believe that we had a good chance to get away from most of them. To improve our speed and wind, we often took long runs into the country. Tam o' Shanter's mare outran a lot of witches,—at least until she reached a place of safety beyond the keystone of the bridge,—and we thought perhaps we also might be able to outrun them.

Our house formerly belonged to a physician, and a servant girl told us that the ghost of the dead doctor haunted one of the unoccupied rooms in the second story that was kept dark on account of a heavy window-tax. Our bedroom was adjacent to the ghost room, which had in it a lot of chemical apparatus,—glass tubing, glass and brass retorts, test-tubes, flasks, etc.,—and we thought that those strange articles were still used by the old dead doctor in compounding physic. In the long summer days David and I were put to bed several hours before sunset. Mother tucked us in carefully, drew the curtains of the big old-fashioned bed, and told us to lie still and sleep like gude bairns; but we were usually out of bed, playing games of daring called "scootchers," about as soon as our loving mother reached the foot of the stairs, for we couldn't lie still, however hard we might try. Going into the ghost room was regarded as a very great scootcher. After venturing in a few steps and rushing back in terror, I used to dare David to go as far without getting caught.

The roof of our house, as well as the crags and walls of the old castle, offered fine mountaineering exercise. Our bedroom was lighted by a dormer window. One night I opened it in search of good scootchers and hung myself out over the slates, holding on to the sill, while the wind was making a balloon of my nightgown. I then dared David to try the adventure, and he did. Then I went out again and hung by one hand, and David did the same. Then I hung by one finger, being careful not to slip, and he did that too. Then I stood on the sill and examined the edge of the left wall of the window, crept up the slates along its side by slight finger-holds, got astride of the roof, sat there a few minutes looking at the scenery over the garden wall while the wind was howling and threatening to blow me off, then managed to slip down, catch hold of the sill, and get safely back into the room. But before attempting this scootcher, recognizing its dangerous character, with commendable caution I warned David that in case I should happen to slip I would grip the rain-trough when I was going over the eaves and hang on, and that he must then run fast downstairs and tell father to get a ladder for me, and tell him to be quick because I would soon be tired hanging dangling in the wind by my hands. After my return from this capital scootcher, David, not to be outdone, crawled up to the top of the window-roof, and got bravely astride of it; but in trying to return he lost courage and began to greet (to cry), "I canna get doon. Oh, I canna get doon." I leaned out of the window and shouted encouragingly, "Dinna greet, Davie, dinna greet, I'll help ye doon. If you greet, fayther will hear, and gee us baith an awfu' skelping." Then, standing on the sill and holding on by one hand to the window-casing, I directed him to slip his feet down within reach, and, after securing a good hold, I jumped inside and dragged him in by his heels. This finished scootcher-scrambling for the night and frightened us into bed.

In the short winter days, when it was dark even at our early bed-time, we usually spent the hours before going to sleep playing voyages around the world under the bed-clothing. After mother had carefully covered us, bade us good-night and gone downstairs, we set out on our travels. Burrowing like moles, we visited France, India, America, Australia, New Zealand, and all the places we had ever heard of; our travels never ending until we fell asleep. When mother came to take a last look at us, before she went to bed, to see that we were covered, we were oftentimes covered so well that she had difficulty in finding us, for we were hidden in all sorts of positions where sleep happened to overtake us, but in the morning we always found ourselves in good order, lying straight like gude bairns, as she said.

Some fifty years later, when I visited Scotland, I got one of my Dunbar schoolmates to introduce me to the owners of our old home, from whom I obtained permission to go upstairs to examine our bedroom window and judge what sort of adventure getting on its roof must have been, and with all my after experience in mountaineering, I found that what I had done in daring boyhood was now beyond my skill.

Boys are often at once cruel and merciful, thoughtlessly hard-hearted and tender-hearted, sympathetic, pitiful, and kind in ever changing contrasts. Love of neighbors, human or animal, grows up amid savage traits, coarse and fine. When father made out to get us securely locked up in the back yard to prevent our shore and field wanderings, we had to play away the comparatively dull time as best we could. One of our amusements was hunting cats without seriously hurting them. These sagacious animals knew, however, that, though not very dangerous, boys were not to be trusted. One time in particular I remember, when we began throwing stones at an experienced old Tom, not wishing to hurt him much, though he was a tempting mark. He soon saw what we were up to, fled to the stable, and climbed to the top of the hay manger. He was still within range, however, and we kept the stones flying faster and faster, but he just blinked and played possum without wincing either at our best shots or at the noise we made. I happened to strike him pretty hard with a good-sized pebble, but he still blinked and sat still as if without feeling. "He must be mortally wounded," I said, "and now we must kill him to put him out of pain," the savage in us rapidly growing with indulgence. All took heartily to this sort of cat mercy and began throwing the heaviest stones we could manage, but that old fellow knew what characters we were, and just as we imagined him mercifully dead he evidently thought the play was becoming too serious and that it was time to retreat; for suddenly with a wild whirr and gurr of energy he launched himself over our heads, rushed across the yard in a blur of speed, climbed to the roof of another building and over the garden wall, out of pain and bad company, with all his lives wideawake and in good working order.

After we had thus learned that Tom had at least nine lives, we tried to verify the common saying that no matter how far cats fell they always landed on their feet unhurt. We caught one in our back yard, not Tom but a smaller one of manageable size, and somehow got him smuggled up to the top story of the house. I don't know how in the world we managed to let go of him, for as soon as we opened the window and held him over the sill he knew his danger and made violent efforts to scratch and bite his way back into the room; but we determined to carry the thing through, and at last managed to drop him. I can remember to this day how the poor creature in danger of his life strained and balanced as he was falling and managed to alight on his feet. This was a cruel thing for even wild boys to do, and we never tried the experiment again, for we sincerely pitied the poor fellow when we saw him creeping slowly away, stunned and frightened, with a swollen black and blue chin.

Again—showing the natural savagery of boys—we delighted in dog-fights, and even in the horrid red work of slaughter-houses, often running long distances and climbing over walls and roofs to see a pig killed, as soon as we heard the desperately earnest squealing. And if the butcher was good-natured, we begged him to let us get a near view of the mysterious insides and to give us a bladder to blow up for a foot-ball.

But here is an illustration of the better side of boy nature. In our back yard there were three elm trees and in the one nearest the house a pair of robin-redbreasts had their nest. When the young were almost able to fly, a troop of the celebrated "Scottish Grays," visited Dunbar, and three or four of the fine horses were lodged in our stable. When the soldiers were polishing their swords and helmets, they happened to notice the nest, and just as they were leaving, one of them climbed the tree and robbed it. With sore sympathy we watched the young birds as the hard-hearted robber pushed them one by one beneath his jacket,—all but two that jumped out of the nest and tried to fly, but they were easily caught as they fluttered on the ground, and were hidden away with the rest. The distress of the bereaved parents, as they hovered and screamed over the frightened crying children they so long had loved and sheltered and fed, was pitiful to see; but the shining soldier rode grandly away on his big gray horse, caring only for the few pennies the young songbirds would bring and the beer they would buy, while we all, sisters and brothers, were crying and sobbing. I remember, as if it happened this day, how my heart fairly ached and choked me. Mother put us to bed and tried to comfort us, telling us that the little birds would be well fed and grow big, and soon learn to sing in pretty cages; but again and again we rehearsed the sad story of the poor bereaved birds and their frightened children, and could not be comforted. Father came into the room when we were half asleep and still sobbing, and I heard mother telling him that, "a' the bairns' hearts were broken over the robbing of the nest in the elm."

After attaining the manly, belligerent age of five or six years, very few of my schooldays passed without a fist fight, and half a dozen was no uncommon number. When any classmate of our own age questioned our rank and standing as fighters, we always made haste to settle the matter at a quiet place on the Davel Brae. To be a "gude fechter" was our highest ambition, our dearest aim in life in or out of school. To be a good scholar was a secondary consideration, though we tried hard to hold high places in our classes and gloried in being Dux. We fairly reveled in the battle stories of glorious William Wallace and Robert the Bruce, with which every breath of Scotch air is saturated, and of course we were all going to be soldiers. On the Davel Brae battleground we often managed to bring on something like real war, greatly more exciting than personal combat. Choosing leaders, we divided into two armies. In winter damp snow furnished plenty of ammunition to make the thing serious, and in summer sand and grass sods. Cheering and shouting some battle-cry such as "Bannockburn! Bannockburn! Scotland forever! The Last War in India!" we were led bravely on. For heavy battery work we stuffed our Scotch blue bonnets with snow and sand, sometimes mixed with gravel, and fired them at each other as cannon-balls.

Of course we always looked eagerly forward to vacation days and thought them slow in coming. Old Mungo Siddons gave us a lot of gooseberries or currants and wished us a happy time. Some sort of special closing-exercises—singing, recitations, etc.—celebrated the great day, but I remember only the berries, freedom from school work, and opportunities for run-away rambles in the fields and along the wave-beaten seashore.

An exciting time came when at the age of seven or eight years I left the auld Davel Brae school for the grammar school. Of course I had a terrible lot of fighting to do, because a new scholar had to meet every one of his age who dared to challenge him, this being the common introduction to a new school. It was very strenuous for the first month or so, establishing my fighting rank, taking up new studies, especially Latin and French, getting acquainted with new classmates and the master and his rules. In the first few Latin and French lessons the new teacher, Mr. Lyon, blandly smiled at our comical blunders, but pedagogical weather of the severest kind quickly set in, when for every mistake, everything short of perfection, the taws was promptly applied. We had to get three lessons every day in Latin, three in French, and as many in English, besides spelling, history, arithmetic, and geography. Word lessons in particular, the wouldst-couldst-shouldst-have-loved kind, were kept up, with much warlike thrashing, until I had committed the whole of the French, Latin, and English grammars to memory, and in connection with reading-lessons we were called on to recite parts of them with the rules over and over again, as if all the regular and irregular incomprehensible verb stuff was poetry. In addition to all this, father made me learn so many Bible verses every day that by the time I was eleven years of age I had about three fourths of the Old Testament and all of the New by heart and by sore flesh. I could recite the New Testament from the beginning of Matthew to the end of Revelation without a single stop. The dangers of cramming and of making scholars study at home instead of letting their little brains rest were never heard of in those days. We carried our school-books home in a strap every night and committed to memory our next day's lessons before we went to bed, and to do that we had to bend our attention as closely on our tasks as lawyers on great million-dollar cases. I can't conceive of anything that would now enable me to concentrate my attention more fully than when I was a mere stripling boy, and it was all done by whipping,—thrashing in general. Old-fashioned Scotch teachers spent no time in seeking short roads to knowledge, or in trying any of the new-fangled psychological methods so much in vogue nowadays. There was nothing said about making the seats easy or the lessons easy. We were simply driven pointblank against our books like soldiers against the enemy, and sternly ordered, "Up and at 'em. Commit your lessons to memory!" If we failed in any part, however slight, we were whipped; for the grand, simple, all-sufficing Scotch discovery had been made that there was a close connection between the skin and the memory, and that irritating the skin excited the memory to any required degree.

Fighting was carried on still more vigorously in the high school than in the common school. Whenever any one was challenged, either the challenge was allowed or it was decided by a battle on the seashore, where with stubborn enthusiasm we battered each other as if we had not been sufficiently battered by the teacher. When we were so fortunate as to finish a fight without getting a black eye, we usually escaped a thrashing at home and another next morning at school, for other traces of the fray could be easily washed off at a well on the church brae, or concealed, or passed as results of playground accidents; but a black eye could never be explained away from downright fighting. A good double thrashing was the inevitable penalty, but all without avail; fighting went on without the slightest abatement, like natural storms; for no punishment less than death could quench the ancient inherited belligerence burning in our pagan blood. Nor could we be made to believe it was fair that father and teacher should thrash us so industriously for our good, while begrudging us the pleasure of thrashing each other for our good. All these various thrashings, however, were admirably influential in developing not only memory but fortitude as well. For if we did not endure our school punishments and fighting pains without flinching and making faces, we were mocked on the playground, and public opinion on a Scotch playground was a powerful agent in controlling behavior; therefore we at length managed to keep our features in smooth repose while enduring pain that would try anybody but an American Indian. Far from feeling that we were called on to endure too much pain, one of our playground games was thrashing each other with whips about two feet long made from the tough, wiry stems of a species of polygonum fastened together in a stiff, firm braid. One of us handing two of these whips to a companion to take his choice, we stood up close together and thrashed each other on the legs until one succumbed to the intolerable pain and thus lost the game. Nearly all of our playground games were strenuous,—shin-battering shinny, wrestling, prisoners' base, and dogs and hares,—all augmenting in no slight degree our lessons in fortitude. Moreover, we regarded our punishments and pains of every sort as training for war, since we were all going to be soldiers. Besides single combats we sometimes assembled on Saturdays to meet the scholars of another school, and very little was required for the growth of strained relations, and war. The immediate cause might be nothing more than a saucy stare. Perhaps the scholar stared at would insolently inquire, "What are ye glowerin' at, Bob?" Bob would reply, "I'll look where I hae a mind and hinder me if ye daur." "Weel, Bob," the outraged stared-at scholar would reply, "I'll soon let ye see whether I daur or no!" and give Bob a blow on the face. This opened the battle, and every good scholar belonging to either school was drawn into it. After both sides were sore and weary, a strong-lunged warrior would be heard above the din of battle shouting, "I'll tell ye what we'll dae wi' ye. If ye'll let us alane we'll let ye alane!" and the school war ended as most wars between nations do; and some of them begin in much the same way.

Notwithstanding the great number of harshly enforced rules, not very good order was kept in school in my time. There were two schools within a few rods of each other, one for mathematics, navigation, etc., the other, called the grammar school, that I attended. The masters lived in a big freestone house within eight or ten yards of the schools, so that they could easily step out for anything they wanted or send one of the scholars. The moment our master disappeared, perhaps for a book or a drink, every scholar left his seat and his lessons, jumped on top of the benches and desks or crawled beneath them, tugging, rolling, wrestling, accomplishing in a minute a depth of disorder and din unbelievable save by a Scottish scholar. We even carried on war, class against class, in those wild, precious minutes. A watcher gave the alarm when the master opened his house-door to return, and it was a great feat to get into our places before he entered, adorned in awful majestic authority, shouting "Silence!" and striking resounding blows with his cane on a desk or on some unfortunate scholar's back.

Forty-seven years after leaving this fighting school, I returned on a visit to Scotland, and a cousin in Dunbar introduced me to a minister who was acquainted with the history of the school, and obtained for me an invitation to dine with the new master. Of course I gladly accepted, for I wanted to see the old place of fun and pain, and the battleground on the sands. Mr. Lyon, our able teacher and thrasher, I learned, had held his place as master of the school for twenty or thirty years after I left it, and had recently died in London, after preparing many young men for the English Universities. At the dinner-table, while I was recalling the amusements and fights of my old schooldays, the minister remarked to the new master, "Now, don't you wish that you had been teacher in those days, and gained the honor of walloping John Muir?" This pleasure so merrily suggested showed that the minister also had been a fighter in his youth. The old freestone school building was still perfectly sound, but the carved, ink-stained desks were almost whittled away.

The highest part of our playground back of the school commanded a view of the sea, and we loved to watch the passing ships and, judging by their rigging, make guesses as to the ports they had sailed from, those to which they were bound, what they were loaded with, their tonnage, etc. In stormy weather they were all smothered in clouds and spray, and showers of salt scud torn from the tops of the waves came flying over the playground wall. In those tremendous storms many a brave ship foundered or was tossed and smashed on the rocky shore.

When a wreck occurred within a mile or two of the town, we often managed by running fast to reach it and pick up some of the spoils. In particular I remember visiting the battered fragments of an unfortunate brig or schooner that had been loaded with apples, and finding fine unpitiful sport in rushing into the spent waves and picking up the red-cheeked fruit from the frothy, seething foam.

All our school-books were extravagantly illustrated with drawings of every kind of sailing-vessel, and every boy owned some sort of craft whittled from a block of wood and trimmed with infinite pains,—sloops, schooners, brigs, and full-rigged ships, with their sails and string ropes properly adjusted and named for us by some old sailor. These precious toy craft with lead keels we learned to sail on a pond near the town. With the sails set at the proper angle to the wind, they made fast straight voyages across the pond to boys on the other side, who readjusted the sails and started them back on the return voyages. Oftentimes fleets of half a dozen or more were started together in exciting races.

Our most exciting sport, however, was playing with gunpowder. We made guns out of gas-pipe, mounted them on sticks of any shape, clubbed our pennies together for powder, gleaned pieces of lead here and there and cut them into slugs, and, while one aimed, another applied a match to the touch-hole. With these awful weapons we wandered along the beach and fired at the gulls and solan-geese as they passed us. Fortunately we never hurt any of them that we knew of. We also dug holes in the ground, put in a handful or two of powder, tamped it well around a fuse made of a wheat-stalk, and, reaching cautiously forward, touched a match to the straw. This we called making earthquakes. Oftentimes we went home with singed hair and faces well peppered with powder-grains that could not be washed out. Then, of course, came a correspondingly severe punishment from both father and teacher.

Another favorite sport was climbing trees and scaling garden-walls. Boys eight or ten years of age could get over almost any wall by standing on each other's shoulders, thus making living ladders. To make walls secure against marauders, many of them were finished on top with broken bottles imbedded in lime, leaving the cutting edges sticking up; but with bunches of grass and weeds we could sit or stand in comfort on top of the jaggedest of them.

Like squirrels that begin to eat nuts before they are ripe, we began to eat apples about as soon as they were formed, causing, of course, desperate gastric disturbances to be cured by castor oil. Serious were the risks we ran in climbing and squeezing through hedges, and, of course, among the country folk we were far from welcome. Farmers passing us on the roads often shouted by way of greeting: "Oh, you vagabonds! Back to the toon wi' ye. Gang back where ye belang.

You're up to mischief, Ise warrant. I can see it. The gamekeeper'll catch ye, and maist like ye'll a' be hanged some day."

Breakfast in those auld-lang-syne days was simple oatmeal porridge, usually with a little milk or treacle, served in wooden dishes called "luggies," formed of staves hooped together like miniature tubs about four or five inches in diameter. One of the staves, the lug or ear, a few inches longer than the others, served as a handle, while the number of luggies ranged in a row on a dresser indicated the size of the family. We never dreamed of anything to come after the porridge, or of asking for more. Our portions were consumed in about a couple of minutes; then off to school. At noon we came racing home ravenously hungry. The midday meal, called dinner, was usually vegetable broth, a small piece of boiled mutton, and barley-meal scone. None of us liked the barley scone bread, therefore we got all we wanted of it, and in desperation had to eat it, for we were always hungry, about as hungry after as before meals. The evening meal was called "tea" and was served on our return from school. It consisted, as far as we children were concerned, of half a slice of white bread without butter, barley scone, and warm water with a little milk and sugar in it, a beverage called "content," which warmed but neither cheered nor inebriated. Immediately after tea we ran across the street with our books to Grandfather Gilrye, who took pleasure in seeing us and hearing us recite our next day's lessons. Then back home to supper, usually a boiled potato and piece of barley scone. Then family worship, and to bed.

Our amusements on Saturday afternoons and vacations depended mostly on getting away from home into the country, especially in the spring when the birds were calling loudest. Father sternly forbade David and me from playing truant in the fields with plundering wanderers like ourselves, fearing we might go on from bad to worse, get hurt in climbing over walls, caught by gamekeepers, or lost by falling over a cliff into the sea. "Play as much as you like in the back yard and garden," he said, "and mind what you'll get when you forget and disobey." Thus he warned us with an awfully stern countenance, looking very hard-hearted, while naturally his heart was far from hard, though he devoutly believed in eternal punishment for

bad boys both here and hereafter. Nevertheless, like devout mar-
tyrs of wildness, we stole away to the seashore or the green, sunny
fields with almost religious regularity, taking advantage of opportunities when father was very busy, to join our companions, oftenest
to hear the birds sing and hunt their nests, glorying in the number
we had discovered and called our own. A sample of our nest chatter
was something like this: Willie Chisholm would proudly exclaim—
"I ken (know) seventeen nests, and you, Johnnie, ken only fifteen."

"But I wouldna gie my fifteen for your seventeen, for five of
mine are larks and mavises. You ken only three o' the best singers."

"Yes, Johnnie, but I ken six goldies and you ken only one. Maist
of yours are only sparrows and linties and robin-redbreasts."

Then perhaps Bob Richardson would loudly declare that he
"kenned mair nests than onybody, for he kenned twenty-three, with
about fifty eggs in them and mair than fifty young birds—maybe
a hundred. Some of them naething but raw gorblings but lots of
them as big as their mithers and ready to flee. And aboot fifty craw's
nests and three fox dens."

"Oh, yes, Bob, but that's no fair, for naebody counts craw's nests
and fox holes, and then you live in the country at Belle-haven where
ye have the best chance."

"Yes, but I ken a lot of bumbee's nests, baith the red-legged and
the yellow-legged kind."

"Oh, wha cares for bumbee's nests!"

"Weel, but here's something! Ma father let me gang to a fox hunt,
and man, it was grand to see the hounds and the lang-legged horses
lowpin the dykes and burns and hedges!"

The nests, I fear, with the beautiful eggs and young birds, were
prized quite as highly as the songs of the glad parents, but no Scotch
boy that I know of ever failed to listen with enthusiasm to the songs
of the skylarks. Oftentimes on a broad meadow near Dunbar we
stood for hours enjoying their marvelous singing and soaring. From
the grass where the nest was hidden the male would suddenly rise, as
straight as if shot up, to a height of perhaps thirty or forty feet, and,
sustaining himself with rapid wing-beats, pour down the most delicious melody, sweet and clear and strong, overflowing all bounds,

then suddenly he would soar higher again and again, ever higher and higher, soaring and singing until lost to sight even on perfectly clear days, and oftentimes in cloudy weather "far in the downy cloud," as the poet says.

To test our eyes we often watched a lark until he seemed a faint speck in the sky and finally passed beyond the keenest-sighted of us all. "I see him yet!" we would cry, "I see him yet!" "I see him yet!" "I see him yet!" as he soared. And finally only one of us would be left to claim that he still saw him. At last he, too, would have to admit that the singer had soared beyond his sight, and still the music came pouring down to us in glorious profusion, from a height far above our vision, requiring marvelous power of wing and marvelous power of voice, for that rich, delicious, soft, and yet clear music was distinctly heard long after the bird was out of sight. Then, suddenly ceasing, the glorious singer would appear, falling like a bolt straight down to his nest, where his mate was sitting on the eggs.

It was far too common a practice among us to carry off a young lark just before it could fly, place it in a cage, and fondly, laboriously feed it. Sometimes we succeeded in keeping one alive for a year or two, and when awakened by the spring weather it was pitiful to see the quivering imprisoned soarer of the heavens rapidly beating its wings and singing as though it were flying and hovering in the air like its parents. To keep it in health we were taught that we must supply it with a sod of grass the size of the bottom of the cage, to make the poor bird feel as though it were at home on its native meadow,—a meadow perhaps a foot or at most two feet square. Again and again it would try to hover over that miniature meadow from its miniature sky just underneath the top of the cage. At last, conscience-stricken, we carried the beloved prisoner to the meadow west of Dunbar where it was born, and, blessing its sweet heart, bravely set it free, and our exceeding great reward was to see it fly and sing in the sky.

In the winter, when there was but little doing in the fields, we organized running-matches. A dozen or so of us would start out on races that were simply tests of endurance, running on and on along a public road over the breezy hills like hounds, without stopping or getting tired. The only serious trouble we ever felt in these long races was an occasional stitch in our sides. One of the boys started the story that sucking raw eggs was a sure cure for the stitches. We had hens in our back yard, and on the next Saturday we managed to swallow a couple of eggs apiece, a disgusting job, but we would do almost anything to mend our speed, and as soon as we could get away after taking the cure we set out on a ten or twenty mile run to prove its worth. We thought nothing of running right ahead ten or a dozen miles before turning back; for we knew nothing about taking time by the sun, and none of us had a watch in those days. Indeed, we never cared about time until it began to get dark. Then we thought of home and the thrashing that awaited us. Late or early, the thrashing was sure, unless father happened to be away. If he was expected to return soon, mother made haste to get us to bed before his arrival. We escaped the thrashing next morning, for father never felt like thrashing us in cold blood on the calm holy Sabbath. But no punishment, however sure and severe, was of any avail against the attraction of the fields and woods. It had other uses, developing memory, etc., but in keeping us at home it was of no use at all. Wildness was ever sounding in our ears, and

Nature saw to it that besides school lessons and church lessons some of her own lessons should be learned, perhaps with a view to the time when we should be called to wander in wildness to our heart's content. Oh, the blessed enchantment of those Saturday runaways in the prime of the spring! How our young wondering eyes reveled in the sunny, breezy glory of the hills and the sky, every particle of us thrilling and tingling with the bees and glad birds and glad streams! Kings may be blessed; we were glorious, we were free,— school cares and scoldings, heart thrashings and flesh thrashings alike, were forgotten in the fullness of Nature's glad wildness. These were my first excursions,—the beginnings of lifelong wanderings.

A New World

❦

Our grammar-school reader, called, I think, "Maccoulough's Course of Reading," contained a few natural-history sketches that excited me very much and left a deep impression, especially a fine description of the fish hawk and the bald eagle by the Scotch ornithologist Wilson, who had the good fortune to wander for years in the American woods while the country was yet mostly wild. I read his description over and over again, till I got the vivid picture he drew by heart,—the long-winged hawk circling over the heaving waves, every motion watched by the eagle perched on the top of a crag or dead tree; the fish hawk poising for a moment to take aim at a fish and plunging under the water; the eagle with kindling eye spreading his wings ready for instant flight in case the attack should prove successful; the hawk emerging with a struggling fish in his talons, and proud flight; the eagle launching himself in pursuit; the wonderful wing-work in the sky, the fish hawk, though encumbered with his prey, circling higher, higher, striving hard to keep above the robber eagle; the eagle at length soaring above him, compelling him with a cry of despair to drop his hard-won prey; then the eagle steadying himself for a moment to take aim, descending swift as a lightning-bolt, and seizing the falling fish before it reached the sea.

Not less exciting and memorable was Audubon's wonderful story of the passenger pigeon, a beautiful bird flying in vast flocks that darkened the sky like clouds, countless millions assembling to rest and sleep and rear their young in certain forests, miles in length and breadth, fifty or a hundred nests on a single tree; the overloaded branches bending low and often breaking; the farmers gathering from far and near, beating down countless thousands of the young and old birds from their nests and roosts with long poles at night, and in the morning driving their bands of hogs, some of them brought from farms a hundred miles distant, to fatten on the dead and wounded covering the ground.

In another of our reading-lessons some of the American forests were described. The most interesting of the trees to us boys was the sugar maple, and soon after we had learned this sweet story we heard everybody talking about the discovery of gold in the same wonder-filled country.

One night, when David and I were at grandfather's fireside solemnly learning our lessons as usual, my father came in with news, the most wonderful, most glorious, that wild boys ever heard. "Bairns," he said, "you needna learn your lessons the nicht, for we're gan to America the morn!" No more grammar, but boundless woods full of mysterious good things; trees full of sugar, growing in ground full of gold; hawks, eagles, pigeons, filling the sky; millions of birds' nests, and no gamekeepers to stop us in all the wild, happy land. We were utterly, blindly glorious. After father left the room, grandfather gave David and me a gold coin apiece for a keepsake, and looked very serious, for he was about to be deserted in his lonely old age. And when we in fullness of young joy spoke of what we were going to do, of the wonderful birds and their nests that we should find, the sugar and gold, etc., and promised to send him a big box full of that tree sugar packed in gold from the glorious paradise over the sea, poor lonely grandfather, about to be forsaken, looked with downcast eyes on the floor and said in a low, trembling, troubled voice, "Ah, poor laddies, poor laddies, you'll find something else ower the sea forbye gold and sugar, birds' nests and freedom fra lessons and schools. You'll find plenty hard, hard work." And so we did. But nothing he could say could cloud our joy or abate the fire of youthful, hopeful, fearless adventure. Nor could we in the midst of such measureless excitement see or feel the shadows and sorrows of his darkening old age. To my schoolmates, met that night on the street, I shouted the glorious news, "I'm gan to Amaraka the morn!" None could believe it. I said, "Weel, just you see if I am at the skule the morn!"

Next morning we went by rail to Glasgow and thence joyfully sailed away from beloved Scotland, flying to our fortunes on the wings of the winds, care-free as thistle seeds. We could not then know what we were leaving, what we were to encounter in the New World, nor what our gains were likely to be. We were too young and full of hope for fear or regret, but not too young to look forward with eager enthusiasm to the wonderful schoolless bookless American wilderness. Even the natural heart-pain of parting from grandfather and grandmother Gilrye, who loved us so well, and from mother and sisters and brother was quickly quenched in young joy. Father took with him only my sister Sarah (thirteen years of age), myself (eleven), and brother David (nine), leaving my eldest sister, Margaret, and the three youngest of the family, Daniel, Mary, and Anna, with mother, to join us after a farm had been found in the wilderness and a comfortable house made to receive them.

In crossing the Atlantic before the days of steamships, or even the American clippers, the voyages made in old-fashioned sailing-vessels were very long. Ours was six weeks and three days. But because we had no lessons to get, that long voyage had not a dull moment for us boys. Father and sister Sarah, with most of the old folk, stayed below in rough weather, groaning in the miseries of seasickness, many of the passengers wishing they had never ventured in "the auld rockin' creel," as they called our bluff-bowed, wave-beating ship, and, when the weather was moderately calm, singing songs in the evenings,— "The Youthful Sailor Frank and Bold," "Oh, why left I my hame, why did I cross the deep," etc. But no matter how much the old tub tossed about and battered the waves, we were on deck every day, not in the least seasick, watching the sailors at their rope-hauling and climbing work; joining in their songs, learning the names of the ropes and sails, and helping them as far as they would let us; playing games with other boys in calm weather when the deck was dry, and in stormy weather rejoicing in sympathy with the big curly-topped waves.

The captain occasionally called David and me into his cabin and asked us about our schools, handed us books to read, and seemed surprised to find that Scotch boys could read and pronounce English with perfect accent and knew so much Latin and French. In Scotch schools only pure English was taught, although not a word of English was spoken out of school. All through life, however well educated, the

Scotch spoke Scotch among their own folk, except at times when unduly excited on the only two subjects on which Scotchmen get much excited, namely religion and politics. So long as the controversy went on with fairly level temper, only gude braid Scots was used, but if one became angry, as was likely to happen, then he immediately began speaking severely correct English, while his antagonist, drawing himself up, would say: "Weel, there's na use pursuing this subject ony further, for I see ye hae gotten to your English."

As we neared the shore of the great new land, with what eager wonder we watched the whales and dolphins and porpoises and seabirds, and made the good-natured sailors teach us their names and tell us stories about them!

There were quite a large number of emigrants aboard, many of them newly married couples, and the advantages of the different parts of the New World they expected to settle in were often discussed. My father started with the intention of going to the backwoods of Upper Canada. Before the end of the voyage, however, he was persuaded that the States offered superior advantages, especially Wisconsin and Michigan, where the land was said to be as good as in Canada and far more easily brought under cultivation; for in Canada the woods were so close and heavy that a man might wear out his life in getting a few acres cleared of trees and stumps. So he changed his mind and concluded to go to one of the Western States.

On our wavering westward way a grain-dealer in Buffalo told father that most of the wheat he handled came from Wisconsin; and this influential information finally determined my father's choice. At Milwaukee a farmer who had come in from the country near Fort Winnebago with a load of wheat agreed to haul us and our formidable load of stuff to a little town called Kingston for thirty dollars. On that hundred-mile journey, just after the spring thaw, the roads over the prairies were heavy and miry, causing no end of lamentation, for we often got stuck in the mud, and the poor farmer sadly declared that never, never again would he be tempted to try to haul such a cruel, heart-breaking, wagon-breaking, horse-killing load, no, not for a hundred dollars.

In leaving Scotland, father, like many other homeseekers, burdened himself with far too much luggage, as if all America were still a wilderness in which little or nothing could be bought. One of his big iron-bound boxes must have weighed about four hundred pounds, for it contained an old-fashioned beam-scales with a complete set of cast-iron counterweights, two of them fifty-six pounds each, a twenty-eight, and so on down to a single pound. Also a lot of iron wedges, carpenter's tools, and so forth, and at Buffalo, as if on the very edge of the wilderness, he gladly added to his burden a big cast-iron stove with pots and pans, provisions enough for a long siege, and a scythe and cumbersome cradle for cutting wheat, all of which he succeeded in landing in the primeval Wisconsin woods.

A land-agent at Kingston gave father a note to a farmer by the name of Alexander Gray, who lived on the border of the settled part of the country, knew the section-lines, and would probably help him to find a good place for a farm. So father went away to spy out the land, and in the mean time left us children in Kingston in a rented room. It took us less than an hour to get acquainted with some of the boys in the village; we challenged them to wrestle, run races, climb trees, etc., and in a day or two we felt at home, carefree and happy, notwithstanding our family was so widely divided. When father returned he told us that he had found fine land for a farm in sunny open woods on the side of a lake, and that a team of three yoke of oxen with a big wagon was coming to haul us to Mr. Gray's place.

We enjoyed the strange ten-mile ride through the woods very much, wondering how the great oxen could be so strong and wise and tame as to pull so heavy a load with no other harness than a chain and a crooked piece of wood on their necks, and how they could sway so obediently to right and left past roadside trees and stumps when the driver said *haw* and *gee*. At Mr. Gray's house, father again left us for a few days to build a shanty on the quarter-section he had selected four or five miles to the westward. In the mean while we enjoyed our freedom as usual, wandering in the fields and meadows, looking at the trees and flowers, snakes and birds and squirrels. With the help of the nearest neighbors the little shanty was built in less than a day after the rough bur-oak logs for the walls and the white-oak boards for the floor and roof were got together.

To this charming hut, in the sunny woods, overlooking a flowery glacier meadow and a lake rimmed with white water-lilies, we were hauled by an ox-team across trackless carex swamps and low rolling hills sparsely dotted with round-headed oaks. Just as we arrived at the shanty, before we had time to look at it or the scenery about it, David and I jumped down in a hurry off the load of household goods, for we had discovered a blue jay's nest, and in a minute or so we were up the tree beside it, feasting our eyes on the beautiful green eggs and beautiful birds,—our first memorable discovery. The handsome birds had not seen Scotch boys before and made a desperate screaming as if we were robbers like themselves; though we left the eggs untouched, feeling that we were already beginning to get rich, and wondering how many more nests we should find in the grand sunny woods. Then we ran along the brow of the hill that the shanty stood on, and down to the meadow, searching the trees and grass tufts and bushes, and soon discovered a bluebird's and a woodpecker's nest, and began an acquaintance with the frogs and snakes and turtles in the creeks and springs.

Muir's Lake (Fountain Lake) and the Garden

This sudden plash into pure wildness—baptism in Nature's warm heart—how utterly happy it made us! Nature streaming into us, wooingly teaching her wonderful glowing lessons, so unlike the dismal grammar ashes and cinders so long thrashed into us. Here without knowing it we still were at school; every wild lesson a love lesson, not whipped but charmed into us. Oh, that glorious Wisconsin wilderness! Everything new and pure in the very prime of the spring when Nature's pulses were beating highest and mysteriously keeping time with our own! Young hearts, young leaves, flowers, animals, the winds and the streams and the sparkling lake, all wildly, gladly rejoicing together!

Next morning, when we climbed to the precious jay nest to take another admiring look at the eggs, we found it empty. Not a shell-fragment was left, and we wondered how in the world the birds were able to carry off their thin-shelled eggs either in their bills or in their feet without breaking them, and how they could be kept warm while a new nest was being built. Well, I am still asking these questions. When I was on the Harriman Expedition I asked Robert Ridgway, the eminent ornithologist, how these sudden flittings were accomplished, and he frankly confessed that he didn't know, but guessed that jays and many other birds carried their eggs in their mouths; and when I objected that a jay's mouth seemed too small to hold its eggs, he replied that birds' mouths were larger than the narrowness of their bills indicated. Then I asked him what he thought they did with the eggs while a new nest was being prepared. He didn't know; neither do I to this day. A specimen of the many puzzling problems presented to the naturalist.

We soon found many more nests belonging to birds that were not half so suspicious. The handsome and notorious blue jay plunders the nests of other birds and of course he could not trust us. Almost all the others—brown thrushes, bluebirds, song sparrows, kingbirds, hen-hawks, nighthawks, whip-poor-wills, woodpeckers, etc.—simply tried to avoid being seen, to draw or drive us away, or paid no attention to us.

We used to wonder how the woodpeckers could bore holes so perfectly round, true mathematical circles. We ourselves could not have done it even with gouges and chisels. We loved to watch them feeding their young, and wondered how they could glean food enough for so many clamorous, hungry, unsatisfiable babies, and how they managed to give each one its share; for after the young grew strong, one would get his head out of the door-hole and try to hold possession of it to meet the food-laden parents. How hard they worked to support their families, especially the red-headed and speckledy woodpeckers and flickers; digging, hammering on scaly bark and decaying trunks and branches from dawn to dark, coming and going at intervals of a few minutes all the livelong day!

We discovered a hen-hawk's nest on the top of a tall oak thirty or forty rods from the shanty and approached it cautiously. One of the pair always kept watch, soaring in wide circles high above the tree, and when we attempted to climb it, the big dangerous-looking bird came swooping down at us and drove us away.

We greatly admired the plucky kingbird. In Scotland our great ambition was to be good fighters, and we admired this quality in the handsome little chattering flycatcher that whips all the other birds. He was particularly angry when plundering jays and hawks came near his home, and took pains to thrash them not only away from the nest-tree but out of the neighborhood. The nest was usually built on a bur oak near a meadow where insects were abundant, and where no undesirable visitor could approach without being discovered. When a hen-hawk hove in sight, the male immediately set off after him, and it was ridiculous to see that great, strong bird hurrying away as fast as his clumsy wings would carry him, as soon as he saw the little, waspish kingbird coming. But the kingbird easily overtook him, flew just a few feet above him, and with a lot of chattering, scolding notes kept diving and striking him on the back of the head until tired; then he alighted to rest on the hawk's broad shoulders, still scolding and chattering as he rode along, like an angry boy pouring out vials of wrath. Then, up and at him again with his sharp bill; and after he had thus driven and ridden his big enemy a mile or so from the nest, he went home to his mate, chuckling and bragging as if trying to tell her what a wonderful fellow he was.

This first spring, while some of the birds were still building their nests and very few young ones had yet tried to fly, father hired a Yankee to assist in clearing eight or ten acres of the best ground for a field. We found new wonders every day and often had to call on this Yankee to solve puzzling questions. We asked him one day if there was any bird in America that the kingbird couldn't whip. What about the sandhill crane? Could he whip that long-legged, long-billed fellow?

"A crane never goes near kingbirds' nests or notices so small a bird," he said, "and therefore there could be no fighting between them." So we hastily concluded that our hero could whip every bird in the country except perhaps the sandhill crane.

We never tired listening to the wonderful whip-poor-will. One came every night about dusk and sat on a log about twenty or thirty feet from our cabin door and began shouting "Whip poor Will! Whip poor Will!" with loud emphatic earnestness. "What's that? What's that?" we cried when this startling visitor first announced himself. "What do you call it?"

"Why, it's telling you its name," said the Yankee. "Don't you hear it and what he wants you to do? He says his name is 'Poor Will' and he wants you to whip him, and you may if you are able to catch him." Poor Will seemed the most wonderful of all the strange creatures we had seen. What a wild, strong, bold voice he had, unlike any other we had ever heard on sea or land!

A near relative, the bull-bat, or nighthawk, seemed hardly less wonderful. Towards evening scattered flocks kept the sky lively as they circled around on their long wings a hundred feet or more above the ground, hunting moths and beetles, interrupting their rather slow but strong, regular wing-beats at short intervals with quick quivering strokes while uttering keen, squeaky cries something like *pfee, pfee,* and every now and then diving nearly to the ground with a loud ripping, bellowing sound, like bull-roaring, suggesting its name; then turning and gliding swiftly up again. These fine wild gray birds, about the size of a pigeon, lay their two eggs on bare ground without anything like a nest or even a concealing bush or grass-tuft. Nevertheless they are not easily seen, for they are colored like the ground. While sitting on their eggs, they depend so much upon not being noticed that if you are walking rapidly ahead they allow you to step within an inch or two of them without flinching. But if they see by your looks that you have discovered them, they leave their eggs or young, and, like a good many other birds, pretend that they are sorely wounded, fluttering and rolling over on the ground and gasping as if dying, to draw you away. When pursued we were surprised to find that just when we were on the point of overtaking them they were always able to flutter a few yards farther, until they had led us about a quarter of a mile from the nest; then, suddenly getting well, they quietly flew home by a roundabout way to their precious babies or eggs, o'er a' the ills of life victorious, bad boys among the worst. The Yankee took particular pleasure in encouraging us to pursue them.

Everything about us was so novel and wonderful that we could hardly believe our senses except when hungry or while father was thrashing us. When we first saw Fountain Lake Meadow, on a sultry evening, sprinkled with millions of lightning-bugs throbbing with light, the effect was so strange and beautiful that it seemed far too marvelous to be real. Looking from our shanty on the hill, I thought that the whole wonderful fairy show must be in my eyes; for only in fighting, when my eyes were struck, had I ever seen anything in the least like it. But when I asked my brother if he saw anything strange in the meadow he said, "Yes, it's all covered with shaky fire-sparks." Then I guessed that it might be something outside of us, and applied to our all-knowing Yankee to explain it. "Oh, it's nothing but lightnin'-bugs," he said, and kindly led us down the hill to the edge of the fiery meadow, caught a few of the wonderful bugs, dropped them into a cup, and carried them to the shanty, where we watched them throbbing and flashing out their mysterious light at regular intervals, as if each little passionate glow were caused by the beating of a heart. Once I saw a splendid display of glow-worm light in the foothills of the Himalayas, north of Calcutta, but glorious as it appeared in pure starry radiance, it was far less impressive than the extravagant abounding, quivering, dancing fire on our Wisconsin meadow.

Partridge drumming was another great marvel. When I first heard the low, soft, solemn sound I thought it must be made by some strange disturbance in my head or stomach, but as all seemed serene within, I asked David whether he heard anything queer. "Yes," he said, "I hear something saying *boomp, boomp, boomp,* and I'm wondering at it." Then I was half satisfied that the source of the mysterious sound must be in something outside of us, coming perhaps from the ground or from some ghost or bogie or woodland fairy. Only after long watching and listening did we at last discover it in the wings of the plump brown bird.

The love-song of the common jack snipe seemed not a whit less mysterious than partridge drumming. It was usually heard on cloudy evenings, a strange, unearthly, winnowing, spiritlike sound, yet easily heard at a distance of a third of a mile. Our sharp eyes soon detected the bird while making it, as it circled high in the air over the meadow with wonderfully strong and rapid wing-beats, suddenly descending and rising, again and again, in deep, wide loops; the tones being very low and smooth at the beginning of the descent, rapidly increasing to a curious little whirling storm-roar at the bottom, and gradually fading lower and lower until the top was reached. It was long, however, before we identified this mysterious wing-singer as the little brown jack snipe that we knew so well and had so often watched as he silently probed the mud around the edges of our meadow stream and spring-holes, and made short zigzag flights over the grass uttering only little short, crisp quacks and chucks.

The love-songs of the frogs seemed hardly less wonderful than those of the birds, their musical notes varying from the sweet, tranquil, soothing peeping and purring of the hylas to the awfully deep low-bass blunt bellowing of the bullfrogs. Some of the smaller species have wonderfully clear, sharp voices and told us their good Bible names in musical tones about as plainly as the whip-poor-will. *Isaac, Isaac; Yacob, Yacob; Israel, Israel;* shouted in sharp, ringing, far-reaching tones, as if they had all been to school and severely drilled in elocution. In the still, warm evenings, big bunchy bullfrogs bellowed, *Drunk! Drunk! Drunk! Jug o' rum! Jug o' rum!* and early in the spring, countless thousands of the commonest species, up to the throat in cold water, sang in concert, making a mass of music, such as it was, loud enough to be heard at a distance of more than half a mile.

We reveled in the glory of the sky scenery as well as that of the woods and meadows and rushy, lily-bordered lakes. The great thunderstorms in particular interested us, so unlike any seen in Scotland, exciting awful, wondering admiration. Gazing awe-stricken, we watched the upbuilding of the sublime cloud-mountains,—glowing, sun-beaten pearl and alabaster cumuli, glorious in beauty and majesty and looking so firm and lasting that birds, we thought, might build their nests amid their downy bosses; the black-browed storm-clouds marching in awful grandeur across the landscape, trailing broad gray sheets of hail and rain like vast cataracts, and ever and anon flashing down vivid zigzag lightning followed by terrible crashing thunder. We saw several trees shattered, and one of them, a punky old oak, was set on fire, while we wondered why all the trees and everybody and everything did not share the same fate, for oftentimes the whole sky blazed. After sultry storm days, many of the nights were darkened by smooth black apparently structureless cloud-mantles which at short intervals were illumined with startling suddenness to a fiery glow by quick, quivering lightning-flashes, revealing the landscape in almost noonday brightness, to be instantly quenched in solid blackness.

But those first days and weeks of unmixed enjoyment and freedom, reveling in the wonderful wildness about us, were soon to be mingled with the hard work of making a farm. I was first put to burning brush in clearing land for the plough. Those magnificent brush fires with great white hearts and red flames, the first big, wild outdoor fires I had ever seen, were wonderful sights for young eyes. Again and again, when they were burning fiercest so that we could hardly approach near enough to throw on another branch, father put them to awfully practical use as warning lessons, comparing their heat with that of hell, and the branches with bad boys. "Now, John," he would say,—"now, John, just think what an awful thing it would be to be thrown into that fire:—and then think of hellfire, that is so many times hotter. Into that fire all bad boys, with

sinners of every sort who disobey God, will be cast as we are casting branches into this brush fire, and although suffering so much,
their sufferings will never never end, because neither the fire nor the
sinners can die." But those terrible fire lessons quickly faded away in
the blithe wilderness air; for no fire can be hotter than the heavenly
fire of faith and hope that burns in every healthy boy's heart.

Soon after our arrival in the woods some one added a cat and
puppy to the animals father had bought. The cat soon had kittens,
and it was interesting to watch her feeding, protecting, and training
them. After they were able to leave their nest and play, she went
out hunting and brought in many kinds of birds and squirrels for
them, mostly ground squirrels (spermophiles), called "gophers" in
Wisconsin.

When she got within a dozen yards or so of the shanty, she
announced her approach by a peculiar call, and the sleeping kittens
immediately bounced up and ran to meet her, all racing for the first
bite of they knew not what, and we too ran to see what she brought.
She then lay down a few minutes to rest and enjoy the enjoyment
of her feasting family, and again vanished in the grass and flowers,
coming and going every half-hour or so. Sometimes she brought in
birds that we had never seen before, and occasionally a flying squirrel, chipmunk, or big fox squirrel. We were just old enough, David
and I, to regard all these creatures as wonders, the strange inhabitants of our new world.

The pup was a common cur, though very uncommon to us, a
black and white short-haired mongrel that we named "Watch." We
always gave him a pan of milk in the evening just before we knelt
in family worship, while daylight still lingered in the shanty. And,
instead of attending to the prayers, I too often studied the small
wild creatures playing around us. Field mice scampered about the
cabin as though it had been built for them alone, and their performances were very amusing. About dusk, on one of the calm, sultry
nights so grateful to moths and beetles, when the puppy was lapping his milk, and we were on our knees, in through the door came
a heavy broad-shouldered beetle about as big as a mouse, and after
it had droned and boomed round the cabin two or three times, the

pan of milk, showing white in the gloaming, caught its eyes, and, taking good aim, it alighted with a slanting, glinting plash in the middle of the pan like a duck alighting in a lake. Baby Watch, having never before seen anything like that beetle, started back, gazing in dumb astonishment and fear at the black sprawling monster trying to swim. Recovering somewhat from his fright, he began to bark at the creature, and ran round and round his milk-pan, wouf-woufing, gurring, growling, like an old dog barking at a wild-cat or a bear. The natural astonishment and curiosity of that boy dog getting his first entomological lesson in this wonderful world was so immoderately funny that I had great difficulty in keeping from laughing out loud.

Snapping turtles were common throughout the woods, and we were delighted to find that they would snap at a stick and hang on like bull-dogs; and we amused ourselves by introducing Watch to them, enjoying his curious behavior and theirs in getting acquainted with each other. One day we assisted one of the smallest of the turtles to get a good grip of poor Watch's ear. Then away he rushed, holding his head sidewise, yelping and terror-stricken, with the strange buglike reptile biting hard and clinging fast,—a shameful amusement even for wild boys.

As a playmate Watch was too serious, though he learned more than any stranger would judge him capable of, was a bold, faithful watch-dog, and in his prime a grand fighter, able to whip all the other dogs in the neighborhood. Comparing him with ourselves, we soon learned that although he could not read books he could read faces, was a good judge of character, always knew what was going on and what we were about to do, and liked to help us. We could run nearly as fast as he could, see about as far, and perhaps hear as well, but in sense of smell his nose was incomparably better than ours. One sharp winter morning when the ground was covered with snow, I noticed that when he was yawning and stretching himself after leaving his bed he suddenly caught the scent of something that excited him, went round the corner of the house, and looked intently to the westward across a tongue of land that we called West Bank, eagerly questioning the air with quivering nostrils, and bristling up as though he felt sure that there was something dangerous in that direction and had actually caught sight of it. Then he ran toward the Bank, and I followed him, curious to see what his nose had discovered. The top of the Bank commanded a view of the north end of our lake and meadow, and when we got there we saw an Indian hunter with a long spear, going from one muskrat cabin to another, approaching cautiously, careful to make no noise, and then suddenly thrusting his spear down through the house. If well aimed, the spear went through the poor beaver rat as it lay cuddled up in the snug nest it had made for itself in the fall with so much far-seeing care, and when the hunter felt the spear quivering, he dug down the mossy hut with his tomahawk and secured his prey,—the flesh for food, and the skin to sell for a dime or so. This was a clear object lesson on dogs' keenness of scent. That Indian was more than half a mile away across a wooded ridge. Had the hunter been a white man, I suppose Watch would not have noticed him.

When he was about six or seven years old, he not only became cross, so that he would do only what he liked, but he fell on evil ways, and was accused by the neighbors who had settled around us of catching and devouring whole broods of chickens, some of them only a day or two out of the shell. We never imagined he would do anything so grossly undoglike. He never did at home. But several of the neighbors declared over and over again that they had caught him in the act, and insisted that he must be shot. At last, in spite of tearful protests, he was condemned and executed. Father examined the poor fellow's stomach in search of sure evidence, and discovered the heads of eight chickens that he had devoured at his last meal. So poor Watch was killed simply because his taste for chickens was too much like our own. Think of the millions of squabs that preaching, praying men and women kill and eat, with all sorts of other animals great and small, young and old, while eloquently discoursing on the coming of the blessed peaceful, bloodless millennium! Think of the passenger pigeons that fifty or sixty years ago filled the woods and sky over half the continent, now exterminated by beating down the young from the nests together with the brooding parents, before they could try their wonderful wings; by trapping them in nets, feeding them to hogs, etc. None of our fellow mortals is safe who eats what we eat, who in any way interferes with our pleasures, or who may be used for work or food, clothing or ornament, or mere cruel, sportish amusement. Fortunately many are too small to be seen, and therefore enjoy life beyond our reach. And in looking through God's great stone books made up of records reaching back millions and millions of years, it is a great comfort to learn that vast multitudes of creatures, great and small and infinite in number, lived and had a good time in God's love before man was created.

The old Scotch fashion of whipping for every act of disobedience or of simple, playful forgetfulness was still kept up in the wilderness, and of course many of those whippings fell upon me. Most of them were outrageously severe, and utterly barren of fun. But here is one that was nearly all fun.

Father was busy hauling lumber for the frame house that was to be got ready for the arrival of my mother, sisters, and brother, left behind in Scotland. One morning, when he was ready to start for another load, his ox-whip was not to be found. He asked me if I knew anything about it. I told him I didn't know where it was, but Scotch conscience compelled me to confess that when I was playing with it I had tied it to Watch's tail, and that he ran away, dragging it through the grass, and came back without it. "It must have slipped off his tail," I said, and so I didn't know where it was. This honest, straightforward little story made father so angry that he exclaimed with heavy, foreboding emphasis: "The very deevil's in that boy!" David, who had been playing with me and was perhaps about as responsible for the loss of the whip as I was, said never a word, for he was always prudent enough to hold his tongue when the parental weather was stormy, and so escaped nearly all punishment. And, strange to say, this time I also escaped, all except a terrible scolding, though the thrashing weather seemed darker than ever. As if unwilling to let the sun see the shameful job, father took me into the cabin where the storm was to fall, and sent David to the woods for a switch. While he was out selecting the switch, father put in the spare time sketching my play-wickedness in awful colors, and of course referred again and again to the place prepared for bad boys. In the midst of this terrible word-storm, dreading most the impending thrashing, I whimpered that I was only playing because I couldn't help it; didn't know I was doing wrong; wouldn't do it again, and so forth. After this miserable dialogue was about exhausted, father became impatient at my brother for taking so long to find the switch; and so was I, for I wanted to have the thing over and done with. At last, in came David, a picture of open-hearted innocence, solemnly dragging a young bur-oak sapling, and handed the end of it to father, saying it was the best switch he could find. It was an awfully heavy one, about two and a half inches thick at the butt and ten feet long, almost big enough for a fence-pole. There wasn't room enough in the cabin to swing it, and the moment I saw it I burst out laughing in the midst of my fears. But father failed to see the fun and was very angry at David, heaved the bur-oak outside and passionately demanded his reason for fetching "sic a muckle rail like that instead o' a switch? Do ye ca' that a switch? I have a gude mind to thrash you insteed o' John." David, with demure, downcast eyes, looked preternaturally righteous, but as usual prudently answered never a word.

It was a hard job in those days to bring up Scotch boys in the way they should go; and poor overworked father was determined to do it if enough of the right kind of switches could be found. But this time, as the sun was getting high, he hitched up old Tom and Jerry and made haste to the Kingston lumber-yard, leaving me unscathed and as innocently wicked as ever; for hardly had father got fairly out of sight among the oaks and hickories, ere all our troubles, hell-threatenings, and exhortations were forgotten in the fun we had lassoing a stubborn old sow and laboriously trying to teach her to go reasonably steady in rope harness. She was the first hog that father bought to stock the farm, and we boys regarded her as a very wonderful beast. In a few weeks she had a lot of pigs, and of all the queer, funny, animal children we had yet seen, none amused us more. They were so comic in size and shape, in their gait and gestures, their merry sham fights, and the false alarms they got up for the fun of scampering back to their mother and begging her in most persuasive little squeals to lie down and give them a drink.

After her darling short-snouted babies were about a month old, she took them out to the woods and gradually roamed farther and farther from the shanty in search of acorns and roots. One afternoon we heard a rifle-shot, a very noticeable thing, as we had no near neighbors, as yet. We thought it must have been fired by an Indian on the trail that followed the right bank of the Fox River between Portage and Packwaukee Lake and passed our shanty at a distance of about three quarters of a mile. Just a few minutes after that shot was heard, along came the poor mother rushing up to the shanty for protection, with her pigs, all out of breath and terror-stricken. One of them was missing, and we supposed of course that an Indian had shot it for food. Next day, I discovered a blood-puddle where the Indian trail crossed the outlet of our lake. One of father's hired men told us that the Indians thought nothing of levying this sort of blackmail whenever they were hungry. The solemn awe and fear in the eyes of that old mother and those little pigs I never can forget; it was as unmistakable and deadly a fear as I ever saw expressed by any human eye, and corroborates in no uncertain way the oneness of all of us.

Life On A Wisconsin Farm

∾

Coming direct from school in Scotland while we were still hopefully ignorant and far from tame,—notwithstanding the unnatural profusion of teaching and thrashing lavished upon us,—getting acquainted with the animals about us was a never-failing source of wonder and delight. At first my father, like nearly all the backwoods settlers, bought a yoke of oxen to do the farm work, and as field after field was cleared, the number was gradually increased until we had five yoke. These wise, patient, plodding animals did all the ploughing, logging, hauling, and hard work of every sort for the first four or five years, and, never having seen oxen before, we looked at them with the same eager freshness of conception as we did at the wild animals. We worked with them, sympathized with them in their rest and toil and play, and thus learned to know them far better than we should had we been only trained scientific naturalists. We soon learned that each ox and cow and calf had individual character. Old white-faced Buck, one of the second yoke of oxen we owned, was a notably sagacious fellow. He seemed to reason sometimes almost like ourselves. In the fall we fed the cattle lots of pumpkins and had to split them open so that mouthfuls could be readily broken off. But Buck never waited for us to come to his help. The others, when they were hungry and impatient, tried to break through the hard rind with their teeth, but seldom with success if the pumpkin was full grown. Buck never wasted time in this mumbling, slavering way, but crushed them with his head. He went to the pile, picked out a good one, like a boy choosing an orange or apple, rolled it down on to the open ground, deliberately kneeled in front of it, placed his broad, flat brow on top of it, brought his weight hard down and crushed it, then quietly arose and went on with his meal in comfort.

Some would call this "instinct," as if so-called "blind instinct" must necessarily make an ox stand on its head to break pumpkins when its teeth got sore, or when nobody came with an axe to split them. Another fine ox showed his skill when hungry by opening all the fences that stood in his way to the corn-fields.

The humanity we found in them came partly through the expression of their eyes when tired, their tones of voice when hungry and calling for food, their patient plodding and pulling in hot weather, their long-drawn-out sighing breath when exhausted and suffering like ourselves, and their enjoyment of rest with the same grateful looks as ours. We recognized their kinship also by their yawning like ourselves when sleepy and evidently enjoying the same peculiar pleasure at the roots of their jaws; by the way they stretched themselves in the morning after a good rest; by learning languages,—Scotch, English, Irish, French, Dutch,—a smattering of each as required in the faithful service they so willingly, wisely rendered; by their intelligent, alert curiosity, manifested in listening to strange sounds; their love of play; the attachments they made; and their mourning, long continued, when a companion was killed.

When we went to Portage, our nearest town, about ten or twelve miles from the farm, it would oftentimes be late before we got back, and in the summer-time, in sultry, rainy weather, the clouds were full of sheet lightning which every minute or two would suddenly illumine the landscape, revealing all its features, the hills and valleys, meadows and trees, about as fully and clearly as the noonday sunshine; then as suddenly the glorious light would be quenched, making the darkness seem denser than before. On such nights the cattle had to find the way home without any help from us, but they never got off the track, for they followed it by scent like dogs. Once, father, returning late from Portage or Kingston, compelled Tom and Jerry, our first oxen, to leave the dim track, imagining they must be going wrong. At last they stopped and refused to go farther. Then father unhitched them from the wagon, took hold of Tom's tail, and was thus led straight to the shanty. Next morning he set out to seek his wagon and found it on the brow of a steep hill above an impassable swamp. We learned less from the cows, because we did not enter so far into their lives, working with them, suffering heat and cold, hunger and thirst, and almost deadly weariness with them; but none with natural charity could fail to sympathize with them in their love for their calves, and to feel that it in no way differed from the divine mother-love of a woman in thoughtful, self-sacrificing care; for they would brave every danger, giving their lives for their offspring. Nor could we fail to sympathize with their awkward, blunt-nosed baby calves, with such beautiful, wondering eyes looking out on the world and slowly getting acquainted with things, all so strange to them, and awkwardly learning to use their legs, and play and fight.

Before leaving Scotland, father promised us a pony to ride when we got to America, and we saw to it that this promise was not forgotten. Only a week or two after our arrival in the woods he bought us a little Indian pony for thirteen dollars from a store-keeper in Kingston who had obtained him from a Winnebago or Menominee Indian in trade for goods. He was a stout handsome bay with long black mane and tail, and, though he was only two years old, the Indians had already taught him to carry all sorts of burdens, to stand without being tied, to go anywhere over all sorts of ground fast or slow, and to jump and swim and fear nothing,—a truly wonderful creature, strangely different from shy, skittish, nervous, superstitious civilized beasts. We turned him loose, and, strange to say, he never ran away from us or refused to be caught, but behaved as if he had known Scotch boys all his life; probably because we were about as wild as young Indians.

One day when father happened to have a little leisure, he said, "Noo, bairns, rin doon the meadow and get your powny and learn to ride him." So we led him out to a smooth place near an Indian mound back of the shanty, where father directed us to begin. I mounted for the first memorable lesson, crossed the mound, and set out at a slow walk along the wagon-track made in hauling lumber; then father shouted: "Whup him up, John, whup him up! Make him gallop; gallopin' is easier and better than walkin' or trottin'." Jack was willing, and away he sped at a good fast gallop. I managed to keep my balance fairly well by holding fast to the mane, but could not keep from bumping up and down, for I was plump and elastic and so was Jack; therefore about half of the time I was in the air.

After a quarter of a mile or so of this curious transportation, I cried, "Whoa, Jack!" The wonderful creature seemed to understand Scotch, for he stopped so suddenly I flew over his head, but he stood perfectly still as if that flying method of dismounting were the regular way. Jumping on again, I bumped and bobbed back along the grassy, flowery track, over the Indian mound, cried, "Whoa, Jack!" flew over his head, and alighted in father's arms as gracefully as if it were all intended for circus work.

After going over the course five or six times in the same free, picturesque style, I gave place to brother David, whose performances were much like my own. In a few weeks, however, or a month, we were taking adventurous rides more than a mile long out to a big meadow frequented by sandhill cranes, and returning safely with wonderful stories of the great long-legged birds we had seen, and how on the whole journey away and back we had fallen off only five or six times. Gradually we learned to gallop through the woods without roads of any sort, bareback and without rope or bridle, guiding only by leaning from side to side or by slight knee pressure. In this free way we used to amuse ourselves, riding at full speed across a big "kettle" that was on our farm, without holding on by either mane or tail.

These so-called "kettles" were formed by the melting of large detached blocks of ice that had been buried in moraine material thousands of years ago when the ice-sheet that covered all this region was receding. As the buried ice melted, of course the moraine material above and about it fell in, forming hopper-shaped hollows, while the grass growing on their sides and around them prevented the rain and wind from filling them up. The one we performed in was perhaps seventy or eighty feet wide and twenty or thirty feet deep; and without a saddle or hold of any kind it was not easy to keep from slipping over Jack's head in diving into it, or over his tail climbing out. This was fine sport on the long summer Sundays when we were able to steal away before meeting-time without being seen. We got very warm and red at it, and oftentimes poor Jack, dripping with sweat like his riders, seemed to have been boiled in that kettle.

In Scotland we had often been admonished to be bold, and this advice we passed on to Jack, who had already got many a wild lesson from Indian boys. Once, when teaching him to jump muddy streams, I made him try the creek in our meadow at a place where it is about twelve feet wide. He jumped bravely enough, but came down with a grand splash hardly more than halfway over. The water was only about a foot in depth, but the black vegetable mud half afloat was unfathomable. I managed to wallow ashore, but poor Jack sank deeper and deeper until only his head was visible in the black abyss, and his Indian fortitude was desperately tried. His foundering so suddenly in the treacherous gulf recalled the story of the Abbot of Aberbrothok's bell, which went down with a gurgling sound while bubbles rose and burst around. I had to go to father for help. He tied a long hemp rope brought from Scotland around Jack's neck, and Tom and Jerry seemed to have all they could do to pull him out. After which I got a solemn scolding for asking the "puir beast to jump intil sic a saft bottomless place."

We moved into our frame house in the fall, when mother with the rest of the family arrived from Scotland, and, when the winter snow began to fly, the bur-oak shanty was made into a stable for Jack. Father told us that good meadow hay was all he required, but we fed him corn, lots of it, and he grew very frisky and fat. About the middle of winter his long hair was full of dust and, as we thought, required washing. So, without taking the frosty weather into account, we gave him a thorough soap and water scouring, and as we failed to get him rubbed dry, a row of icicles formed under his belly. Father happened to see him in this condition and angrily asked what we had been about. We said Jack was dirty and we had washed him to make him healthy. He told us we ought to be ashamed of ourselves, "soaking the puir beast in cauld water at this time o' year"; that when we wanted to clean him we should have sense enough to use the brush and curry-comb.

In summer Dave or I had to ride after the cows every evening about sundown, and Jack got so accustomed to bringing in the drove that

Our first Wisconsin Home, built in 1849

when we happened to be a few minutes late he used to go off alone at the regular time and bring them home at a gallop. It used to make father very angry to see Jack chasing the cows like a shepherd dog, running from one to the other and giving each a bite on the rump to keep them on the run, flying before him as if pursued by wolves. Father would declare at times that the wicked beast had the deevil in him and would be the death of the cattle. The corral and barn were just at the foot of a hill, and he made a great display of the drove on the home stretch as they walloped down that hill with their tails on end.

One evening when the pell-mell Wild West show was at its wildest, it made father so extravagantly mad that he ordered me to "Shoot Jack!" I went to the house and brought the gun, suffering most horrible mental anguish, such as I suppose unhappy Abraham felt when commanded to slay Isaac. Jack's life was spared, however, though I can't tell what finally became of him. I wish I could. After father bought a span of work horses he was sold to a man who said he was going to ride him across the plains to California. We had him, I think, some five or six years. He was the stoutest, gentlest, bravest little horse I ever saw. He never seemed tired, could canter all day with a man about as heavy as himself on his back, and feared nothing. Once fifty or sixty pounds of beef that was tied on his back slid over his shoulders along his neck and weighed down his head to the ground, fairly anchoring him; but he stood patient and still for half an hour or so without making the slightest struggle to free himself, while I was away getting help to untie the pack-rope and set the load back in its place.

As I was the eldest boy I had the care of our first span of work horses. Their names were Nob and Nell. Nob was very intelligent, and even affectionate, and could learn almost anything. Nell was entirely different; balky and stubborn, though we managed to teach her a good many circus tricks; but she never seemed to like to play with us in anything like an affectionate way as Nob did. We turned them out one day into the pasture, and an Indian, hiding in the brush that had sprung up after the grass fires had been kept out, managed to catch Nob, tied a rope to her jaw for a bridle, rode her to Green Lake, about thirty or forty miles away, and tried to sell her for fifteen dollars. All our hearts were sore, as if one of the family had been lost. We hunted everywhere and could not at first imagine what had become of her. We discovered her track where the fence was broken down, and, following it for a few miles, made sure the track was Nob's; and a neighbor told us he had seen an Indian riding fast through the woods on a horse that looked like Nob. But we could find no farther trace of her until a month or two after she was lost, and we had given up hope of ever seeing her again. Then we learned that she had been taken from an Indian by a farmer at Green Lake because he saw that she had been shod and had worked in harness. So when the Indian tried to sell her the farmer said: "You are a thief. That is a white man's horse. You stole her."

"No," said the Indian, "I brought her from Prairie du Chien and she has always been mine."

The man, pointing to her feet and the marks of the harness, said: "You are lying. I will take that horse away from you and put her in my pasture, and if you come near it I will set the dogs on you." Then he advertised her. One of our neighbors happened to see the advertisement and brought us the glad news, and great was our rejoicing when father brought her home. That Indian must have treated her with terrible cruelty, for when I was riding her through the pasture several years afterward, looking for another horse that we wanted to catch, as we approached the place where she had been captured she stood stock still gazing through the bushes, fearing the Indian might still be hiding there ready to spring; and she was so excited that she trembled, and her heartbeats were so loud that I could hear them distinctly as I sat on her back, *boomp, boomp, boomp,* like the drumming of a partridge. So vividly had she remembered her terrible experiences.

She was a great pet and favorite with the whole family, quickly learned playful tricks, came running when we called, seemed to know everything we said to her, and had the utmost confidence in our friendly kindness.

We used to cut and shock and husk the Indian corn in the fall, until a keen Yankee stopped overnight at our house and among other labor-saving notions convinced father that it was better to let it stand, and husk it at his leisure during the winter, then turn in the cattle to eat the leaves and trample down the stalks, so that they could be ploughed under in the spring. In this winter method each of us took two rows and husked into baskets, and emptied the corn on the ground in piles of fifteen to twenty basketfuls, then loaded it into the wagon to be hauled to the crib. This was cold, painful work, the temperature being oftentimes far below zero and the ground covered with dry, frosty snow, giving rise to miserable crops of chilblains and frosted fingers,—a sad change from the merry Indian-summer husking, when the big yellow pumpkins covered the cleared fields;—golden corn, golden pumpkins, gathered in the hazy golden weather. Sad change, indeed, but we occasionally got some fun out of the nipping, shivery work from hungry prairie chickens, and squirrels and mice that came about us.

The piles of corn were often left in the field several days, and while loading them into the wagon we usually found field mice in them,—big, blunt-nosed, strong-scented fellows that we were taught to kill just because they nibbled a few grains of corn. I used to hold one while it was still warm, up to Nob's nose for the fun of seeing her make faces and snort at the smell of it; and I would say: "Here, Nob," as if offering her a lump of sugar. One day I offered her an extra fine, fat, plump specimen, something like a little woodchuck, or muskrat, and to my astonishment, after smelling it curiously and doubtfully, as if wondering what the gift might be, and rubbing it back and forth in the palm of my hand with her upper lip, she deliberately took it into her mouth, crunched and munched and chewed it fine and swallowed it, bones, teeth, head, tail, everything. Not a single hair of that mouse was wasted. When she was chewing it she nodded and grunted, as though critically tasting and relishing it.

My father was a steadfast enthusiast on religious matters, and, of course, attended almost every sort of church-meeting, especially revival meetings. They were occasionally held in summer, but mostly in winter when the sleighing was good and plenty of time available. One hot summer day father drove Nob to Portage and back, twenty-four miles over a sandy road. It was a hot, hard, sultry day's work, and she had evidently been over-driven in order to get home in time for one of these meetings. I shall never forget how tired and wilted she looked that evening when I unhitched her; how she drooped in her stall, too tired to eat or even to lie down. Next morning it was plain that her lungs were inflamed; all the dreadful symptoms were just the same as my own when I had pneumonia. Father sent for a Methodist minister, a very energetic, resourceful man, who was a blacksmith, farmer, butcher, and horse-doctor as well as minister; but all his gifts and skill were of no avail. Nob was doomed. We bathed her head and tried to get her to eat something, but she couldn't eat, and in about a couple of weeks we turned her loose to let her come around the house and see us in the weary suffering and loneliness of the shadow of death. She tried to follow us children, so long her friends and workmates and playmates. It was awfully touching. She had several hemorrhages, and in the forenoon of her last day, after she had had one of her dreadful spells of bleeding and gasping for breath, she came to me trembling, with beseeching, heartbreaking looks, and after I had bathed her head and tried to soothe and pet her, she lay down and gasped and died. All the family gathered about her, weeping, with aching hearts. Then dust to dust.

She was the most faithful, intelligent, playful, affectionate, human-like horse I ever knew, and she won all our hearts. Of the many advantages of farm life for boys one of the greatest is the gaining a real knowledge of animals as fellow-mortals, learning to respect them and love them, and even to win some of their love. Thus god-like sympathy grows and thrives and spreads far beyond the teachings of churches and schools, where too often the mean, blinding, loveless doctrine is taught that animals have neither mind nor soul, have no rights that we are bound to respect, and were made only for man, to be petted, spoiled, slaughtered, or enslaved.

At first we were afraid of snakes, but soon learned that most of them were harmless. The only venomous species seen on our farm were the rattlesnake and the copperhead, one of each. David saw the rattler, and we both saw the copperhead. One day, when my brother came in from his work, he reported that he had seen a snake that made a queer buzzy noise with its tail. This was the only rattlesnake seen on our farm, though we heard of them being common on limestone hills eight or ten miles distant. We discovered the copperhead when we were ploughing, and we saw and felt at the first long, fixed, half-charmed, admiring stare at him that he was an awfully dangerous fellow. Every fibre of his strong, lithe, quivering body, his burnished copper-colored head, and above all his fierce, able eyes, seemed to be overflowing full of deadly power, and bade us beware. And yet it is only fair to say that this terrible, beautiful reptile showed no disposition to hurt us until we threw clods at him and tried to head him off from a log fence into which he was trying to escape. We were barefooted and of course afraid to let him get very near, while we vainly battered him with the loose sandy clods of the freshly ploughed field to hold him back until we could get a stick. Looking us in the eyes after a moment's pause, he probably saw we were afraid, and he came right straight at us, snapping and looking terrible, drove us out of his way, and won his fight.

Out on the open sandy hills there were a good many thick burly blow snakes, the kind that puff themselves up and hiss. Our Yankee declared that their breath was very poisonous and that we must not go near them. A handsome ringed species common in damp, shady places was, he told us, the most wonderful of all the snakes, for if chopped into pieces, however small, the fragments would wriggle themselves together again, and the restored snake would go on about its business as if nothing had happened. The commonest kinds were the striped slender species of the meadows and streams, good swimmers, that lived mostly on frogs.

Once I observed one of the larger ones, about two feet long, pursuing a frog in our meadow, and it was wonderful to see how fast the legless, footless, wingless, finless hunter could run. The frog, of course, knew its enemy and was making desperate efforts to escape to the water and hide in the marsh mud. He was a fine, sleek yellow muscular fellow and was springing over the tall grass in wide-arching jumps. The green-striped snake, gliding swiftly and steadily, was keeping the frog in sight and, had I not interfered, would probably have tired out the poor jumper. Then, perhaps, while digesting and enjoying his meal, the happy snake would himself be swallowed frog and all by a hawk. Again, to our astonishment, the small specimens were attacked by our hens. They pursued and pecked away at them until they killed and devoured them, oftentimes quarreling over the division of the spoil, though it was not easily divided.

We watched the habits of the swift-darting dragonflies, wild bees, butterflies, wasps, beetles, etc., and soon learned to discriminate between those that might be safely handled and the pinching or stinging species. But of all our wild neighbors the mosquitoes were the first with which we became very intimately acquainted.

The beautiful meadow lying warm in the spring sunshine, outspread between our lily-rimmed lake and the hill-slope that our shanty stood on, sent forth thirsty swarms of the little gray, speckledy, singing, stinging pests; and how tellingly they introduced themselves! Of little avail were the smudges that we made on muggy evenings to drive them away; and amid the many lessons which they insisted upon teaching us we wondered more and more at the extent of their knowledge, especially that in their tiny, flimsy bodies room could be found for such cunning palates. They would drink their fill from brown, smoky Indians, or from old white folk flavored with tobacco and whiskey, when no better could be had. But the surpassing fineness of their taste was best manifested by their enthusiastic appreciation of boys full of lively red blood, and of girls in full bloom fresh from cool Scotland or England. On these it was pleasant to witness their enjoyment as they feasted. Indians, we were told, believed that if they were brave fighters they would go after death to a happy country abounding in game, where there were no mosquitoes and no cowards. For cowards were driven away by themselves to a miserable country where there was no game fit to eat, and where the sky was always dark with huge gnats and mosquitoes as big as pigeons.

We were great admirers of the little black water-bugs. Their whole lives seemed to be play, skimming, swimming, swirling, and waltzing together in little groups on the edge of the lake and in the meadow springs, dancing to music we never could hear. The long-legged skaters, too, seemed wonderful fellows, shuffling about on top of the water, with air-bubbles like little bladders tangled under their hairy feet; and we often wished that we also might be shod in the same way to enable us to skate on the lake in summer as well as in icy winter. Not less wonderful were the boatmen, swimming on their backs, pulling themselves along with a pair of oar-like legs.

Great was the delight of brothers David and Daniel and myself when father gave us a few pine boards for a boat, and it was a memorable day when we got that boat built and launched into the lake. Never shall I forget our first sail over the gradually deepening water, the sunbeams pouring through it revealing the strange plants covering the bottom, and the fishes coming about us, staring and wondering as if the boat were a monstrous strange fish.

The water was so clear that it was almost invisible, and when we floated slowly out over the plants and fishes, we seemed to be miraculously sustained in the air while silently exploring a veritable fairyland.

We always had to work hard, but if we worked still harder we were occasionally allowed a little spell in the long summer evenings about sundown to fish, and on Sundays an hour or two to sail quietly without fishing-rod or gun when the lake was calm. Therefore we gradually learned something about its inhabitants,— pickerel, sunfish, black bass, perch, shiners, pumpkin-seeds, ducks, loons, turtles, muskrats, etc. We saw the sunfishes making their nests in little openings in the rushes where the water was only a few feet deep, ploughing up and shoving away the soft gray mud with their noses, like pigs, forming round bowls five or six inches in depth and about two feet in diameter, in which their eggs were deposited. And with what beautiful, unweariable devotion they watched and hovered over them and chased away prowling spawn-eating enemies that ventured within a rod or two of the precious nest!

The pickerel is a savage fish endowed with marvelous strength and speed. It lies in wait for its prey on the bottom, perfectly motionless like a waterlogged stick, watching everything that moves, with fierce, hungry eyes. Oftentimes when we were fishing for some other kinds over the edge of the boat, a pickerel that we had not noticed would come like a bolt of lightning and seize the fish we had caught before we could get it into the boat. The very first pickerel that I ever caught jumped into the air to seize a small fish dangling on my line, and, missing its aim, fell plump into the boat as if it had dropped from the sky.

Some of our neighbors fished for pickerel through the ice in midwinter. They usually drove a wagon out on the lake, set a large number of lines baited with live minnows, hung a loop of the lines over a small bush planted at the side of each hole, and watched to see the loops pulled off when a fish had taken the bait. Large quantities of pickerel were often caught in this cruel way.

Our beautiful lake, named Fountain Lake by father, but Muir's Lake by the neighbors, is one of the many small glacier lakes that adorn the Wisconsin landscapes. It is fed by twenty or thirty meadow springs, is about half a mile long, half as wide, and surrounded by low finely-modeled hills dotted with oak and hickory, and meadows full of grasses and sedges and many beautiful orchids and ferns. First there is a zone of green, shining rushes, and just beyond the rushes a zone of white and orange water-lilies fifty or sixty feet wide forming a magnificent border. On bright days, when the lake was rippled by a breeze, the lilies and sun-spangles danced together in radiant beauty, and it became difficult to discriminate between them.

On Sundays, after or before chores and sermons and Bible-lessons, we drifted about on the lake for hours, especially in lily time, getting finest lessons and sermons from the water and flowers, ducks, fishes, and muskrats. In particular we took Christ's advice and devoutly "considered the lilies"—how they grow up in beauty out of gray lime mud, and ride gloriously among the breezy sun-spangles. On our way home we gathered grand bouquets of them to be kept fresh all the week.

Early in summer we feasted on strawberries, that grew in rich beds beneath the meadow grasses and sedges as well as in the dry sunny woods. And in different bogs and marshes, and around their borders on our own farm and along the Fox River, we found dew-berries and cranberries, and a glorious profusion of huckleberries, the fountain-heads of pies of wondrous taste and size, colored in the heart like sunsets. Nor were we slow to discover the value of the hickory trees yielding both sugar and nuts. We carefully counted the different kinds on our farm, and every morning when we could steal a few minutes before breakfast after doing the chores, we visited the trees that had been wounded by the axe, to scrape off and enjoy the thick white delicious syrup that exuded from them, and gathered the nuts as they fell in the mellow Indian summer, making haste to get a fair share with the sapsuckers and squirrels. The hickory makes fine masses of color in the fall, every leaf a flower, but it was the sweet sap and sweet nuts that first interested us. No harvest in the Wisconsin woods was ever gathered with more pleasure and care. Also, to our delight, we found plenty of hazelnuts, and in a few places abundance of wild apples. They were desperately sour, and we used to fill our pockets with them and dare each other to eat one without making a face,—no easy feat.

One hot summer day father told us that we ought to learn to swim. This was one of the most interesting suggestions he had ever offered, but precious little time was allowed for trips to the lake, and he seldom tried to show us how. "Go to the frogs," he said, "and they will give you all the lessons you need. Watch their arms and legs and see how smoothly they kick themselves along and dive and come up. When you want to dive, keep your arms by your side or over your head, and kick, and when you want to come up, let your legs drag and paddle with your hands."

We found a little basin among the rushes at the south end of the lake, about waist-deep and a rod or two wide, shaped like a sunfish's nest. Here we kicked and plashed for many a lesson, faithfully trying to imitate frogs; but the smooth, comfortable sliding gait of our amphibious teachers seemed hopelessly hard to learn. When we tried to kick frog-fashion, down went our heads as if weighted with lead the moment our feet left the ground. One day it occurred to me to hold my breath as long as I could and let my head sink as far as it liked without paying any attention to it, and try to swim under the water instead of on the surface. This method was a great success, for at the very first trial I managed to cross the basin without touching bottom, and soon learned the use of my limbs. Then, of course, swimming with my head above water soon became so easy that it seemed perfectly natural. David tried the plan with the same success. Then we began to count the number of times that we could swim around the basin without stopping to rest, and after twenty or thirty rounds failed to tire us, we proudly thought that a little more practice would make us about as amphibious as frogs.

On the fourth of July of this swimming year one of the Lawson boys came to visit us, and we went down to the lake to spend the great warm day with the fishes and ducks and turtles. After gliding about on the smooth mirror water, telling stories and enjoying the company of the happy creatures about us, we rowed to our bathing-pool, and David and I went in for a swim, while our companion fished from the boat a little way out beyond the rushes. After a few turns in the pool, it occurred to me that it was now about time to try deep water. Swimming through the thick growth of rushes and lilies was somewhat dangerous, especially for a beginner, because one's arms and legs might be entangled among the long, limber stems; nevertheless I ventured and struck out boldly enough for the boat, where the water was twenty or thirty feet deep. When I reached the end of the little skiff I raised my right hand to take hold of it to surprise Lawson, whose back was toward me and who was not aware of my approach; but I failed to reach high enough, and, of course, the weight of my arm and the stroke against the overleaning stern of the boat shoved me down and I sank, struggling, frightened and confused. As soon as my feet touched the bottom, I slowly rose to the surface, but before I could get breath enough to call for help, sank back again and lost all control of myself. After sinking and rising I don't know how many times, some water got into my lungs and I began to drown. Then suddenly my mind seemed to clear. I remembered that I could swim under water, and, making a desperate struggle toward the shore, I reached a point where with my toes on the bottom I got my mouth above the surface, gasped for help, and was pulled into the boat.

This humiliating accident spoiled the day, and we all agreed to keep it a profound secret. My sister Sarah had heard my cry for help, and on our arrival at the house inquired what had happened. "Were you drowning, John? I heard you cry you couldna get oot." Lawson made haste to reply, "Oh, no! He was juist haverin (making fun)."

I was very much ashamed of myself, and at night, after calmly reviewing the affair, concluded that there had been no reasonable cause for the accident, and that I ought to punish myself for so nearly losing my life from unmanly fear. Accordingly at the very first opportunity, I stole away to the lake by myself, got into my boat, and instead of going back to the old swimming-bowl for further practice, or to try to do sanely and well what I had so ignominiously failed to do in my first adventure, that is, to swim out through the rushes and lilies, I rowed directly out to the middle of the lake, stripped, stood up on the seat in the stern, and with grim deliberation took a header and dove straight down thirty or forty feet, turned easily, and, letting my feet drag, paddled straight to the surface with my hands as father had at first directed me to do. I then swam round the boat, glorying in my suddenly acquired confidence and victory over myself, climbed into it, and dived again, with the same triumphant success. I think I went down four or five times, and each time as I made the dive-spring shouted aloud, "Take that!" feeling that I was getting most gloriously even with myself.

Never again from that day to this have I lost control of myself in water. If suddenly thrown overboard at sea in the dark, or even while asleep, I think I would immediately right myself in a way some would call "instinct," rise among the waves, catch my breath, and try to plan what would better be done. Never was victory over self more complete. I have been a good swimmer ever since. At a slow gait I think I could swim all day in smooth water moderate in temperature. When I was a student at Madison, I used to go on long swimming-journeys, called exploring expeditions, along the south shore of Lake Mendota, on Saturdays, sometimes alone, sometimes with another amphibious explorer by the name of Fuller.

My adventures in Fountain Lake call to mind the story of a boy who in climbing a tree to rob a crow's nest fell and broke his leg, but as soon as it healed compelled himself to climb to the top of the tree he had fallen from.

Like Scotch children in general we were taught grim self-denial, in season and out of season, to mortify the flesh, keep our bodies in subjection to Bible laws, and mercilessly punish ourselves for every fault imagined or committed. A little boy, while helping his sister to drive home the cows, happened to use a forbidden word. "I'll have to tell fayther on ye," said the horrified sister. "I'll tell him that ye said a bad word." "Weel," said the boy, by way of excuse, "I couldna help the word comin' into me, and it's na waur to speak it oot than to let it rin through ye."

A Scotch fiddler playing at a wedding drank so much whiskey that on the way home he fell by the roadside. In the morning he was ashamed and angry and determined to punish himself. Making haste to the house of a friend, a gamekeeper, he called him out, and requested the loan of a gun. The alarmed gamekeeper, not liking the fiddler's looks and voice, anxiously inquired what he was going to do with it. "Surely," said he, "you're no gan to shoot yoursel." "No-o," with characteristic candor replied the penitent fiddler, "I dinna think that I'll juist exactly kill mysel, but I'm gaun to tak a dander doon the burn (brook) wi' the gun and gie mysel a deevil o' a fleg (fright)."

One calm summer evening a red-headed woodpecker was drowned in our lake. The accident happened at the south end, opposite our memorable swimming-hole, a few rods from the place where I came so near being drowned years before. I had returned to the old home during a summer vacation of the State University, and, having made a beginning in botany, I was, of course, full of enthusiasm and ran eagerly to my beloved pogonia, calopogon, and cypripedium gardens, osmunda ferneries, and the lake lilies and pitcher-plants. A little before sundown the day-breeze died away, and the lake, reflecting the wooded hills like a mirror, was dimpled and dotted and streaked here and there where fishes and turtles were poking out their heads and muskrats were sculling themselves along with their flat tails making glittering tracks. After lingering a while, dreamily recalling the old, hard, half-happy days, and watching my favorite red-headed woodpeckers pursuing moths like regular flycatchers, I swam out through the rushes and up the middle of the lake to the north end and back, gliding slowly, looking about me, enjoying the scenery as I would in a saunter along the shore, and studying the habits of the animals as they were explained and recorded on the smooth glassy water.

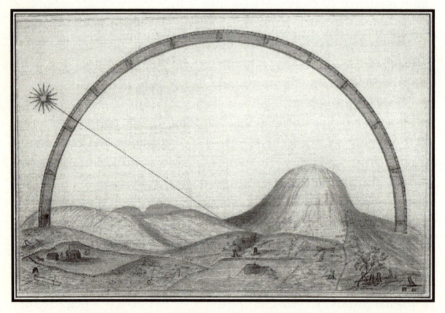

Clock. The Star Hand Rising and Setting with the Sun all Year
Invented by the author in his boyhood

On the way back, when I was within a hundred rods or so of the end of my voyage, I noticed a peculiar plashing disturbance that could not, I thought, be made by a jumping fish or any other inhabitant of the lake; for instead of low regular out-circling ripples such as are made by the popping up of a head, or like those raised by the quick splash of a leaping fish, or diving loon or muskrat, a continuous struggle was kept up for several minutes ere the outspreading, interfering ring-waves began to die away. Swimming hastily to the spot to try to discover what had happened, I found one of my woodpeckers floating motionless with outspread wings. All was over. Had I been a minute or two earlier, I might have saved him. He had glanced on the water I suppose in pursuit of a moth, was unable to rise from it, and died struggling, as I nearly did at this same spot. Like me he seemed to have lost his mind in blind confusion and fear. The water was warm, and had he kept still with his head a little above the surface, he would sooner or later have been wafted ashore. The best aimed flights of birds and man "gang aft agley," but this was the first case I had witnessed of a bird losing its life by drowning.

Doubtless accidents to animals are far more common than is generally known. I have seen quails killed by flying against our house when suddenly startled. Some birds get entangled in hairs of their own nests and die. Once I found a poor snipe in our meadow that was unable to fly on account of difficult egg-birth. Pitying the poor mother, I picked her up out of the grass and helped her as gently as I could, and as soon as the egg was born she flew gladly away. Oftentimes I have thought it strange that one could walk through the woods and mountains and plains for years without seeing a single blood-spot. Most wild animals get into the world and out of it without being noticed. Nevertheless we at last sadly learn that they are all subject to the vicissitudes of fortune like ourselves. Many birds lose their lives in storms. I remember a particularly severe Wisconsin winter, when the temperature was many degrees below zero and the snow was deep, preventing the quail, which feed on the ground, from getting anything like enough of food, as was pitifully shown by a flock I found on our farm frozen solid in a thicket of oak sprouts. They were in a circle about a foot wide, with their heads outward, packed close together for warmth. Yet all had died without a struggle, perhaps more from starvation than frost. Many small birds lose their lives in the storms of early spring, or even summer. One mild spring morning I picked up more than a score out of the grass and flowers, most of them darling singers that had perished in a sudden storm of sleety rain and hail.

In a hollow at the foot of an oak tree that I had chopped down one cold winter day, I found a poor ground squirrel frozen solid in its snug grassy nest, in the middle of a store of nearly a peck of wheat it had carefully gathered. I carried it home and gradually thawed and warmed it in the kitchen, hoping it would come to life like a pickerel I caught in our lake through a hole in the ice, which, after being frozen as hard as a bone and thawed at the fireside, squirmed itself out of the grasp of the cook when she began to scrape it, bounced off the table, and danced about on the floor, making wonderful springy jumps as if trying to find its way back home to the lake. But for the poor spermophile nothing I could do in the way of revival was of any avail. Its life had passed away without the slightest struggle, as it lay asleep curled up like a ball, with its tail wrapped about it.

Young Hunters

∽

I n the older eastern States it used to be considered great sport for an army of boys to assemble to hunt birds, squirrels, and every other unclaimed, unprotected live thing of shootable size. They divided into two squads, and, choosing leaders, scattered through the woods in different directions, and the party that killed the greatest number enjoyed a supper at the expense of the other. The whole neighborhood seemed to enjoy the shameful sport especially the farmers afraid of their crops. With a great air of importance, laws were enacted to govern the gory business. For example, a gray squirrel must count four heads, a woodchuck six heads, common red squirrel two heads, black squirrel ten heads, a partridge five heads, the larger birds, such as whip-poor-wills and nighthawks two heads each, the wary crows three, and bob-whites three. But all the blessed company of mere songbirds, warblers, robins, thrushes, orioles, with nuthatches, chickadees, blue jays, woodpeckers, etc., counted only one head each. The heads of the birds were hastily wrung off and thrust into the game-bags to be counted, saving the bodies only of what were called game, the larger squirrels, bob-whites, partridges, etc. The blood-stained bags of the best slayers were soon bulging full. Then at a given hour all had to stop and repair to the town, empty their dripping sacks, count the heads, and go rejoicing to their dinner. Although, like other wild boys, I was fond of shooting, I never had anything to do with these abominable head-hunts. And now the farmers having learned that birds are their friends wholesale slaughter has been abolished.

We seldom saw deer, though their tracks were common. The Yankee explained that they traveled and fed mostly at night, and hid in tamarack swamps and brushy places in the daytime, and how the

Indians knew all about them and could find them whenever they were hungry.

Indians belonging to the Menominee and Winnebago tribes occasionally visited us at our cabin to get a piece of bread or some matches, or to sharpen their knives on our grindstone, and we boys watched them closely to see that they didn't steal Jack. We wondered at their knowledge of animals when we saw them go direct to trees on our farm, chop holes in them with their tomahawks and take out coons, of the existence of which we had never noticed the slightest trace. In winter, after the first snow, we frequently saw three or four Indians hunting deer in company, running like hounds on the fresh, exciting tracks. The escape of the deer from these noiseless, tireless hunters was said to be well-nigh impossible; they were followed to the death.

Most of our neighbors brought some sort of gun from the old country, but seldom took time to hunt, even after the first hard work of fencing and clearing was over, except to shoot a duck or prairie chicken now and then that happened to come in their way. It was only the less industrious American settlers who left their work to go far a-hunting. Two or three of our most enterprising American neighbors went off every fall with their teams to the pine regions and cranberry marshes in the northern part of the State to hunt and gather berries. I well remember seeing their wagons loaded with game when they returned from a successful hunt. Their loads consisted usually of half a dozen deer or more, one or two black bears, and fifteen or twenty bushels of cranberries; all solidly frozen. Part of both the berries and meat was usually sold in Portage; the balance furnished their families with abundance of venison, bear grease, and pies.

Winter wheat is sown in the fall, and when it is a month or so old the deer, like the wild geese, are very fond of it, especially since other kinds of food are then becoming scarce. One of our neighbors across the Fox River killed a large number, some thirty or forty, on a small patch of wheat, simply by lying in wait for them every night. Our wheat-field was the first that was sown in the neighborhood. The deer soon found it and came in every night to feast, but it was eight or nine years before we ever disturbed them. David then killed one deer, the only one killed by any of our family. He went out shortly after sundown at the time of full moon to one of our wheat-fields, carrying a double-barreled shotgun loaded with buckshot. After lying in wait an hour or so, he saw a doe and her fawn jump the fence and come cautiously into the wheat. After they were within sixty or seventy yards of him, he was surprised when he tried to take aim that about half of the moon's disc was mysteriously darkened as if covered by the edge of a dense cloud. This proved to be an eclipse. Nevertheless, he fired at the mother, and she immediately ran off, jumped the fence, and took to the woods by the way she came. The fawn danced about bewildered, wondering what had become of its mother, but finally fled to the woods. David fired at the poor deserted thing as it ran past him but happily missed it. Hearing the shots, I joined David to learn his luck. He said he thought he must have wounded the mother, and when we were strolling about in the woods in search of her we saw three or four deer on their way to the wheat-field, led by a fine buck. They were walking rapidly, but cautiously halted at intervals of a few rods to listen and look ahead and scent the air. They failed to notice us, though by this time the moon was out of the eclipse shadow and we were standing only about fifty yards from them. I was carrying the gun. David had fired both barrels but when he was reloading one of them he happened to put the wad intended to cover the shot into the empty barrel, and so when we were climbing over the fence the buckshot had rolled out, and when I fired at the big buck I knew by the report that there was nothing but powder in the charge. The startled deer danced about in confusion for a few seconds, uncertain which way to run until they caught sight of us, when they bounded off through the woods. Next morning we found the poor mother lying about three hundred yards from the place where she was shot. She had run this distance and jumped a high fence after one of the buckshot had passed through her heart.

Excepting Sundays we boys had only two days of the year to ourselves, the 4th of July and the 1st of January. Sundays were less than half our own, on account of Bible lessons, Sunday-school lessons and church services; all the others were labor days, rain or shine, cold or warm. No wonder, then, that our two holidays were precious and that it was not easy to decide what to do with them. They were usually spent on the highest rocky hill in the neighborhood, called the Observatory; in visiting our boy friends on adjacent farms to hunt, fish, wrestle, and play games; in reading some new favorite book we had managed to borrow or buy; or in making models of machines I had invented.

One of our July days was spent with two Scotch boys of our own age hunting redwing blackbirds then busy in the corn-fields. Our party had only one single-barreled shotgun, which, as the oldest and perhaps because I was thought to be the best shot, I had the honor of carrying. We marched through the corn without getting sight of a single redwing, but just as we reached the far side of the field, a red-headed woodpecker flew up, and the Lawson boys cried: "Shoot him! Shoot him! He is just as bad as a blackbird. He eats corn!" This memorable woodpecker alighted in the top of a white oak tree about fifty feet high. I fired from a position almost immediately beneath him, and he fell straight down at my feet. When I picked him up and was admiring his plumage, he moved his legs slightly, and I said, "Poor bird, he's no deed yet and we'll hae to kill him to put him oot o' pain,"—sincerely pitying him, after we had taken pleasure in shooting him. I had seen servant girls wringing chicken necks, so with desperate humanity I took the limp unfortunate by the head, swung him around three or four times thinking I was wringing his neck, and then threw him hard on the ground to quench the last possible spark of life and make quick death doubly sure. But to our astonishment the moment he struck the ground he gave a cry of alarm and flew right straight up like a rejoicing lark into the top of the same tree, and perhaps to the same branch he had fallen from, and began to adjust his ruffled feathers, nodding and chirping and looking down at us as if wondering what in the bird world we had been doing to him. This of course banished all thought of killing, as far as that revived woodpecker was concerned, no matter how many ears of corn he might spoil, and we all heartily congratulated him on his wonderful, triumphant resurrection from three kinds of death,—shooting, neck-wringing, and destructive concussion. I suppose only one pellet had touched him, glancing on his head.

Another extraordinary shooting-affair happened one summer morning shortly after daybreak. When I went to the stable to feed the horses I noticed a big white-breasted hawk on a tall oak in front of the chicken-house, evidently waiting for a chicken breakfast. I ran to the house for the gun, and when I fired he fell about halfway down the tree, caught a branch with his claws, hung back downward and fluttered a few seconds, then managed to stand erect. I fired again to put him out of pain, and to my surprise the second shot seemed to restore his strength instead of killing him, for he flew out of the tree and over the meadow with strong and regular wing-beats for thirty or forty rods apparently as well as ever, but died suddenly in the air and dropped like a stone.

We hunted muskrats whenever we had time to run down to the lake. They are brown bunchy animals about twenty-three inches long, the tail being about nine inches in length, black in color and flattened vertically for sculling, and the hind feet are half-webbed. They look like little beavers, usually have from ten to a dozen young, are easily tamed and make interesting pets. We liked to watch them at their work and at their meals. In the spring when the snow vanishes and the lake ice begins to melt, the first open spot is always used as a feeding-place, where they dive from the edge of the ice and in a minute or less reappear with a mussel or a mouthful of pontederia or water-lily leaves, climb back on to the ice and sit up to nibble their food, handling it very much like squirrels or marmots. It is then that they are most easily shot, a solitary hunter oftentimes shooting thirty or forty in a single day. Their nests on the rushy margins of lakes and streams, far from being hidden like those of most birds, are conspicuously large, and conical in shape like Indian wigwams. They are built of plants—rushes, sedges, mosses, etc.—and ornamented around the base with mussel-shells. It was always pleasant and interesting to see them in the fall as soon as the nights began to be frosty, hard at work cutting sedges on the edge of the meadow or swimming out through the rushes, making long glittering ripples as they sculled themselves along, diving where the water is perhaps six or eight feet deep and reappearing in a minute or so with large mouthfuls of the weedy tangled plants gathered from the bottom, returning to their big wigwams, climbing up and depositing their loads where most needed to make them yet larger and firmer and warmer, foreseeing the freezing weather just like ourselves when we banked up our house to keep out the frost.

They lie snug and invisible all winter but do not hibernate. Through a channel carefully kept open they swim out under the ice for mussels, and the roots and stems of water-lilies, etc., on which they feed just as they do in summer. Sometimes the oldest and most enterprising of them venture to orchards near the water in search of fallen apples; very seldom, however, do they interfere with anything belonging to their mortal enemy man. Notwithstanding they are so well hidden and protected during the winter, many of them are killed by Indian hunters, who creep up softly and spear them through the thick walls of their cabins. Indians are fond of their flesh, and so are some of the wildest of the white trappers. They are easily caught in steel traps, and after vainly trying to drag their feet from the cruel crushing jaws, they sometimes in their agony gnaw them off. Even after having gnawed off a leg they are so guileless that they never seem to learn to know and fear traps, for some are occasionally found that have been caught twice and have gnawed off a second foot. Many other animals suffering excruciating pain in these cruel traps gnaw off their legs. Crabs and lobsters are so fortunate as to be able to shed their limbs when caught or merely frightened, apparently without suffering any pain, simply by giving themselves a little shivery shake.

The muskrat is one of the most notable and widely distributed of American animals, and millions of the gentle, industrious, beaver-like creatures are shot and trapped and speared every season for their skins, worth a dime or so,—like shooting boys and girls for their garments.

Surely a better time must be drawing nigh when godlike human beings will become truly humane, and learn to put their animal fellow mortals in their hearts instead of on their backs or in their dinners. In the mean time we may just as well as not learn to live clean, innocent lives instead of slimy, bloody ones. All hale, red-blooded boys are savage, the best and boldest the savagest, fond of hunting and fishing. But when thoughtless childhood is past, the best rise the highest above all this bloody flesh and sport business, the wild foundational animal dying out day by day, as divine uplifting, transfiguring charity grows in.

Hares and rabbits were seldom seen when we first settled in the Wisconsin woods, but they multiplied rapidly after the animals that preyed upon them had been thinned out or exterminated, and food and shelter supplied in grain-fields and log fences and the thickets of young oaks that grew up in pastures after the annual grass fires were kept out. Catching hares in the winter-time, when they were hidden in hollow fence-logs, was a favorite pastime with many of the boys whose fathers allowed them time to enjoy the sport. Occasionally a stout, lithe hare was carried out into an open snow-covered field, set free, and given a chance for its life in a race with a dog. When the snow was not too soft and deep, it usually made good its escape, for our dogs were only fat, short-legged mongrels. We sometimes discovered hares in standing hollow trees, crouching on decayed punky wood at the bottom, as far back as possible from the opening, but when alarmed they managed to climb to a considerable height if the hollow was not too wide, by bracing themselves against the sides.

Foxes, though not uncommon, we boys held steadily to work seldom saw, and as they found plenty of prairie chickens for themselves and families, they did not often come near the farmer's hen-roosts. Nevertheless the discovery of their dens was considered important. No matter how deep the den might be, it was thoroughly explored with pick and shovel by sport-loving settlers at a time when they judged the fox was likely to be at home, but I cannot remember any case in our neighborhood where the fox was actually captured. In one of the dens a mile or two from our farm a lot of prairie chickens were found and some smaller birds.

Badger dens were far more common than fox dens. One of our fields was named Badger Hill from the number of badger holes in a hill at the end of it, but I cannot remember seeing a single one of the inhabitants.

On a stormy day in the middle of an unusually severe winter, a black bear, hungry, no doubt, and seeking something to eat, came strolling down through our neighborhood from the northern pine woods. None had been seen here before, and it caused no little excitement and alarm, for the European settlers imagined that these poor, timid, bashful bears were as dangerous as man-eating lions and tigers, and that they would pursue any human being that came in their way. This species is common in the north part of the State, and few of our enterprising Yankee hunters who went to the pineries in the fall failed to shoot at least one of them.

We saw very little of the owlish, serious-looking coons, and no wonder, since they lie hidden nearly all day in hollow trees and we never had time to hunt them. We often heard their curious, quavering, whinnying cries on still evenings, but only once succeeded in tracing an unfortunate family through our corn-field to their den in a big oak and catching them all. One of our neighbors, Mr. McRath, a Highland Scotchman, caught one and made a pet of it. It became very tame and had perfect confidence in the good intentions of its kind friend and master. He always addressed it in speaking to it as a "little man." When it came running to him and jumped on his lap or climbed up his trousers, he would say, while patting its head as if it were a dog or a child, "Coonie, ma mannie, Coonie, ma mannie, hoo are ye the day? I think you're hungry,"—as the comical pet began to examine his pockets for nuts and bits of bread,—"Na, na, there's nathing in my pooch for ye the day, my wee mannie, but I'll get ye something." He would then fetch something it liked,—bread, nuts, a carrot, or perhaps a piece of fresh meat. Anything scattered for it on the floor it felt with its paw instead of looking at it, judging of its worth more by touch than sight.

The outlet of our Fountain Lake flowed past Mr. McRath's door, and the coon was very fond of swimming in it and searching for frogs and mussels. It seemed perfectly satisfied to stay about the house without being confined, occupied a comfortable bed in a section of a hollow tree, and never wandered far. How long it lived after the death of its kind master I don't know.

I suppose that almost any wild animal may be made a pet, simply by sympathizing with it and entering as much as possible into its life. In Alaska I saw one of the common gray mountain marmots kept as a pet in an Indian family. When its master entered the house it always seemed glad, almost like a dog, and when cold or tired it snuggled up in a fold of his blanket with the utmost confidence.

We have all heard of ferocious animals, lions and tigers, etc., that were fed and spoken to only by their masters, becoming perfectly tame; and, as is well known, the faithful dog that follows man and serves him, and looks up to him and loves him as if he were a god, is a descendant of the blood-thirsty wolf or jackal. Even frogs and toads and fishes may be tamed, provided they have the uniform sympathy of one person, with whom they become intimately acquainted without the distracting and varying attentions of strangers. And surely all God's people, however serious and savage, great or small, like to play. Whales and elephants, dancing, humming gnats, and invisibly small mischievous microbes,—all are warm with divine radium and must have lots of fun in them.

As far as I know, all wild creatures keep themselves clean. Birds, it seems to me, take more pains to bathe and dress themselves than any other animals. Even ducks, though living so much in water, dip and scatter cleansing showers over their backs, and shake and preen their feathers as carefully as land-birds. Watching small singers taking their morning baths is very interesting, particularly when the weather is cold. Alighting in a shallow pool, they oftentimes show a sort of dread of dipping into it, like children hesitating about taking a plunge, as if they felt the same kind of shock, and this makes it easy for us to sympathize with the little feathered people.

Occasionally I have seen from my study-window red-headed linnets bathing in dew when water elsewhere was scarce. A large Monterey cypress with broad branches and innumerable leaves on which the dew lodges in still nights made favorite bathing-places.

Alighting gently, as if afraid to waste the dew, they would pause and fidget as they do before beginning to plash in pools, then dip and scatter the drops in showers and get as thorough a bath as they would in a pool. I have also seen the same kind of baths taken by birds on the boughs of silver firs on the edge of a glacier meadow, but nowhere have I seen the dewdrops so abundant as on the Monterey cypress; and the picture made by the quivering wings and irised dew was memorably beautiful. Children, too, make fine pictures plashing and crowing in their little tubs. How widely different from wallowing pigs, bathing with great show of comfort and rub-bing themselves dry against rough-barked trees!

Some of our own species seem fairly to dread the touch of water. When the necessity of absolute cleanliness by means of frequent baths was being preached by a friend who had been reading Combe's Physiology, in which he had learned something of the wonders of the skin with its millions of pores that had to be kept open for health, one of our neighbors remarked: "Oh! that's unnatural. It's well enough to wash in a tub maybe once or twice a year, but not to be paddling in the water all the time like a frog in a spring-hole." Another neighbor, who prided himself on his knowledge of big words, said with great solemnity: "I never can believe that man is amphibious!"

Natives of tropic islands pass a large part of their lives in water, and seem as much at home in the sea as on the land; swim and dive, pursue fishes, play in the waves like surf-ducks and seals, and explore the coral gardens and groves and seaweed meadows as if truly amphibious. Even the natives of the far north bathe at times. I once saw a lot of Eskimo boys ducking and plashing right merrily in the Arctic Ocean.

It seemed very wonderful to us that the wild animals could keep themselves warm and strong in winter when the temperature was far below zero. Feeble-looking rabbits scud away over the snow, lithe and elastic, as if glorying in the frosty, sparkling weather and sure of their dinners. I have seen gray squirrels dragging ears of corn about as heavy as themselves out of our field through loose snow and up a tree, balancing them on limbs and eating in comfort with their dry, electric tails spread airily over their backs. Once I saw a fine hardy fellow go into a knot-hole. Thrusting in my hand I caught him and pulled him out. As soon as he guessed what I was up to, he took the end of my thumb in his mouth and sunk his teeth right through it, but I gripped him hard by the neck, carried him home, and shut him up in a box that contained about half a bushel of hazel-and hickory-nuts, hoping that he would not be too much frightened and discouraged to eat while thus imprisoned after the rough handling he had suffered. I soon learned, however, that sympathy in this direction was wasted, for no sooner did I pop him in than he fell to with right hearty appetite, gnawing and munching the nuts as if he had gathered them himself and was very hungry that day. Therefore, after allowing time enough for a good square meal, I made haste to get him out of the nut-box and shut him up in a spare bedroom, in which father had hung a lot of selected ears of Indian corn for seed. They were hung up by the husks on cords stretched across from side to side of the room. The squirrel managed to jump from the top of one of the bed-posts to the cord, cut off an ear, and let it drop to the floor. He then jumped down, got a good grip of the heavy ear, carried it to the top of one of the slippery, polished bed-posts, seated himself comfortably, and, holding it well balanced, deliberately pried out one kernel at a time with his long chisel teeth, ate the soft, sweet germ, and dropped the hard part of the kernel. In this masterly way, working at high speed, he demolished several ears a day, and with a good warm bed in a box made himself at home and grew fat. Then naturally, I suppose, free romping in the snow and tree-tops with companions came to mind. Anyhow he began to look for a way of escape. Of course he first tried the window, but found that his teeth made no impression on the glass. Next he tried the sash and gnawed the wood off level with the glass; then father happened to come upstairs and discovered the mischief that was being done to his seed corn and window and immediately ordered him out of the house.

The flying squirrel was one of the most interesting of the little animals we found in the woods, a beautiful brown creature, with fine eyes and smooth, soft fur like that of a mole or field mouse. He is about half as long as the gray squirrel, but his wide-spread tail and the folds of skin along his sides that form the wings make him look broad and flat, something like a kite. In the evenings our cat often brought them to her kittens at the shanty, and later we saw them fly during the day from the trees we were chopping. They jumped and glided off smoothly and apparently without effort, like birds, as soon as they heard and felt the breaking shock of the strained fibres at the stump, when the trees they were in began to totter and groan. They can fly, or rather glide, twenty or thirty yards from the top of a tree twenty or thirty feet high to the foot of another, gliding upward as they reach the trunk, or if the distance is too great they alight comfortably on the ground and make haste to the nearest tree, and climb just like the wingless squirrels.

Every boy and girl loves the little fairy, airy striped chipmunk, half squirrel, half spermophile. He is about the size of a field mouse, and often made us think of linnets and song sparrows as he frisked about gathering nuts and berries. He likes almost all kinds of grain, berries, and nuts,—hazel-nuts, hickory-nuts, strawberries, huckleberries, wheat, oats, corn,—he is fond of them all and thrives on them. Most of the hazel bushes on our farm grew along the fences as if they had been planted for the chipmunks alone, for the rail fences were their favorite highways. We never wearied watching them, especially when the hazel-nuts were ripe and the little fellows were sitting on the rails nibbling and handling them like tree-squirrels. We used to notice too that, although they are very neat animals, their lips and fingers were dyed red like our own, when the strawberries and huckleberries were ripe. We could always tell when the wheat and oats were in the milk by seeing the chipmunks feeding on the ears. They kept nibbling at the wheat until it was harvested and then gleaned in the stubble, keeping up a careful watch for their enemies,—dogs, hawks, and shrikes. They are as widely distributed over the continent as the squirrels, various species inhabiting different regions on the mountains and lowlands, but all the different kinds have the same general characteristics of light, airy cheerfulness and good nature.

Before the arrival of farmers in the Wisconsin woods the small ground squirrels, called "gophers," lived chiefly on the seeds of wild grasses and weeds, but after the country was cleared and ploughed no feasting animal fell to more heartily on the farmer's wheat and corn. Increasing rapidly in numbers and knowledge, they became very destructive, especially in the spring when the corn was planted, for they learned to trace the rows and dig up and eat the three or four seeds in each hill about as fast as the poor farmers could cover them. And unless great pains were taken to diminish the numbers of the cunning little robbers, the fields had to be planted two or three times over, and even then large gaps in the rows would be found. The loss of the grain they consumed after it was ripe, together with the winter stores laid up in their burrows, amounted to little as compared with the loss of the seed on which the whole crop depended.

One evening about sundown, when my father sent me out with the shotgun to hunt them in a stubble field, I learned something curious and interesting in connection with these mischievous gophers, though just then they were doing no harm. As I strolled through the stubble watching for a chance for a shot, a shrike flew past me and alighted on an open spot at the mouth of a burrow about thirty yards ahead of me. Curious to see what he was up to, I stood still to

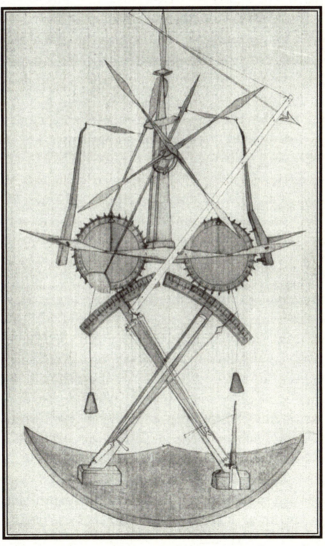

Combined Thermometer, Hygrometer, Barometer and Pyrometer
Invented by the author in his boyhood

watch him. He looked down the gopher hole in a listening attitude, then looked back at me to see if I was coming, looked down again and listened, and looked back at me. I stood perfectly still, and he kept twitching his tail, seeming uneasy and doubtful about venturing to do the savage job that I soon learned he had in his mind. Finally, encouraged by my keeping so still, to my astonishment he suddenly vanished in the gopher hole.

A bird going down a deep narrow hole in the ground like a ferret or a weasel seemed very strange, and I thought it would be a fine thing to run forward, clap my hand over the hole, and have the fun of imprisoning him and seeing what he would do when he tried to get out. So I ran forward but stopped when I got within a dozen or fifteen yards of the hole, thinking it might perhaps be more interesting to wait and see what would naturally happen without my interference. While I stood there looking and listening, I heard a great disturbance going on in the burrow, a mixed lot of keen squeaking, shrieking, distressful cries, telling that down in the dark something terrible was being done. Then suddenly out popped a half-grown gopher, four and a half or five inches long, and, without stopping a single moment to choose a way of escape, ran screaming through the stubble straight away from its home, quickly followed by another and another, until some half-dozen were driven out, all of them crying and running in different directions as if at this dreadful time home, sweet home, was the most dangerous and least desirable of any place in the wide world. Then out came the shrike, flew above the run-away gopher children, and, diving on them, killed them one after another with blows at the back of the skull. He then seized one of them, dragged it to the top of a small clod so as to be able to get a start, and laboriously made out to fly with it about ten or fifteen yards, when he alighted to rest. Then he dragged it to the top of another clod and flew with it about the same distance, repeating this hard work over and over again until he managed to get one of the gophers on to the top of a log fence. How much he ate of his hard-won prey, or what he did with the others, I can't tell, for by this time the sun was down and I had to hurry home to my chores.

The Hickory Hill House, built in 1857

Knowledge And Inventions

ᖗᗢᖘ

I learned arithmetic in Scotland without understanding any of it, though I had the rules by heart. But when I was about fifteen or sixteen years of age, I began to grow hungry for real knowledge, and persuaded father, who was willing enough to have me study provided my farm work was kept up, to buy me a higher arithmetic. Beginning at the beginning, in one summer I easily finished it without assistance, in the short intervals between the end of dinner and the afternoon start for the harvest-and hay-fields, accomplishing more without a teacher in a few scraps of time than in years in school before my mind was ready for such work. Then in succession

I took up algebra, geometry, and trigonometry and made some little progress in each, and reviewed grammar. I was fond of reading, but father had brought only a few religious books from Scotland. Fortunately, several of our neighbors had brought a dozen or two of all sorts of books, which I borrowed and read, keeping all of them except the religious ones carefully hidden from father's eye. Among these were Scott's novels, which, like all other novels, were strictly forbidden, but devoured with glorious pleasure in secret. Father was easily persuaded to buy Josephus' "Wars of the Jews," and D'Aubigné's "History of the Reformation," and I tried hard to get him to buy Plutarch's Lives, which, as I told him, everybody, even religious people, praised as a grand good book; but he would have nothing to do with the old pagan until the graham bread and anti-flesh doctrines came suddenly into our backwoods neighborhood, making a stir something like phrenology and spirit-rappings, which were as mysterious in their attacks as influenza. He then thought it possible that Plutarch might be turned to account on the food question by revealing what those old Greeks and Romans ate to make them strong; and so at last we gained our glorious Plutarch. Dick's "Christian Philosopher," which I borrowed from a neighbor, I thought I might venture to read in the open, trusting that the word "Christian" would be proof against its cautious condemnation. But father balked at the word "Philosopher," and quoted from the Bible a verse which spoke of "philosophy falsely so-called." I then ventured to speak in defense of the book, arguing that we could not do without at least a little of the most useful kinds of philosophy.

"Yes, we can," he said with enthusiasm, "the Bible is the only book human beings can possibly require throughout all the journey from earth to heaven."

"But how," I contended, "can we find the way to heaven without the Bible, and how after we grow old can we read the Bible without a little helpful science? Just think, father, you cannot read your Bible without spectacles, and millions of others are in the same fix; and spectacles cannot be made without some knowledge of the science of optics."

"Oh!" he replied, perceiving the drift of the argument, "there will always be plenty of worldly people to make spectacles."

To this I stubbornly replied with a quotation from the Bible with reference to the time coming when "all shall know the Lord from the least even to the greatest," and then who will make the spectacles? But he still objected to my reading that book, called me a contumacious quibbler too fond of disputation, and ordered me to return it to the accommodating owner. I managed, however, to read it later.

On the food question father insisted that those who argued for a vegetable diet were in the right, because our teeth showed plainly that they were made with reference to fruit and grain and not for flesh like those of dogs and wolves and tigers. He therefore promptly adopted a vegetable diet and requested mother to make the bread from graham flour instead of bolted flour. Mother put both kinds on the table, and meat also, to let all the family take their choice, and while father was insisting on the foolishness of eating flesh, I came to her help by calling father's attention to the passage in the Bible which told the story of Elijah the prophet who, when he was pursued by enemies who wanted to take his life, was hidden by the Lord by the brook Cherith, and fed by ravens; and surely the Lord knew what was good to eat, whether bread or meat. And on what, I asked, did the Lord feed Elijah? On vegetables or graham bread? No, he directed the ravens to feed his prophet on flesh. The Bible being the sole rule, father at once acknowledged that he was mistaken. The Lord never would have sent flesh to Elijah by the ravens if graham bread were better.

I remember as a great and sudden discovery that the poetry of the Bible, Shakespeare, and Milton was a source of inspiring, exhilarating, uplifting pleasure; and I became anxious to know all the poets, and saved up small sums to buy as many of their books as possible. Within three or four years I was the proud possessor of parts of Shakespeare's, Milton's, Cowper's, Henry Kirke White's, Campbell's, and Akenside's works, and quite a number of others seldom read nowadays. I think it was in my fifteenth year that I began to relish good literature with enthusiasm, and smack my lips over favorite lines, but there was desperately little time for reading, even in the winter evenings,—only a few stolen minutes now and then. Father's strict rule was, straight to bed immediately after family worship, which in winter was usually over by eight o'clock. I was in the habit of lingering in the kitchen with a book and candle after the rest of the family had retired, and considered myself fortunate if I got five minutes' reading before father noticed the light and ordered me to bed; an order that of course I immediately obeyed. But night after night I tried to steal minutes in the same lingering way, and how keenly precious those minutes were, few nowadays can know. Father failed perhaps two or three times in a whole winter to notice my light for nearly ten minutes, magnificent golden blocks of time, long to be remembered like holidays or geological periods. One evening when I was reading Church history father was particularly irritable, and called out with hope-killing emphasis, "*John go to bed!* Must I give you a separate order every night to get you to go to bed? Now, I will have no irregularity in the family; you *must* go when the rest go, and without my having to tell you." Then, as an afterthought, as if judging that his words and tone of voice were too severe for so pardonable an offense as reading a religious book he unwarily added: "If you *will* read, get up in the morning and read. You may get up in the morning as early as you like."

That night I went to bed wishing with all my heart and soul that somebody or something might call me out of sleep to avail myself of this wonderful indulgence; and next morning to my joyful surprise I awoke before father called me. A boy sleeps soundly after working all day in the snowy woods, but that frosty morning I sprang out of bed as if called by a trumpet blast, rushed downstairs, scarce feeling my chilblains, enormously eager to see how much time I had won; and when I held up my candle to a little clock that stood on a bracket in the kitchen I found that it was only one o'clock. I had gained five hours, almost half a day "Five hours to myself!" I said, "five huge, solid hours!" I can hardly think of any other event in my life, any discovery I ever made that gave birth to joy so transportingly glorious as the possession of these five frosty hours.

In the glad, tumultuous excitement of so much suddenly acquired time-wealth, I hardly knew what to do with it. I first thought of going on with my reading, but the zero weather would make a fire necessary, and it occurred to me that father might object to the cost of firewood that took time to chop. Therefore, I prudently decided to go down cellar, and begin work on a model of a self-setting sawmill I had invented. Next morning I managed to get up at the same gloriously early hour, and though the temperature of the cellar was a little below the freezing point, and my light was only a tallow candle the mill work went joyfully on. There were a few tools in a corner of the cellar,—a vise, files, a hammer, chisels, etc., that father had brought from Scotland, but no saw excepting a coarse crooked one that was unfit for sawing dry hickory or oak. So I made a fine-tooth saw suitable for my work out of a strip of steel that had formed part of an old-fashioned corset, that cut the hardest wood smoothly. I also made my own bradawls, punches, and a pair of compasses, out of wire and old files.

My workshop was immediately under father's bed, and the filing and tapping in making cogwheels, journals, cams, etc., must, no doubt, have annoyed him, but with the permission he had granted in his mind, and doubtless hoping that I would soon tire of getting up at one o'clock, he impatiently waited about two weeks before saying a word. I did not vary more than five minutes from one o'clock all winter, nor did I feel any bad effects whatever, nor did I think at all about the subject as to whether so little sleep might be in any way injurious; it was a grand triumph of will-power over cold and common comfort and work-weariness in abruptly cutting down my ten hours' allowance of sleep to five. I simply felt that I was rich beyond anything I could have dreamed of or hoped for. I was far more than happy. Like Tam o' Shanter I was glorious, "O'er a' the ills o' life victorious."

Father, as was customary in Scotland, gave thanks and asked a blessing before meals, not merely as a matter of form and decent Christian manners, for he regarded food as a gift derived directly from the hands of the Father in heaven. Therefore every meal to him was a sacrament requiring conduct and attitude of mind not unlike that befitting the Lord's Supper. No idle word was allowed to be spoken at our table, much less any laughing or fun or story-telling. When we were at the breakfast-table, about two weeks after the great golden time-discovery, father cleared his throat preliminary, as we all knew, to saying something considered important. I feared that it was to be on the subject of my early rising, and dreaded the withdrawal of the permission he had granted on account of the noise I made, but still hoping that, as he had given his word that I might get up as early as I wished, he would as a Scotchman stand to it, even though it was given in an unguarded moment and taken in a sense unreasonably far-reaching. The solemn sacramental silence was broken by the dreaded question:—

"John, what time is it when you get up in the morning?"

"About one o'clock," I replied in a low, meek, guilty tone of voice.

"And what kind of a time is that, getting up in the middle of the night and disturbing the whole family?"

I simply reminded him of the permission he had freely granted me to get up as early as I wished.

"I *know* it," he said, in an almost agonized tone of voice, "I *know* I gave you that miserable permission, but I never imagined that you would get up in the middle of the night."

To this I cautiously made no reply, but continued to listen for the heavenly one-o'clock call, and it never failed.

After completing my self-setting sawmill I dammed one of the streams in the meadow and put the mill in operation. This invention was speedily followed by a lot of others,—water-wheels, curious doorlocks and latches, thermometers, hygrometers, pyrometers, clocks, a barometer, an automatic contrivance for feeding the horses at any required hour, a lamp-lighter and fire-lighter, an early-or-late-rising machine, and so forth.

After the sawmill was proved and discharged from my mind, I happened to think it would be a fine thing to make a timekeeper which would tell the day of the week and the day of the month, as well as strike like a common clock and point out the hours; also to have an attachment whereby it could be connected with a bedstead to set me on my feet at any hour in the morning; also to start fires, light lamps, etc. I had learned the time laws of the pendulum from a book, but with this exception I knew nothing of timekeepers, for I had never seen the inside of any sort of clock or watch. After long brooding, the novel clock was at length completed in my mind, and was tried and found to be durable and to work well and look well before I had begun to build it in wood. I carried small parts of it in my pocket to whittle at when I was out at work on the farm, using every spare or stolen moment within reach without father's knowing anything about it. In the middle of summer, when harvesting was in progress, the novel time-machine was nearly completed. It was hidden upstairs in a spare bedroom where some tools were kept. I did the making and mending on the farm, but one day at noon, when I happened to be away, father went upstairs for a hammer or something and discovered the mysterious machine back of the bedstead. My sister Margaret saw him on his knees examining it, and at the first opportunity whispered in my ear, "John, fayther saw that thing you're making upstairs." None of the family knew what I was doing, but they knew very well that all such work was frowned on by father, and kindly warned me of any danger that threatened my plans. The fine invention seemed doomed to destruction before its time-ticking commenced, though I thought it handsome, had so long carried it in my mind, and like the nest of Burns's wee mousie it had cost me mony a weary whittling nibble. When we were at dinner several days after the sad discovery, father began to clear his throat to speak, and I feared the doom of martyrdom was about to be pronounced on my grand clock.

"John," he inquired, "what is that thing you are making upstairs?"

I replied in desperation that I didn't know what to call it.

"What! You mean to say you don't know what you are trying to do?"

"Oh, yes," I said, "I know very well what I am doing."

"What, then, is the thing for?"

"It's for a lot of things," I replied, "but getting people up early in the morning is one of the main things it is intended for; therefore it might perhaps be called an early-rising machine."

After getting up so extravagantly early, all the last memorable winter to make a machine for getting up perhaps still earlier seemed so ridiculous that he very nearly laughed. But after controlling himself and getting command of a sufficiently solemn face and voice he said severely, "Do you not think it is very wrong to waste your time on such nonsense?"

"No," I said meekly, "I don't think I'm doing any wrong."

"Well," he replied, "I assure you I do; and if you were only half as zealous in the study of religion as you are in contriving and whittling these useless, nonsensical things, it would be infinitely better for you. I want you to be like Paul, who said that he desired to know nothing among men but Christ and Him crucified."

To this I made no reply, gloomily believing my fine machine was to be burned, but still taking what comfort I could in realizing that anyhow I had enjoyed inventing and making it.

After a few days, finding that nothing more was to be said, and that father after all had not had the heart to destroy it, all necessity for secrecy being ended, I finished it in the half-hours that we had at noon and set it in the parlor between two chairs, hung moraine boulders that had come from the direction of Lake Superior on it for weights, and set it running. We were then hauling grain into the barn. Father at this period devoted himself entirely to the Bible and did no farm work whatever. The clock had a good loud tick, and when he heard it strike, one of my sisters told me that he left his study, went to the parlor, got down on his knees and carefully examined the machinery, which was all in plain sight, not being enclosed in a case. This he did repeatedly, and evidently seemed a little proud of my ability to invent and whittle such a thing, though careful to give no encouragement for anything more of the kind in future.

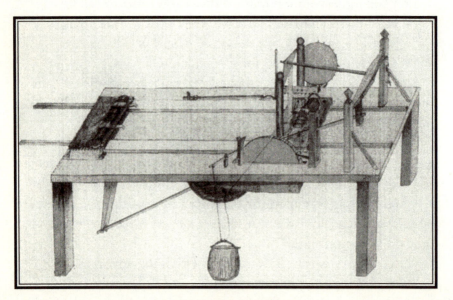

Self-Setting Sawmill

But somehow it seemed impossible to stop. Inventing and whittling faster than ever, I made another hickory clock, shaped like a scythe to symbolize the scythe of Father Time. The pendulum is a bunch of arrows symbolizing the flight of time. It hangs on a leafless mossy oak snag showing the effect of time, and on the snath is written, "All flesh is grass." This, especially the inscription, rather pleased father, and, of course, mother and all my sisters and brothers admired it. Like the first it indicates the days of the week and month, starts fires and beds at any given hour and minute, and, though made more than fifty years ago, is still a good timekeeper.

My mind still running on clocks, I invented a big one like a town clock with four dials, with the time-figures so large they could be read by all our immediate neighbors as well as ourselves when at work in the fields, and on the side next the house the days of the week and month were indicated. It was to be placed on the peak of the barn roof. But just as it was all but finished, father stopped me, saying that it would bring too many people around the barn. I then asked permission to put it on the top of a black-oak tree near the house. Studying the larger main branches, I thought I could secure a sufficiently rigid foundation for it, while the trimmed sprays and leaves would conceal the angles of the cabin required to shelter the works from the weather, and the two-second pendulum, fourteen feet long, could be snugly encased on the side of the trunk. Nothing about the grand, useful timekeeper, I argued, would disfigure the tree, for it would look something like a big hawk's nest. "But that," he objected, "would draw still bigger bothersome trampling crowds about the place, for who ever heard of anything so queer as a big clock on the top of a tree?" So I had to lay aside its big wheels and cams and rest content with the pleasure of inventing it, and looking at it in my mind and listening to the deep solemn throbbing of its long two-second pendulum with its two old axes back to back for the bob.

One of my inventions was a large thermometer made of an iron rod, about three feet long and five eighths of an inch in diameter, that had formed part of a wagon-box. The expansion and contraction of this rod was multiplied by a series of levers made of strips of hoop iron. The pressure of the rod against the levers was kept constant by a small counterweight, so that the slightest change in the length of the rod was instantly shown on a dial about three feet wide multiplied about thirty-two thousand times. The zero-point was gained by packing the rod in wet snow. The scale was so large that the big black hand on the white-painted dial could be seen distinctly and the temperature read while we were ploughing in the field below the house. The extremes of heat and cold caused the hand to make several revolutions. The number of these revolutions was indicated on a small dial marked on the larger one. This

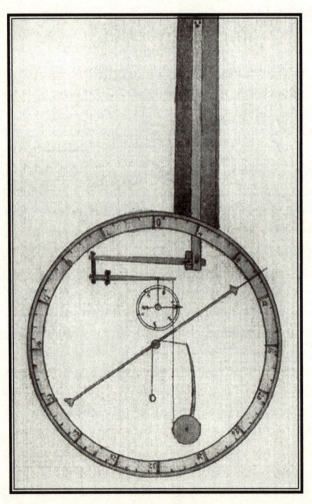

Thermometer

thermometer was fastened on the side of the house, and was so sensitive that when any one approached it within four or five feet the heat radiated from the observer's body caused the hand of the dial to move so fast that the motion was plainly visible, and when he stepped back, the hand moved slowly back to its normal position. It was regarded as a great wonder by the neighbors and even by my own all-Bible father.

Boys are fond of the books of travelers, and I remember that one day, after I had been reading Mungo Park's travels in Africa, mother said: "Weel, John, maybe you will travel like Park and Humboldt some day." Father overheard her and cried out in solemn deprecation,

"Oh, Anne! dinna put sic notions in the laddie's heed." But at this time there was precious little need of such prayers. My brothers left the farm when they came of age, but I stayed a year longer, loath to leave home. Mother hoped I might be a minister some day; my sisters that I would be a great inventor. I often thought I should like to be a physician, but I saw no way of making money and getting the necessary education, excepting as an inventor. So, as a beginning, I decided to try to get into a big shop or factory and live a while among machines. But I was naturally extremely shy and had been taught to have a poor opinion of myself, as of no account, though all our neighbors encouragingly called me a genius, sure to rise in the world. When I was talking over plans one day with a friendly neighbor, he said: "Now, John, if you wish to get into a machine-shop, just take some of your inventions to the State Fair, and you may be sure that as soon as they are seen they will open the door of any shop in the country for you. You will be welcomed everywhere." And when I doubtingly asked if people would care to look at things made of wood, he said, "Made of wood! Made of wood! What does it matter what they're made of when they are so out-and-out original. There's nothing else like them in the world. That is what will attract attention, and besides they're mighty handsome things anyway to come from the backwoods." So I was encouraged to leave home and go at his direction to the State Fair when it was being held in Madison.

The World And The University

∾

W hen I told father that I was about to leave home, and inquired whether, if I should happen to be in need of money, he would send me a little, he said, "No; depend entirely on yourself." Good advice, I suppose, but surely needlessly severe for a bashful, home-loving boy who had worked so hard. I had the gold sovereign that my grandfather had given me when I left Scotland, and a few dollars, perhaps ten, that I had made by raising a few bushels of grain on a little patch of sandy abandoned ground. So when I left home to try the world I had only about fifteen dollars in my pocket.

Strange to say, father carefully taught us to consider ourselves very poor worms of the dust, conceived in sin, etc., and devoutly believed that quenching every spark of pride and self-confidence was a sacred duty, without realizing that in so doing he might at the same time be quenching everything else. Praise he considered most venomous, and tried to assure me that when I was fairly out in the wicked world making my own way I would soon learn that although I might have thought him a hard taskmaster at times, strangers were far harder. On the contrary, I found no lack of kindness and sympathy. All the baggage I carried was a package made up of the two clocks and a small thermometer made of a piece of old wash-board, all three tied together, with no covering or case of any sort, the whole looking like one very complicated machine.

The aching parting from mother and my sisters was, of course, hard to bear. Father let David drive me down to Pardeeville, a place I had never before seen, though it was only nine miles south of the Hickory Hill home. When we arrived at the village tavern, it seemed deserted. Not a single person was in sight. I set my clock baggage on the rickety platform. David said good-bye and started for home, leaving me alone in the world. The grinding noise made by the wagon in turning short brought out the landlord, and the first thing that caught his eye was my strange bundle. Then he looked at me and said, "Hello, young man, what's this?"

"Machines," I said, "for keeping time and getting up in the morning, and so forth."

"Well! Well! That's a mighty queer get-up. You must be a Down-East Yankee. Where did you get the pattern for such a thing?"

"In my head," I said.

Some one down the street happened to notice the landlord looking intently at something and came up to see what it was. Three or four people in that little village formed an attractive crowd, and in fifteen or twenty minutes the greater part of the population of Pardeeville stood gazing in a circle around my strange hickory belongings. I kept outside of the circle to avoid being seen, and had the advantage of hearing the remarks without being embarrassed. Almost every one as he came up would say, "What's that? What's it for? Who made it?" The landlord would answer them all alike, "Why, a young man that lives out in the country somewhere made it, and he says it's a thing for keeping time, getting up in the morning, and something that I didn't understand. I don't know what he meant." "Oh, no!" one of the crowd would say, "that can't be. It's for something else—something mysterious. Mark my words, you'll see all about it in the newspapers some of these days." A curious little fellow came running up the street, joined the crowd, stood on tiptoe to get sight of the wonder, quickly made up his mind, and shouted in crisp, confident, cock-crowing style, "I know what that contraption's for. It's a machine for taking the bones out of fish."

This was in the time of the great popular phrenology craze, when the fences and barns along the roads throughout the country were plastered with big skull-bump posters, headed, "Know Thyself," and advising everybody to attend schoolhouse lectures to have their heads explained and be told what they were good for and whom they ought to marry. My mechanical bundle seemed to bring a good deal of this phrenology to mind, for many of the onlookers would say, "I wish I could see that boy's head,—he must have a tremendous bump of invention." Others complimented me by saying, "I wish I had that fellow's head. I'd rather have it than the best farm in the State."

I stayed overnight at this little tavern, waiting for a train. In the morning I went to the station, and set my bundle on the platform. Along came the thundering train, a glorious sight, the first train I had ever waited for. When the conductor saw my queer baggage, he cried, "Hello! What have we here?"

"Inventions for keeping time, early rising, and so forth. May I take them into the car with me?"

"You can take them where you like," he replied, "but you had better give them to the baggage-master. If you take them into the car they will draw a crowd and might get broken."

So I gave them to the baggage-master and made haste to ask the conductor whether I might ride on the engine. He good-naturedly said: "Yes, it's the right place for you. Run ahead, and tell the engineer what I say." But the engineer bluntly refused to let me on, saying: "It don't matter what the conductor told you. *I* say you can't ride on my engine."

By this time the conductor, standing ready to start his train, was watching to see what luck I had, and when he saw me returning came ahead to meet me.

"The engineer won't let me on," I reported.

"Won't he?" said the kind conductor. "Oh! I guess he will. You come down with me." And so he actually took the time and patience to walk the length of that long train to get me on to the engine.

"Charlie," said he, addressing the engineer, "don't you ever take a passenger?"

"Very seldom," he replied.

"Anyhow, I wish you would take this young man on. He has the strangest machines in the baggage-car I ever saw in my life. I believe he could make a locomotive. He wants to see the engine running. Let him on." Then in a low whisper he told me to jump on, which I did gladly, the engineer offering neither encouragement nor objection.

As soon as the train was started, the engineer asked what the "strange thing" the conductor spoke of really was.

"Only inventions for keeping time, getting folk up in the morning, and so forth," I hastily replied, and before he could ask any more questions I asked permission to go outside of the cab to see the machinery. This he kindly granted, adding, "Be careful not to fall off, and when you hear me whistling for a station you come back, because if it is reported against me to the superintendent that I allow boys to run all over my engine I might lose my job."

Assuring him that I would come back promptly, I went out and walked along the foot-board on the side of the boiler, watching the magnificent machine rushing through the landscapes as if glorying in its strength like a living creature. While seated on the cow-catcher platform, I seemed to be fairly flying, and the wonderful display of power and motion was enchanting. This was the first time I had ever been on a train, much less a locomotive, since I had left Scotland. When I got to Madison, I thanked the kind conductor and engineer for my glorious ride, inquired the way to the Fair, shouldered my inventions, and walked to the Fair Ground.

When I applied for an admission ticket at a window by the gate I told the agent that I had something to exhibit.

"What is it?" he inquired.

"Well, here it is. Look at it."

When he craned his neck through the window and got a glimpse of my bundle, he cried excitedly, "Oh! *you* don't need a ticket,—come right in."

When I inquired of the agent where such things as mine should be exhibited, he said, "You see that building up on the hill with a big flag on it? That's the Fine Arts Hall, and it's just the place for your wonderful invention."

So I went up to the Fine Arts Hall and looked in, wondering if they would allow wooden things in so fine a place.

I was met at the door by a dignified gentleman, who greeted me kindly and said, "Young man, what have we got here?"

"Two clocks and a thermometer," I replied.

"Did you make these? They look wonderfully beautiful and novel and must, I think, prove the most interesting feature of the fair."

"Where shall I place them?" I inquired.

"Just look around, young man, and choose the place you like best, whether it is occupied or not. You can have your pick of all the building, and a carpenter to make the necessary shelving and assist you every way possible!"

So I quickly had a shelf made large enough for all of them, went out on the hill and picked up some glacial boulders of the right size for weights, and in fifteen or twenty minutes the clocks were running. They seemed to attract more attention than anything else in the hall I got lots of praise from the crowd and the newspaper-reporters. The local press reports were copied into the Eastern papers. It was considered wonderful that a boy on a farm had been able to invent and make such things, and almost every spectator foretold good fortune. But I had been so lectured by my father above all things to avoid praise that I was afraid to read those kind newspaper notices, and never clipped out or preserved any of them, just glanced at them and turned away my eyes from beholding vanity. They gave me a prize of ten or fifteen dollars and a diploma for wonderful things not down in the list of exhibits.

Many years later, after I had written articles and books, I received a letter from the gentleman who had charge of the Fine Arts Hall. He proved to be the Professor of English Literature in the University of Wisconsin at this Fair time, and long afterward he sent me clippings of reports of his lectures. He had a lecture on me, discussing style, etcetera, and telling how well he remembered my arrival at the Hall in my shirt-sleeves with those mechanical wonders on my shoulder, and so forth, and so forth. These inventions, though of little importance, opened all doors for me and made marks that have lasted many years, simply, I suppose, because they were original and promising.

I was looking around in the mean time to find out where I should go to seek my fortune. An inventor at the Fair, by the name of Wiard, was exhibiting an iceboat he had invented to run on the upper Mississippi from Prairie du Chien to St. Paul during the winter months, explaining how useful it would be thus to make a highway of the river while it was closed to ordinary navigation by ice. After he saw my inventions he offered me a place in his foundry and machine-shop in Prairie du Chien and promised to assist me all he could. So I made up my mind to accept his offer and rode with him to Prairie du Chien in his iceboat, which was mounted on a flat car. I soon found, however, that he was seldom at home and that I was not likely to learn much at his small shop. I found a place where I could work for my board and devote my spare hours to mechanical drawing, geometry, and physics, making but little headway, however, although the Pelton family, for whom I worked, were very kind. I made up my mind after a few months' stay in Prairie du Chien to return to Madison, hoping that in some way I might be able to gain an education.

At Madison I raised a few dollars by making and selling a few of those bedsteads that set the sleepers on their feet in the morning,— inserting in the footboard the works of an ordinary clock that could be bought for a dollar. I also made a few dollars addressing circulars in an insurance office, while at the same time I was paying my board by taking care of a pair of horses and going errands. This is of no great interest except that I was thus winning my bread while hoping that something would turn up that might enable me to make money enough to enter the State University. This was my ambition, and it never wavered no matter what I was doing. No University, it seemed to me, could be more admirably, situated, and as I sauntered about it, charmed with its fine lawns and trees and beautiful lakes, and saw the students going and coming with their books, and occasionally practicing with a theodolite in measuring distances, I thought that if I could only join them it would be the greatest joy of life. I was desperately hungry and thirsty for knowledge and willing to endure anything to get it.

One day I chanced to meet a student who had noticed my inventions at the Fair and now recognized me. And when I said, "You are fortunate fellows to be allowed to study in this beautiful place. I wish I could join you." "Well, why don't you?" he asked. "I haven't money enough," I said. "Oh, as to money," he reassuringly explained, "very little is required. I presume you're able to enter the Freshman class, and you can board yourself as quite a number of us do at a cost of about a dollar a week. The baker and milkman come every day. You can live on bread and milk." Well, I thought, maybe I have money enough for at least one beginning term. Anyhow I couldn't help trying.

With fear and trembling, overladen with ignorance, I called on Professor Stirling, the Dean of the Faculty, who was then Acting President, presented my case, and told him how far I had got on with my studies at home, and that I hadn't been to school since leaving Scotland at the age of eleven years, excepting one short term of a couple of months at a district school, because I could not be spared from the farm work. After hearing my story, the kind professor welcomed me to the glorious University—next, it seemed to me, to the Kingdom of Heaven. After a few weeks in the preparatory department I entered the Freshman class. In Latin I found that one of the books in use I had already studied in Scotland. So, after an interruption of a dozen years, I began my Latin over again where I had left off; and, strange to say, most of it came back to me, especially the grammar which I had committed to memory at the Dunbar Grammar School.

During the four years that I was in the University, I earned enough in the harvest-fields during the long summer vacations to carry me through the balance of each year, working very hard, cutting with a cradle four acres of wheat a day, and helping to put it in the shock. But, having to buy books and paying, I think, thirty-two dollars a year for instruction, and occasionally buying acids and retorts, glass tubing, bell-glasses, flasks, etc.,

I had to cut down expenses for board now and then to half a dollar a week.

One winter I taught school ten miles south of Madison, earning much-needed money at the rate of twenty dollars a month, "boarding round," and keeping up my University work by studying at night. As I was not then well enough off to own a watch, I used one of my hickory clocks, not only for keeping time, but for starting the school fire in the cold mornings, and regulating class-times. I carried it out on my shoulder to the old log schoolhouse, and set it to work on a little shelf nailed to one of the knotty, bulging logs. The winter was very cold, and I had to go to the schoolhouse and start the fire about eight o'clock to warm it before the arrival of the scholars. This was a rather trying job, and one that my clock might easily be made to do. Therefore, after supper one evening I told the head of the family with whom I was boarding that if he would give me a candle I would go back to the schoolhouse and make arrangements for lighting the fire at eight o'clock, without my having to be present until time to open the school at nine. He said, "Oh! young man, you have some curious things in the school-room, but I don't think you can do that." I said, "Oh, yes! It's easy," and in hardly more than an hour the simple job was completed. I had only to place a teaspoonful of powdered chlorate of potash and sugar on the stove-hearth near a few shavings and kindling, and at the required time make the clock, through a simple arrangement, touch the inflammable mixture with a drop of sulphuric acid. Every evening after school was dismissed, I shoveled out what was left of the fire into the snow, put in a little kindling, filled up the big box stove with heavy oak wood, placed the lighting arrangement on the hearth, and set the clock to drop the acid at the hour of eight; all this requiring only a few minutes.

The first morning after I had made this simple arrangement I invited the doubting farmer to watch the old squat schoolhouse from a window that overlooked it, to see if a good smoke did not rise from the stovepipe. Sure enough, on the minute, he saw a tall column curling gracefully up through the frosty air, but instead of congratulating me on my success he solemnly shook his head and said in a hollow, lugubrious voice, "Young man, you will be setting fire to the schoolhouse." All winter long that faithful clock fire never failed, and by the time I got to the schoolhouse the stove was usually red-hot.

At the beginning of the long summer vacations I returned to the Hickory Hill farm to earn the means in the harvest-fields to continue my University course, walking all the way to save railroad fares. And although I cradled four acres of wheat a day, I made the long, hard, sweaty day's work still longer and harder by keeping up my study of plants. At the noon hour I collected a large handful, put them in water to keep them fresh, and after supper got to work on

the leaf of the locust is made up of several leaflets, and so also
ne leaf of the pea. Now taste the locust leaf."

did so and found that it tasted like the leaf of the pea. Nature
used the same seasoning for both, though one is a straggling
e, the other a big tree.

Now, surely you cannot imagine that all these similar charac-
are mere coincidences. Do they not rather go to show that the
ator in making the pea vine and locust tree had the same idea in
d, and that plants are not classified arbitrarily? Man has nothing
o with their classification. Nature has attended to all that, giving
ntial unity with boundless variety, so that the botanist has only
xamine plants to learn the harmony of their relations."

his fine lesson charmed me and sent me to the woods and mead-
in wild enthusiasm. Like everybody else I was always fond of
ers, attracted by their external beauty and purity. Now my eyes
e opened to their inner beauty, all alike revealing glorious traces
he thoughts of God, and leading on and on into the infinite
nos. I wandered away at every opportunity, making long excur-
s round the lakes, gathering specimens and keeping them fresh
bucket in my room to study at night after my regular class tasks
e learned; for my eyes never closed on the plant glory I had seen.

evertheless, I still indulged my love of mechanical inventions.
ented a desk in which the books I had to study were arranged
der at the beginning of each term. I also made a bed which set
on my feet every morning at the hour determined on, and in
winter mornings just as the bed set me on the floor it lighted
np. Then, after the minutes allowed for dressing had elapsed,
ck was heard and the first book to be studied was pushed up
a rack below the top of the desk, thrown open, and allowed
main there the number of minutes required. Then the machin-
losed the book and allowed it to drop back into its stall, then
ed the rack forward and threw up the next in order, and so on,
e day being divided according to the times of recitation, and
required and allotted to each study. Besides this, I thought it
d be a fine thing in the summer-time when the sun rose early,
ispense with the clock-controlled bed machinery, and make

them and sat up till after midnight, analyzing and
leaving only four hours for sleep; and by the end ⟨...⟩
after taking up botany, I knew the principal floweri⟨...⟩
region.

I received my first lesson in botany from a studen⟨...⟩
Griswold, who is now County Judge of the Count⟨...⟩
Wisconsin. In the University he was often laughe⟨...⟩
of his anxiety to instruct others, and his frequently
emphasis, "Imparting instruction is my greatest e⟨...⟩
memorable day in June, when I was standing on th⟨...⟩
the north dormitory, Mr. Griswold joined me an⟨...⟩
to teach. He reached up, plucked a flower from ⟨...⟩
branch of a locust tree, and, handing it to me, sai⟨...⟩
know what family this tree belongs to?"

"No," I said, "I don't know anything about bota⟨...⟩

"Well, no matter," said he, "what is it like?"

"It's like a pea flower," I replied.

"That's right. You're right," he said, "it belongs t⟨...⟩

"But how can that be," I objected, "when the pe⟨...⟩
ing, straggling herb, and the locust a big, thorny h⟨...⟩

"Yes, that is true," he replied, "as to the diffe⟨...⟩
it is also true that in all their essential characters t⟨...⟩
therefore they must belong to one and the same f⟨...⟩
the peculiar form of the locust flower; you see tha⟨...⟩
called the banner, is broad and erect, and so is t⟨...⟩
the pea flower; the two lower petals, called the wir⟨...⟩
and wing-shaped; so are those of the pea; and the
the wings are united on their edges, curve upwar⟨...⟩
is called the keel, and so you see are the correspon⟨...⟩
pea flower. And now look at the stamens and pi⟨...⟩
nine of the ten stamens have their filaments un⟨...⟩
around the pistil, but the tenth stamen has its fil⟨...⟩
are very marked characters, are they not? And, s⟨...⟩
will find them the same in the tree and in the vine⟨...⟩
ovules or seeds of the locust, and you will see that
in a pod or legume like those of the pea. And look⟨...⟩

use of sunbeams instead. This I did simply by taking a lens out of my small spy-glass, fixing it on a frame on the sill of my bedroom window, and pointing it to the sunrise; the sunbeams focused on a thread burned it through, allowing the bed machinery to put me on my feet. When I wished to arise at any given time after sunrise, I had only to turn the pivoted frame that held the lens the requisite number of degrees or minutes. Thus I took Emerson's advice and hitched my dumping-wagon bed to a star.

I also invented a machine to make visible the growth of plants and the action of the sunlight, a very delicate contrivance, enclosed in glass. Besides this I invented a barometer and a lot of novel scientific apparatus. My room was regarded as a sort of show place by the professors, who oftentimes brought visitors to it on Saturdays and holidays. And when, some eighteen years after I had left the University, I was sauntering over the campus in time of vacation, and spoke to a man who seemed to be taking some charge of the grounds, he informed me that he was the janitor; and when I inquired what had become of Pat, the janitor in my time, and a favorite with the students, he replied that Pat was still alive and well, but now too old to do much work. And when I pointed to the dormitory room that I long ago occupied, he said: "Oh! then I know who you are," and mentioned my name. "How comes it that you know my name?" I inquired. He explained that "Pat always pointed out that room to newcomers and told long stories about the wonders that used to be in it." So long had the memory of my little inventions survived.

Although I was four years at the University, I did not take the regular course of studies, but instead picked out what I thought would be most useful to me, particularly chemistry, which opened a new world, and mathematics and physics, a little Greek and Latin, botany and geology. I was far from satisfied with what I had learned, and should have stayed longer. Anyhow I wandered away on a glorious botanical and geological excursion, which has lasted nearly fifty years and is not yet completed, always happy and free, poor and rich, without thought of a diploma or of making a name, urged on and on through endless, inspiring, Godful beauty.

From the top of a hill on the north side of Lake Mendota I gained a last wistful, lingering view of the beautiful University grounds and buildings where I had spent so many hungry and happy and hopeful days. There with streaming eyes I bade my blessed Alma Mater farewell. But I was only leaving one University for another, the Wisconsin University for the University of the Wilderness.

PART TWO

From *My First Summer in the Sierra*

My Desk, made and used at Wisconsin State University

Through the Foothills With a Flock of Sheep

∞

In the great Central Valley of California there are only two seasons—spring and summer. The spring begins with the first rainstorm, which usually falls in November. In a few months the wonderful flowery vegetation is in full bloom, and by the end of May it is dead and dry and crisp, as if every plant had been roasted in an oven.

Then the lolling, panting flocks and herds are driven to the high, cool, green pastures of the Sierra. I was longing for the mountains about this time, but money was scarce and I couldn't see how a bread supply was to be kept up. While I was anxiously brooding on the bread problem, so troublesome to wanderers, and trying to believe that I might learn to live like the wild animals, gleaning nourishment here and there from seeds, berries, etc., sauntering and climbing in joyful independence of money or baggage, Mr. Delaney, a sheep-owner, for whom I had worked a few weeks, called on me, and offered to engage me to go with his shepherd and flock to the headwaters of the Merced and Tuolumne rivers—the very region I had most in mind. I was in the mood to accept work of any kind that would take me into the mountains whose treasures I had tasted last summer in the Yosemite region. The flock, he explained, would be moved gradually higher through the successive forest belts as the snow melted, stopping for a few weeks at the best places we came to. These I thought would be good centers of observation from which I might be able to make many telling excursions within a radius of eight or ten miles of the camps to learn something of the plants, animals, and rocks; for he assured me that I should be left perfectly free to follow my studies. I judged, however, that I was in no way the right man for the place, and freely explained my shortcomings, confessing that I was wholly unacquainted with the topography of the upper mountains, the streams that would have to be crossed, and the wild sheep-eating animals, etc.; in short that, what with bears, coyotes, rivers, cañons, and thorny, bewildering chaparral, I feared that half or more of his flock would be lost. Fortunately these shortcomings seemed insignificant to Mr. Delaney. The main thing, he said, was to have a man about the camp whom he could trust to see that the shepherd did his duty, and he assured me that the difficulties that seemed so formidable at a distance would vanish as we went on; encouraging me further by saying that the shepherd would do all the herding, that I could study plants and rocks and scenery as much as I liked, and that he would himself accompany us to the first main camp and make occasional visits to our higher ones to replenish our store of provisions and see how we prospered. Therefore I concluded to go, though still fearing, when I saw the silly sheep bouncing one by one through the narrow gate of the home corral to be counted, that of the two thousand and fifty many would never return.

I was fortunate in getting a fine St. Bernard dog for a companion. His master, a hunter with whom I was slightly acquainted, came to me as soon as he heard that I was going to spend the summer in the Sierra and begged me to take his favorite dog, Carlo, with me, for he feared that if he were compelled to stay all summer on the plains the fierce heat might be the death of him. "I think I can trust you to be kind to him," he said, "and I am sure he will be good to you. He knows all about the mountain animals, will guard the camp, assist in managing the sheep, and in every way be found able and faithful." Carlo knew we were talking about him, watched our faces, and listened so attentively that I fancied he understood us. Calling him by name, I asked him if he was willing to go with me. He looked me in the face with eyes expressing wonderful intelligence, then turned to his master, and after permission was given by a wave of the hand toward me and a farewell patting caress, he quietly followed me as if he perfectly understood all that had been said and had known me always.

June 3, 1869. This morning provisions, camp-kettles, blankets, plant-press, etc., were packed on two horses, the flock headed for the tawny foothills, and away we sauntered in a cloud of dust: Mr. Delaney, bony and tall, with sharply hacked profile like Don Quixote, leading the pack-horses, Billy, the proud shepherd, a Chinaman and a Digger Indian to assist in driving for the first few days in the brushy foothills, and myself with notebook tied to my belt.

The home ranch from which we set out is on the south side of the Tuolumne River near French Bar, where the foothills of metamorphic gold-bearing slates dip below the stratified deposits of the Central Valley. We had not gone more than a mile before some of the old leaders of the flock showed by the eager, inquiring way they ran and looked ahead that they were thinking of the high pastures they had enjoyed last summer. Soon the whole flock seemed to be hopefully excited, the mothers calling their lambs, the lambs replying in tones wonderfully human, their fondly quavering calls interrupted now and then by hastily snatched mouthfuls of withered grass. Amid all this seeming babel of baas as they streamed over the hills every mother and child recognized each other's voice. In case a tired lamb, half asleep in the smothering dust, should fail to answer, its mother would come running back through the flock toward the spot whence its last response was heard, and refused to be comforted until she found it, the one of a thousand, though to our eyes and ears all seemed alike.

The flock traveled at the rate of about a mile an hour, outspread in the form of an irregular triangle, about a hundred yards wide at the base, and a hundred and fifty yards long, with a crooked, ever-changing point made up of the strongest foragers, called the "leaders," which, with the most active of those scattered along the ragged sides of the "main body," hastily explored nooks in the rocks and bushes for grass and leaves; the lambs and feeble old mothers dawdling in the rear were called the "tail end."

About noon the heat was hard to bear; the poor sheep panted pitifully and tried to stop in the shade of every tree they came to,

Sheep in the Mountains

while we gazed with eager longing through the dim burning glare toward the snowy mountains and streams, though not one was in sight. The landscape is only wavering foothills roughened here and there with bushes and trees and outcropping masses of slate. The trees, mostly the blue oak (*Quercus Douglasii*), are about thirty to forty feet high, with pale blue-green leaves and white bark, sparsely planted on the thinnest soil or in crevices of rocks beyond the reach of grass fires. The slates in many places rise abruptly through the tawny grass in sharp lichen-covered slabs like tombstones in deserted burying-grounds. With the exception of the oak and four or five species of manzanita and ceanothus, the vegetation of the foothills is mostly the same as that of the plains. I saw this region in the early spring, when it was a charming landscape garden full of birds and bees and flowers. Now the scorching weather makes everything dreary. The ground is full of cracks, lizards glide about on the rocks, and ants in amazing numbers, whose tiny sparks of life only burn the brighter with the heat, fairly quiver with unquenchable energy as they run in long lines to fight and gather food. How it comes that they do not dry to a crisp in a few seconds' exposure to such sun-fire is marvelous. A few rattlesnakes lie coiled in out-of-the-way places, but are seldom seen. Magpies and crows, usually so noisy, are silent now, standing in mixed flocks on the ground beneath the best shade trees, with bills wide open and wings drooped, too breathless to speak; the quails also are trying to keep in the shade about the few tepid alkaline water-holes; cotton-tail rabbits are running from shade to shade among the ceanothus brush, and occasionally the long-eared hare is seen cantering grace-fully across the wider openings.

After a short noon rest in a grove, the poor dust-choked flock was again driven ahead over the brushy hills, but the dim roadway we had been following faded away just where it was most needed, compel-ling us to stop to look about us and get our bearings. The Chinaman seemed to think we were lost, and chattered in pidgin English con-cerning the abundance of "litty stick" (chaparral), while the Indian silently scanned the billowy ridges and gulches for openings. Pushing through the thorny jungle, we at length discovered a road trending toward Coulterville, which we followed until an hour before sunset, when we reached a dry ranch and camped for the night.

Camping in the foothills with a flock of sheep is simple and easy, but far from pleasant. The sheep were allowed to pick what they could find in the neighborhood until after sunset, watched by the shepherd, while the others gathered wood, made a fire, cooked, unpacked and fed the horses, etc. About dusk the weary sheep were gathered on the highest open spot near camp, where they willingly bunched close together, and after each mother had found her lamb and suckled it, all lay down and required no attention until morning.

Supper was announced by the call, "Grub!" Each with a tin plate helped himself direct from the pots and pans while chatting about such camp studies as sheep-feed, mines, coyotes, bears, or adventures during the memorable gold days of pay dirt. The Indian kept in the background, saying never a word, as if he belonged to another species. The meal finished, the dogs were fed, the smokers smoked by the fire, and under the influences of fullness and tobacco the calm that settled on their faces seemed almost divine, something like the mellow meditative glow portrayed on the countenances of saints. Then suddenly, as if awakening from a dream, each with a sigh or a grunt knocked the ashes out of his pipe, yawned, gazed at the fire a few moments, said, "Well, I believe I'll turn in," and straightway vanished beneath his blankets. The fire smouldered and flickered an hour or two longer; the stars shone brighter; coons, coyotes, and owls stirred the silence here and there, while crickets and hylas made a cheerful, continuous music, so fitting and full that it seemed a part of the very body of the night. The only discordance came from a snoring sleeper, and the coughing sheep with dust in their throats. In the starlight the flock looked like a big gray blanket.

June 4. The camp was astir at daybreak; coffee, bacon, and beans formed the breakfast, followed by quick dish-washing and packing. A general bleating began about sunrise. As soon as a mother ewe arose, her lamb came bounding and bunting for its breakfast, and after the thousand youngsters had been suckled the flock began to nibble and spread. The restless wethers with ravenous appetites were the first to move, but dared not go far from the main body.

Billy and the Indian and the Chinaman kept them headed along the weary road, and allowed them to pick up what little they could find on a breadth of about a quarter of a mile. But as several flocks had already gone ahead of us, scarce a leaf, green or dry, was left; therefore the starving flock had to be hurried on over the bare, hot hills to the nearest of the green pastures, about twenty or thirty miles from here.

The pack-animals were led by Don Quixote, a heavy rifle over his shoulder intended for bears and wolves. This day has been as hot and dusty as the first, leading over gently sloping brown hills, with mostly the same vegetation, excepting the strange-looking Sabine pine (*Pinus Sabiniana*), which here forms small groves or is scattered among the blue oaks. The trunk divides at a height of fifteen or twenty feet into two or more stems, outleaning or nearly upright, with many straggling branches and long gray needles, casting but little shade. In general appearance this tree looks more like a palm than a pine. The cones are about six or seven inches long, about five in diameter, very heavy, and last long after they fall, so that the ground beneath the trees is covered with them. They make fine resiny, light-giving camp-fires, next to ears of Indian corn the most beautiful fuel I've ever seen. The nuts, the Don tells me, are gathered in large quantities by the Digger Indians for food. They are about as large and hard-shelled as hazelnuts—food and fire fit for the gods from the same fruit.

June 5. This morning a few hours after setting out with the crawling sheep-cloud, we gained the summit of the first well-defined bench on the mountain-flank at Pino Blanco. The Sabine pines interest me greatly. They are so airy and strangely palm-like I was eager to sketch them, and was in a fever of excitement without accomplishing much. I managed to halt long enough, however, to make a tolerably fair sketch of Pino Blanco peak from the southwest side, where there is a small field and vineyard irrigated by a stream that makes a pretty fall on its way down a gorge by the roadside.

After gaining the open summit of this first bench, feeling the natural exhilaration due to the slight elevation of a thousand feet or so, and the hopes excited concerning the outlook to be obtained, a magnificent section of the Merced Valley at what is called Horseshoe Bend came full in sight—a glorious wilderness that seemed to be calling with a thousand songful voices. Bold, down-sweeping slopes, feathered with pines and clumps of manzanita with sunny, open spaces between them, make up most of the foreground; the middle and background present fold beyond fold of finely modeled hills and ridges rising into mountain-like masses in the distance, all covered with a shaggy growth of chaparral, mostly adenostoma, planted so marvelously close and even that it looks like soft, rich plush without a single tree or bare spot. As far as the eye can reach it extends, a heaving, swelling sea of green as regular and continuous as that produced by the heaths of Scotland. The sculpture of the landscape is as striking in its main lines as in its lavish richness of detail; a grand congregation of massive heights with the river shining between, each carved into smooth, graceful folds without leaving a single rocky angle exposed, as if the delicate fluting and ridging fashioned out of metamorphic slates had been carefully sandpapered. The whole landscape showed design, like man's noblest sculptures. How wonderful the power of its beauty! Gazing awe-stricken, I might have left everything for it. Glad, endless work would then be mine tracing the forces that have brought forth its features, its rocks and plants and animals and glorious weather. Beauty beyond thought everywhere, beneath, above, made and being made forever. I gazed

Horseshoe Bend, Merced River

and gazed and longed and admired until the dusty sheep and packs were far out of sight, made hurried notes and a sketch, though there was no need of either, for the colors and lines and expression of this divine landscape-countenance are so burned into mind and heart they surely can never grow dim.

The evening of this charmed day is cool, calm, cloudless, and full of a kind of lightning I have never seen before—white glowing cloud-shaped masses down among the trees and bushes, like quick-throbbing fireflies in the Wisconsin meadows rather than the so-called "wild fire." The spreading hairs of the horses' tails and sparks from our blankets show how highly charged the air is.

June 6. We are now on what may be called the second bench or plateau of the Range, after making many small ups and downs over belts of hill-waves, with, of course, corresponding changes in the vegetation. In open spots many of the lowland compositæ are still to be found, and some of the Mariposa tulips and other conspicuous members of the lily family; but the characteristic blue oak of the foothills is left below, and its place is taken by a fine large species (*Quercus Californica*) with deeply lobed deciduous leaves, picturesquely divided trunk, and broad, massy, finely lobed and modeled head. Here also at a height of about twenty-five hundred feet we come to the edge of the great coniferous forest, made up mostly of yellow pine with just a few sugar pines. We are now in the mountains and they are in us, kindling enthusiasm, making every nerve quiver, filling every pore and cell of us. Our flesh-and-bone tabernacle seems transparent as glass to the beauty about us, as if truly an inseparable part of it, thrilling with the air and trees, streams and rocks, in the waves of the sun,—a part of all nature, neither old nor young, sick nor well, but immortal. Just now I can hardly conceive of any bodily condition dependent on food or breath any more than the ground or the sky. How glorious a conversion, so complete and wholesome it is, scarce memory enough of old bondage days left as a standpoint to view it from! In this newness of life we seem to have been so always.

Through a meadow opening in the pine woods I see snowy peaks about the headwaters of the Merced above Yosemite. How near they seem and how clear their outlines on the blue air, or rather *in* the blue air; for they seem to be saturated with it. How consuming strong the invitation they extend! Shall I be allowed to go to them? Night and day I'll pray that I may, but it seems too good to be true. Some one worthy will go, able for the Godful work, yet as far as I can I must drift about these love-monument mountains, glad to be a servant of servants in so holy a wilderness.

Found a lovely lily (*Calochortus albus*) in a shady adenostoma thicket near Coulterville, in company with *Adiantum Chilense.* It is white with a faint purplish tinge inside at the base of the petals, a most impressive plant, pure as a snow crystal, one of the plant saints that all must love and be made so much the purer by it every time it is seen. It puts the roughest mountaineer on his good behavior. With this plant the whole world would seem rich though none other existed. It is not easy to keep on with the camp cloud while such plant people are standing preaching by the wayside.

During the afternoon we passed a fine meadow bounded by stately pines, mostly the arrowy yellow pine, with here and there a noble sugar pine, its feathery arms outspread above the spires of its companion species in marked contrast; a glorious tree, its cones fifteen to twenty inches long, swinging like tassels at the ends of the branches with superb ornamental effect. Saw some logs of this species at the Greeley Mill. They are round and regular as if turned in a lathe, excepting the butt cuts, which have a few buttressing projections. The fragrance of the sugary sap is delicious and scents the mill and lumber yard. How beautiful the ground beneath this pine thickly strewn with slender needles and grand cones, and the piles of cone-scales, seed-wings and shells around the instep of each tree where the squirrels have been feasting! They get the seeds by cutting off the scales at the base in regular order, following their spiral arrangement, and the two seeds at the base of each scale, a hundred or two in a cone, must make a good meal. The yellow pine cones and those of most other species and genera are held upside down on the ground by the Douglas squirrel, and turned around gradually until stripped, while he sits usually with his back to a tree, probably for safety. Strange to say, he never seems to get himself smeared with gum, not even his paws or whiskers—and how cleanly and beautiful in color the cone-litter kitchen-middens he makes.

We are now approaching the region of clouds and cool streams. Magnificent white cumuli appeared about noon above the Yosemite region,—floating fountains refreshing the glorious wilderness,—sky mountains in whose pearly hills and dales the streams take their rise,—blessing with cooling shadows and rain. No rock landscape is more varied in sculpture, none more delicately modeled than these landscapes of the sky; domes and peaks rising, swelling, white as finest marble and firmly outlined, a most impressive manifestation of world building. Every rain-cloud, however fleeting, leaves its mark, not only on trees and flowers whose pulses are quickened, and on the replenished streams and lakes, but also on the rocks are its marks engraved whether we can see them or not.

I have been examining the curious and influential shrub *Adenostoma fasciculata*, first noticed about Horseshoe Bend. It is very abundant on the lower slopes of the second plateau near Coulterville, forming a dense, almost impenetrable growth that looks dark in the distance. It belongs to the rose family, is about six or eight feet high, has small white flowers in racemes eight to twelve inches long, round needle-like leaves, and reddish bark that becomes shreddy when old. It grows on sun-beaten slopes, and like grass is often swept away by running fires, but is quickly renewed from the roots. Any trees that may have established themselves in its midst are at length killed by these fires, and this no doubt is the secret of the unbroken character of its broad belts. A few manzanitas, which also rise again from the root after consuming fires, make out to dwell with it, also a few bush compositæ—baccharis and linosyris, and some liliaceous plants, mostly calochortus and brodiæa, with deep-set bulbs safe from fire. A multitude of birds and "wee, sleekit, cow'rin', tim'rous beasties" find good homes in its deepest thickets, and the open bays and lanes that fringe the margins of its main belts offer shelter and food to the deer when winter storms drive them down from their high mountain pastures. A most admirable plant! It is now in bloom, and I like to wear its pretty fragrant racemes in my buttonhole.

Azalea occidentalis, another charming shrub, grows beside cool streams hereabouts and much higher in the Yosemite region. We found it this evening in bloom a few miles above Greeley's Mill, where we are camped for the night. It is closely related to the rhododendrons, is very showy and fragrant, and everybody must like it not only for itself but for the shady alders and willows, ferny meadows, and living water associated with it.

Another conifer was met to-day,—incense cedar (*Libocedrus decurrens*), a large tree with warm yellow-green foliage in flat plumes like those of arborvitæ, bark cinnamon-colored, and as the boles of the old trees are without limbs they make striking pillars in the woods where the sun chances to shine on them—a worthy companion of the kingly sugar and yellow pines. I feel strangely attracted to this tree. The brown close-grained wood, as well as the small scale-like leaves, is fragrant, and the flat overlapping plumes make fine beds, and must shed the rain well. It would be delightful to be storm-bound beneath one of these noble, hospitable, inviting old trees, its broad sheltering arms bent down like a tent, incense rising from the fire made from its dry fallen branches, and a hearty wind chanting overhead. But the weather is calm to-night, and our camp is only a sheep camp. We are near the North Fork of the Merced. The night wind is telling the wonders of the upper mountains, their snow fountains and gardens, forests and groves; even their topography is in its tones. And the stars, the everlasting sky lilies, how bright they are now that we have climbed above the lowland dust! The horizon is bounded and adorned by a spiry wall of pines, every tree harmoniously related to every other; definite symbols, divine hieroglyphics written with sunbeams. Would I could understand them! The stream flowing past the camp through ferns and lilies and alders makes sweet music to the ear, but the pines marshaled around the edge of the sky make a yet sweeter music to the eye. Divine beauty all. Here I could stay tethered forever with just bread and water, nor would I be lonely; loved friends and neighbors, as love for everything increased, would seem all the nearer however many the miles and mountains between us.

June 7. The sheep were sick last night, and many of them are still far from well, hardly able to leave camp, coughing, groaning, looking wretched and pitiful, all from eating the leaves of the blessed azalea. So at least say the shepherd and the Don. Having had but little grass since they left the plains, they are starving, and so eat anything green they can get. "Sheep men" call azalea "sheep-poison," and wonder what the Creator was thinking about when he made it,—so desperately does sheep business blind and degrade, though supposed to have a refining influence in the good old days we read of. The California sheep owner is in haste to get rich, and often does, now that pasturage costs nothing, while the climate is so favorable that no winter food supply, shelter-pens, or barns are required. Therefore large flocks may be kept at slight expense, and large profits realized, the money invested doubling, it is claimed, every other year. This quickly acquired wealth usually creates desire for more. Then indeed the wool is drawn close down over the poor fellow's eyes, dimming or shutting out almost everything worth seeing.

As for the shepherd, his case is still worse, especially in winter when he lives alone in a cabin. For, though stimulated at times by hopes of one day owning a flock and getting rich like his boss, he at the same time is likely to be degraded by the life he leads, and seldom reaches the dignity or advantage—or disadvantage—of ownership. The degradation in his case has for cause one not far to seek. He is solitary most of the year, and solitude to most people seems hard to bear. He seldom has much good mental work or recreation in the way of books. Coming into his dingy hovel-cabin at night, stupidly weary, he finds nothing to balance and level his life with the universe. No, after his dull drag all day after the sheep, he must get his supper; he is likely to slight this task and try to satisfy his hunger with whatever comes handy. Perhaps no bread is baked; then he just makes a few grimy flapjacks in his unwashed frying-pan, boils a handful of tea, and perhaps fries a few strips of rusty bacon. Usually there are dried peaches or apples in the cabin, but he hates to be bothered with the cooking of them, just swallows the bacon and flapjacks, and depends on the genial stupefaction of tobacco for the rest. Then to bed, often without removing the clothing worn during the day. Of course his health suffers, reacting on his mind; and seeing nobody for weeks or months, he finally becomes semi-insane or wholly so.

The shepherd in Scotland seldom thinks of being anything but a shepherd. He has probably descended from a race of shepherds and inherited a love and aptitude for the business almost as marked as that of his collie. He has but a small flock to look after, sees his family and neighbors, has time for reading in fine weather, and often carries books to the fields with which he may converse with kings. The oriental shepherd, we read, called his sheep by name; they knew his voice and followed him. The flocks must have been small and easily managed, allowing piping on the hills and ample leisure for reading and thinking. But whatever the blessings of sheep-culture in other times and countries, the California shepherd, as far as I've seen or heard, is never quite sane for any considerable time. Of all Nature's voices baa is about all he hears. Even the howls and ki-yis of coyotes might be blessings if well heard, but he hears them only through a blur of mutton and wool, and they do him no good.

The sick sheep are getting well, and the shepherd is discoursing on the various poisons lurking in these high pastures—azalea, kalmia, alkali. After crossing the North Fork of the Merced we turned to the left toward Pilot Peak, and made a considerable ascent on a rocky, brush-covered ridge to Brown's Flat, where for the first time since leaving the plains the flock is enjoying plenty of green grass. Mr. Delaney intends to seek a permanent camp somewhere in the neighborhood, to last several weeks.

Before noon we passed Bower Cave, a delightful marble palace, not dark and dripping, but filled with sunshine, which pours into it through its wide-open mouth facing the south. It has a fine, deep, clear little lake with mossy banks embowered with broad-leaved maples, all under ground, wholly unlike anything I have seen in the cave line even in Kentucky, where a large part of the State is honeycombed with caves. This curious specimen of subterranean scenery is located on a belt of marble that is said to extend from the north end of the Range to the extreme south. Many other caves occur on the belt, but none like this, as far as I have learned, combining as it does sunny outdoor brightness and vegetation with the crystalline beauty of the underworld. It is claimed by a Frenchman, who has fenced and locked it, placed a boat on the lakelet and seats on the mossy bank under the maple trees, and charges a dollar admission fee. Being on one of the ways to the Yosemite Valley, a good many tourists visit it during the travel months of summer, regarding it as an interesting addition to their Yosemite wonders.

Poison oak or poison ivy (*Rhus diversiloba*), both as a bush and a scrambler up trees and rocks, is common throughout the foothill region up to a height of at least three thousand feet above the sea. It is somewhat troublesome to most travelers, inflaming the skin and eyes, but blends harmoniously with its companion plants, and many a charming flower leans confidingly upon it for protection and shade. I have oftentimes found the curious twining lily (*Stropholirion Californicum*) climbing its branches, showing no fear but rather congenial companionship. Sheep eat it without apparent ill effects; so do horses to some extent, though not fond of it, and to many persons it is harmless. Like most other things not apparently useful to man, it has few friends, and the blind question, "Why was it made?" goes on and on with never a guess that first of all it might have been made for itself.

On Second Bench, edge of the Main Forest Belt

Brown's Flat is a shallow fertile valley on the top of the divide between the North Fork of the Merced and Bull Creek, commanding magnificent views in every direction. Here the adventurous pioneer David Brown made his headquarters for many years, dividing his time between gold-hunting and bear-hunting. Where could lonely hunter find a better solitude? Game in the woods, gold in the rocks, health and exhilaration in the air, while the colors and cloud furniture of the sky are ever inspiring through all sorts of weather. Though sternly practical, like most pioneers, old David seems to have been uncommonly fond of scenery. Mr. Delaney, who knew him well, tells me that he dearly loved to climb to the summit of a commanding ridge to gaze abroad over the forest to the snow-clad peaks and sources of the rivers, and over the foreground valleys and gulches to note where miners were at work or claims were abandoned, judging by smoke from cabins and camp-fires, the sounds of axes, etc.; and when a rifle-shot was heard, to guess who was the hunter, whether Indian or some poacher on his wide domain. His dog Sandy accompanied him everywhere, and well the little hairy mountaineer knew and loved his master and his master's aims. In deer-hunting he had but little to do, trotting behind his master as he slowly made his way through the wood, careful not to step heavily on dry twigs, scanning open spots in the chaparral, where the game loves to feed in the early morning and towards sunset; peering cautiously over ridges as new outlooks were reached, and along the meadowy borders of streams. But when bears were hunted, little Sandy became more important, and it was as a bear-hunter that Brown became famous. His hunting method, as described by Mr. Delaney, who had passed many a night with him in his lonely cabin and learned his stories, was simply to go slowly and silently through the best bear pastures, with his dog and rifle and a few pounds of flour, until he found a fresh track and then follow it to the death, paying no heed to the time required. Wherever the bear went he followed, led by little Sandy, who had a keen nose and never lost the track, however rocky the ground. When high open points were reached, the likeliest places were carefully scanned. The time of year enabled the hunter to determine approximately where the bear would be found,—in the spring and early summer on open spots about the banks of streams and springy places eating grass and clover and lupines, or in dry meadows feasting on strawberries; toward the end of summer, on dry ridges, feasting on manzanita berries, sitting on his haunches, pulling down the laden branches with his paws, and pressing them together so as to get good compact mouthfuls however much mixed with twigs and leaves; in the Indian summer, beneath the pines, chewing the cones cut off by the squirrels, or occasionally climbing a tree to gnaw and break off the fruitful branches. In late autumn, when acorns are ripe, Bruin's favorite feeding-grounds are groves of the California oak in park-like cañon flats. Always the cunning hunter knew where to look, and seldom came upon Bruin unawares. When the hot scent showed the dangerous game was nigh, a long halt was made, and the intricacies of the topography and vegetation leisurely scanned to catch a glimpse of the shaggy wanderer, or to at least determine where he was most likely to be.

"Whenever," said the hunter, "I saw a bear before it saw me I had no trouble in killing it. I just studied the lay of the land and got to leeward of it no matter how far around I had to go, and then worked up to within a few hundred yards or so, at the foot of a tree that I could easily climb, but too small for the bear to climb. Then I looked well to the condition of my rifle, took off my boots so as to climb well if necessary, and waited until the bear turned its side in clear view when I could make a sure or at least a good shot. In case it showed fight I climbed out of reach. But bears are slow and awkward with their eyes, and being to leeward of them they could not scent me, and I often got in a second shot before they noticed the smoke. Usually, however, they run when wounded and hide in the brush. I let them run a good safe time before I ventured to follow them, and Sandy was pretty sure to find them dead. If not, he barked and drew their attention, and occasionally rushed in for a distracting bite, so that I was able to get to a safe distance for a final shot. Oh yes, bear-hunting is safe enough when followed in a safe way, though like every other business it has its accidents, and little doggie and I have had some close calls. Bears like to keep out of the way of men as a general thing, but if an old, lean, hungry mother with cubs met a man on her own ground she would, in my opinion, try to catch and eat him. This would be only fair play anyhow, for we eat them, but nobody hereabout has been used for bear grub that I know of."

Brown had left his mountain home ere we arrived, but a considerable number of Digger Indians still linger in their cedar-bark huts on the edge of the flat. They were attracted in the first place by the white hunter whom they had learned to respect, and to whom they looked for guidance and protection against their enemies the Pah Utes, who sometimes made raids across from the east side of the Range to plunder the stores of the comparatively feeble Diggers and steal their wives.

Camp, North Fork of the Merced

In Camp on the North Fork of the Merced

June 8. The sheep, now grassy and good-natured, slowly nibbled their way down into the valley of the North Fork of the Merced at the foot of Pilot Peak Ridge to the place selected by the Don for our first central camp, a picturesque hopper-shaped hollow formed by converging hill slopes at a bend of the river. Here racks for dishes and provisions were made in the shade of the river-bank trees, and beds of fern fronds, cedar plumes, and various flowers, each to the taste of its owner, and a corral back on the open flat for the wool.

June 9. How deep our sleep last night in the mountain's heart, beneath the trees and stars, hushed by solemn-sounding waterfalls and many small soothing voices in sweet accord whispering peace! And our first pure mountain day, warm, calm, cloudless,—how immeasurable it seems, how serenely wild! I can scarcely remember its beginning. Along the river, over the hills, in the ground, in the sky, spring work is going on with joyful enthusiasm, new life, new beauty, unfolding, unrolling in glorious exuberant extravagance,— new birds in their nests, new winged creatures in the air, and new leaves, new flowers, spreading, shining, rejoicing everywhere.

The trees about the camp stand close, giving ample shade for ferns and lilies, while back from the bank most of the sunshine reaches the ground, calling up the grasses and flowers in glorious array, tall bromus waving like bamboos, starry compositæ, monardella, Mariposa tulips, lupines, gilias, violets, glad children of light. Soon every fern frond will be unrolled, great beds of common pteris and woodwardia along the river, wreaths and rosettes of pellæa and cheilanthes on sunny rocks. Some of the woodwardia fronds are already six feet high.

A handsome little shrub, *Chamæbatia foliolosa*, belonging to the rose family, spreads a yellow-green mantle beneath the sugar pines for miles without a break, not mixed or roughened with other plants. Only here and there a Washington lily may be seen nodding above its even surface, or a bunch or two of tall bromus as if for ornament. This fine carpet shrub begins to appear at, say, twenty-five hundred or three thousand feet above sea level, is about knee high or less, has brown branches, and the largest stems are only about half an inch in diameter. The leaves, light yellow green, thrice pinnate and finely cut, give them a rich ferny appearance, and they are dotted with minute glands that secrete wax with a peculiar pleasant odor that blends finely with the spicy fragrance of the pines. The flowers are white, five eighths of an inch in diameter, and look like those of the strawberry. Am delighted with this little bush. It is the only true carpet shrub of this part of the Sierra. The manzanita, rhamnus, and most of the species of ceanothus make shaggy rugs and border fringes rather than carpets or mantles.

The sheep do not take kindly to their new pastures, perhaps from being too closely hemmed in by the hills. They are never fully at rest. Last night they were frightened, probably by bears or coyotes prowling and planning for a share of the grand mass of mutton.

June 10. Very warm. We get water for the camp from a rock basin at the foot of a picturesque cascading reach of the river where it is well stirred and made lively without being beaten into dusty foam.

The rock here is black metamorphic slate, worn into smooth knobs in the stream channels, contrasting with the fine gray and white cascading water as it glides and glances and falls in lace-like sheets and braided overfolding currents. Tufts of sedge growing on the rock knobs that rise above the surface produce a charming effect, the long elastic leaves arching over in every direction, the tips of the longest drooping into the current, which dividing against the projecting rocks makes still finer lines, uniting with the sedges to see how beautiful the happy stream can be made. Nor is this all, for the giant saxifrage also is growing on some of the knob rock islets, firmly anchored and displaying their broad, round, umbrella-like leaves in showy groups by themselves, or above the sedge tufts. The flowers of this species (*Saxifraga peltata*) are purple, and form tall glandular racemes that are in bloom before the appearance of the leaves. The fleshy root-stocks grip the rock in cracks and hollows, and thus enable the plant to hold on against occasional floods,—a marked species employed by Nature to make yet more beautiful the most interesting portions of these cool clear streams. Near camp the trees arch over from bank to bank, making a leafy tunnel full of soft subdued light, through which the young river sings and shines like a happy living creature.

Heard a few peals of thunder from the upper Sierra, and saw firm white bossy cumuli rising back of the pines. This was about noon.

June 11. On one of the eastern branches of the river discovered some charming cascades with a pool at the foot of each of them. White dashing water, a few bushes and tufts of carex on ledges leaning over with fine effect, and large orange lilies assembled in superb groups on fertile soil-beds beside the pools.

There are no large meadows or grassy plains near camp to supply lasting pasture for our thousands of busy nibblers. The main dependence is ceanothus brush on the hills and tufted grass patches here and there, with lupines and pea-vines among the flowers on sunny open spaces. Large areas have already been stripped bare, or nearly so, compelling the poor hungry wool bundles to scatter far and wide, keeping the shepherds and dogs at the top of their speed to hold them within bounds. Mr. Delaney has gone back to the plains, taking the Indian and Chinaman with him, leaving instruction to keep the flock here or hereabouts until his return, which he promised would not be long delayed.

How fine the weather is! Nothing more celestial can I conceive. How gently the winds blow! Scarce can these tranquil air-currents be called winds. They seem the very breath of Nature, whispering peace to every living thing. Down in the camp dell there is no swaying of tree-tops; most of the time not a leaf moves. I don't remember having seen a single lily swinging on its stalk, though they are so tall the least breeze would rock them. What grand bells these lilies have! Some of them big enough for children's bonnets. I have been sketching them, and would fain draw every leaf of their wide shining whorls and every curved and spotted petal. More beautiful, better kept gardens cannot be imagined. The species is *Lilium pardalinum*, five to six feet high, leaf-whorls a foot wide, flowers about six inches wide, bright orange, purple spotted in the throat, segments revolute—a majestic plant.

June 12. A slight sprinkle of rain—large drops far apart, falling with hearty pat and plash on leaves and stones and into the mouths of the flowers. Cumuli rising to the eastward. How beautiful their pearly bosses! How well they harmonize with the upswelling rocks beneath them. Mountains of the sky, solid-looking, finely sculptured, their richly varied topography wonderfully defined. Never before have I seen clouds so substantial looking in form and texture. Nearly every day toward noon they rise with visible swelling motion as if new worlds were being created. And how fondly they brood and hover over the gardens and forests with their cooling shadows and showers, keeping every petal and leaf in glad health and heart. One may fancy the clouds themselves are plants, springing up in the sky-fields at the call of the sun, growing in beauty until they reach their prime, scattering rain and hail like berries and seeds, then wilting and dying.

The mountain live oak, common here and a thousand feet or so higher, is like the live oak of Florida, not only in general appearance, foliage, bark, and wide-branching habit, but in its tough, knotty, unwedgeable wood. Standing alone with plenty of elbow room, the largest trees are about seven to eight feet in diameter near the ground, sixty feet high, and as wide or wider across the head. The leaves are small and undivided, mostly without teeth or wavy edging, though on young shoots some are sharply serrated, both kinds being found on the same tree. The cups of the medium-sized acorns are shallow, thick walled, and covered with a golden dust of minute hairs. Some of the trees have hardly any main trunk, dividing near the ground into large wide-spreading limbs, and these, dividing again and again, terminate in long, drooping, cord-like branchlets, many of which reach nearly to the ground, while a dense canopy of short, shining, leafy branchlets forms a round head which looks something like a cumulus cloud when the sunshine is pouring over it.

Mountain Live Oak (Quercus chrysolepis), Eight feet in diameter

A marked plant is the bush poppy (*Dendromecon rigidum*), found on the hot hillsides near camp, the only woody member of the order I have yet met in all my walks. Its flowers are bright orange yellow, an inch to two inches wide, fruit-pods three or four inches long, slender and curving,—height of bushes about four feet, made up of many slim, straight branches, radiating from the root,—a companion of the manzanita and other sun-loving chaparral shrubs.

June 13. Another glorious Sierra day in which one seems to be dissolved and absorbed and sent pulsing onward we know not where.

Life seems neither long nor short, and we take no more heed to save time or make haste than do the trees and stars. This is true freedom, a good practical sort of immortality. Yonder rises another white skyland. How sharply the yellow pine spires and the palm-like crowns of the sugar pines are outlined on its smooth white domes. And hark! the grand thunder billows booming, rolling from ridge to ridge, followed by the faithful shower.

A good many herbaceous plants come thus far up the mountains from the plains, and are now in flower, two months later than their low land relatives. Saw a few columbines to-day. Most of the ferns are in their prime,—rock ferns on the sunny hillsides, cheilanthes, pellæa, gymnogramme; woodwardia, aspidium, woodsia along the stream banks, and the common *Pteris aquilina* on sandy flats. This last, however common, is here making shows of strong, exuberant, abounding beauty to set the botanist wild with admiration. I measured some scarce full grown that are more than seven feet high. Though the commonest and most widely distributed of all the ferns, I might almost say that I never saw it before. The broad-shouldered fronds held high on smooth stout stalks growing close together, overleaning and overlapping, make a complete ceiling, beneath which one may walk erect over several acres without being seen, as if beneath a roof. And how soft and lovely the light streaming through this living ceiling, revealing the arching branching ribs and veins of the fronds as the framework of countless panes of pale green and yellow plant-glass nicely fitted together—a fairyland created out of the commonest fern-stuff.

The smaller animals wander about as if in a tropical forest. I saw the entire flock of sheep vanish at one side of a patch and reappear a hundred yards farther on at the other, their progress betrayed only by the jerking and trembling of the fronds; and strange to say very few of the stout woody stalks were broken. I sat a long time beneath the tallest fronds, and never enjoyed anything in the way of a bower of wild leaves more strangely impressive. Only spread a fern frond over a man's head and worldly cares are cast out, and freedom and beauty and peace come in. The waving of a pine tree on the top of a mountain,— a magic wand in Nature's hand,—every devout mountaineer knows its power; but the marvelous beauty value of what the Scotch call a breckan in a still dell, what poet has sung this? It would seem impossible that any one, however incrusted with care, could escape the Godful influence of these sacred fern forests. Yet this very day I saw a shepherd pass through one of the finest of them without betraying more feeling than his sheep. "What do you think of these grand ferns?" I asked. "Oh, they're only d——d big brakes," he replied.

Lizards of every temper, style, and color dwell here, seemingly as happy and companionable as the birds and squirrels. Lowly, gentle fellow mortals, enjoying God's sunshine, and doing the best they can in getting a living, I like to watch them at their work and play. They bear acquaintance well, and one likes them the better the longer one looks into their beautiful, innocent eyes. They are easily tamed, and one soon learns to love them, as they dart about on the hot rocks, swift as dragon-flies. The eye can hardly follow them; but they never make long-sustained runs, usually only about ten or twelve feet, then a sudden stop, and as sudden a start again; going all their journeys by quick, jerking impulses. These many stops I find are necessary as rests, for they are short-winded, and when pursued steadily are soon out of breath, pant pitifully, and are easily caught. Their bodies are more than half tail, but these tails are well managed, never heavily dragged nor curved up as if hard to carry; on the contrary, they seem to follow the body lightly of their own will. Some are colored like the sky, bright as bluebirds, others gray like the lichened rocks on which they hunt and bask. Even the horned toad of the plains is a mild, harmless creature, and so are the snake-like species which glide in curves with true snake motion, while their small, undeveloped limbs drag as useless appendages. One specimen fourteen inches long which I observed closely made no use whatever of its tender, sprouting limbs, but glided with all the soft, sly ease and grace of a snake. Here comes a little, gray, dusty fellow who seems to know and trust me, running about my feet, and looking up cunningly into my face. Carlo is watching, makes a quick pounce on him, for the fun of the thing I suppose; but Liz has shot away from his paws like an arrow, and is safe in the recesses of a clump of chaparral. Gentle saurians, dragons, descendants of an ancient and mighty race, Heaven bless you all and make your virtues known! for few of us know as yet that scales may cover fellow creatures as gentle and lovable as feathers, or hair, or cloth.

Mastodons and elephants used to live here no great geological time ago, as shown by their bones, often discovered by miners in washing gold-gravel. And bears of at least two species are here now, besides the California lion or panther, and wild cats, wolves, foxes, snakes, scorpions, wasps, tarantulas; but one is almost tempted at times to regard a small savage black ant as the master existence of this vast mountain world. These fearless, restless, wandering imps, though only about a quarter of an inch long, are fonder of fighting and biting than any beast I know. They attack every living thing around their homes, often without cause as far as I can see. Their bodies are mostly jaws curved like ice-hooks, and to get work for these weapons seems to be their chief aim and pleasure. Most of their colonies are established in living oaks somewhat decayed or hollowed, in which they can conveniently build their cells. These are chosen probably because of their strength as opposed to the attacks of animals and storms. They work both day and night, creep into dark caves, climb the highest trees, wander and hunt through cool ravines as well as on hot, unshaded ridges, and extend their highways and byways over everything but water and sky. From the foothills to a mile above the level of the sea nothing can stir without their knowledge; and alarms are spread in an incredibly short time, without any howl or cry that we can hear. I can't understand the need of their ferocious courage; there seems to be no common sense in it. Sometimes, no doubt, they fight in defense of their homes, but they fight anywhere and always wherever they can find anything to bite. As soon as a vulnerable spot is discovered on man or beast, they stand on their heads and sink their jaws, and though torn limb from limb, they will yet hold on and die biting deeper. When I contemplate this fierce creature so widely distributed and strongly intrenched, I see that much remains to be done ere the world is brought under the rule of universal peace and love.

On my way to camp a few minutes ago, I passed a dead pine nearly ten feet in diameter. It has been enveloped in fire from top to bottom so that now it looks like a grand black pillar set up as a monument. In this noble shaft a colony of large jet-black ants have established themselves, laboriously cutting tunnels and cells through the wood, whether sound or decayed. The entire trunk seems to have been honeycombed, judging by the size of the talus of gnawed chips like sawdust piled up around its base. They are more intelligent looking than their small, belligerent, strong-scented brethren, and have better manners, though quick to fight when required. Their towns are carved in fallen trunks as well as in those left standing, but never in sound, living trees or in the ground. When you happen to sit down to rest or take notes near a colony, some wandering hunter is sure to find you and come cautiously forward to discover the nature of the intruder and what ought to be done. If you are not too near the town and keep perfectly still he may run across your feet a few times, over your legs and hands and face, up your trousers, as if taking your measure and getting comprehensive views, then go in peace without raising an alarm. If, however, a tempting spot is offered or some suspicious movement excites him, a bite follows, and such a bite! I fancy that a bear or wolf bite is not to be compared with it. A quick electric flame of pain flashes along the outraged nerves, and you discover for the first time how great is the capacity for sensation you are possessed of. A shriek, a grab for the animal, and a bewildered stare follow this bite of bites as one comes back to consciousness from sudden eclipse. Fortunately, if careful, one need not be bitten oftener than once or twice in a lifetime. This wonderful electric species is about three fourths of an inch long. Bears are fond of them, and tear and gnaw their home-logs to pieces, and roughly devour the eggs, larvæ, parent ants, and the rotten or sound wood of the cells, all in one spicy acid hash. The Digger Indians also are fond of the larvæ and even of the perfect ants, so I have been told by old mountaineers. They bite off and reject the head, and eat the tickly acid body with keen relish. Thus are the poor biters bitten, like every other biter, big or little, in the world's great family.

There is also a fine, active, intelligent-looking red species, inter-mediate in size between the above. They dwell in the ground, and build large piles of seed husks, leaves, straw, etc., over their nests. Their food seems to be mostly insects and plant leaves, seeds and sap. How many mouths Nature has to fill, how many neighbors we have, how little we know about them, and how seldom we get in each other's way! Then to think of the infinite numbers of smaller fellow mortals, invisibly small, compared with which the smallest ants are as mastodons.

June 14. The pool-basins below the falls and cascades here-abouts, formed by the heavy down-plunging currents, are kept nicely clean and clear of detritus. The heavier parts of the material swept over the falls are heaped up a short distance in front of the basins in the form of a dam, thus tending, together with erosion, to increase their size. Sudden changes, however, are effected during the spring floods, when the snow is melting and the upper tributaries are roaring loud from "bank to brae." Then boulders that have fallen into the channels, and which the ordinary summer and winter currents were unable to move, are suddenly swept forward as by a mighty besom, hurled over the falls into these pools, and piled up in a new dam together with part of the old one, while some of the smaller boulders are carried further down stream and variously lodged according to size and shape, all seeking rest where the force of the current is less than the resistance they are able to offer. But the greatest changes made in these relations of fall, pool, and dam are caused, not by the ordinary spring floods, but by extraordinary ones that occur at irregular intervals. The testimony of trees growing on flood boulder deposits shows that a century or more has passed since the last master flood came to awaken everything movable to go swirling and dancing on wonderful journeys. These floods may occur during the summer, when heavy thunder-showers, called "cloud-bursts," fall on wide, steeply inclined stream basins furrowed by converging channels, which suddenly gather the waters together into the main trunk in booming torrents of enormous transporting power, though short lived.

One of these ancient flood boulders stands firm in the middle of the stream channel, just below the lower edge of the pool dam at the foot of the fall nearest our camp. It is a nearly cubical mass of granite about eight feet high, plushed with mosses over the top and down the sides to ordinary high-water mark. When I climbed on top of it to-day and lay down to rest, it seemed the most romantic spot I had yet found—the one big stone with its mossy level top and smooth sides standing square and firm and solitary, like an altar, the fall in front of it bathing it lightly with the finest of the spray, just enough to keep its moss cover fresh; the clear green pool beneath, with its foam-bells and its half circle of lilies leaning forward like a band of admirers, and flowering dogwood and alder trees leaning over all in sun-sifted arches. How soothingly, restfully cool it is beneath that leafy, translucent ceiling, and how delightful the water music—the deep bass tones of the fall, the clashing, ringing spray, and infinite variety of small low tones of the current gliding past the side of the boulder-island, and glinting against a thousand smaller stones down the ferny channel! All this shut in; every one of these influences acting at short range as if in a quiet room. The place seemed holy, where one might hope to see God.

After dark, when the camp was at rest, I groped my way back to the altar boulder and passed the night on it,—above the water, beneath the leaves and stars,—everything still more impressive than by day, the fall seen dimly white, singing Nature's old love song with solemn enthusiasm, while the stars peering through the leaf-roof seemed to join in the white water's song. Precious night, precious day to abide in me forever. Thanks be to God for this immortal gift.

June 15. Another reviving morning. Down the long mountain-slopes the sunbeams pour, gilding the awakening pines, cheering every needle, filling every living thing with joy. Robins are singing in the alder and maple groves, the same old song that has cheered and sweetened countless seasons over almost all of our blessed continent. In this mountain hollow they seem as much at home as in farmers' orchards. Bullock's oriole and the Louisiana tanager are here also, with many warblers and other little mountain troubadours, most of them now busy about their nests.

Discovered another magnificent specimen of the goldcup oak six feet in diameter, a Douglas spruce seven feet, and a twining lily (*Stropholirion*), with rose-colored flowers.

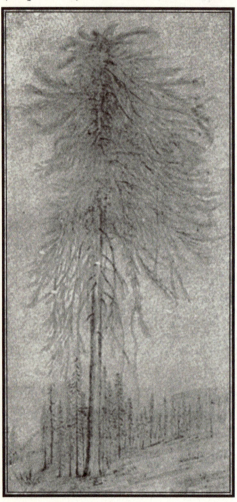

Sugar Pine

Sugar pine cones are cylindrical, slightly tapered at the end and rounded at the base. Found one to-day nearly twenty-four inches long and six in diameter, the scales being open. Another specimen nineteen inches long; the average length of full-grown cones on trees favorably situated is nearly eighteen inches. On the lower edge of the belt at a height of about twenty-five hundred feet above the sea they are smaller, say a foot to fifteen inches long, and at a height of seven thousand feet or more near the upper limits of its growth in the Yosemite region they are about the same size. This noble tree is an inexhaustible study and source of pleasure. I never weary of gazing at its grand tassel cones, its perfectly round bole one hundred feet or more without a limb, the fine purplish color of its bark, and its magnificent outsweeping, down-curving feathery arms forming a crown always bold and striking and exhilarating. In habit and general port it looks somewhat like a palm, but no palm that I have yet seen displays such majesty of form and behavior either when poised silent and thoughtful in sunshine, or wide-awake waving in storm winds with

every needle quivering. When young it is very straight and regular in form like most other conifers; but at the age of fifty to one
hundred years it begins to acquire individuality, so that no two are
alike in their prime or old age. Every tree calls for special admiration. I have been making many sketches, and regret that I cannot
draw every needle. It is said to reach a height of three hundred feet,
though the tallest I have measured falls short of this stature sixty
feet or more. The diameter of the largest near the ground is about
ten feet, though I've heard of some twelve feet thick or even fifteen. The diameter is held to a great height, the taper being almost
imperceptibly gradual. Its companion, the yellow pine, is almost
as large. The long silvery foliage of the younger specimens forms
magnificent cylindrical brushes on the top shoots and the ends of
the upturned branches, and when the wind sways the needles all one
way at a certain angle every tree becomes a tower of white quivering sun-fire. Well may this shining species be called the silver pine.
The needles are sometimes more than a foot long, almost as long
as those of the long-leaf pine of Florida. But though in size the
yellow pine almost equals the sugar pine, and in rugged enduring
strength seems to surpass it, it is far less marked in general habit and
expression, with its regular conventional spire and its comparatively
small cones clustered stiffly among the needles. Were there no sugar
pine, then would this be the king of the world's eighty or ninety species, the brightest of the bright, waving, worshiping multitude. Were
they mere mechanical sculptures, what noble objects they would
still be! How much more throbbing, thrilling, overflowing, full of
life in every fiber and cell, grand glowing silver-rods—the very gods
of the plant kingdom, living their sublime century lives in sight of
Heaven, watched and loved and admired from generation to generation! And how many other radiant resiny sun trees are here and
higher up,—libocedrus, Douglas spruce, silver fir, sequoia. How
rich our inheritance in these blessed mountains, the tree pastures
into which our eyes are turned!

Now comes sundown. The west is all a glory of color transfiguring everything. Far up the Pilot Peak Ridge the radiant host of
trees stand hushed and thoughtful, receiving the Sun's good-night,

as solemn and impressive a leave-taking as if sun and trees were to meet no more. The daylight fades, the color spell is broken, and the forest breathes free in the night breeze beneath the stars.

June 16. One of the Indians from Brown's Flat got right into the middle of the camp this morning, unobserved. I was seated on a stone, looking over my notes and sketches, and happening to look up, was startled to see him standing grim and silent within a few steps of me, as motionless and weather-stained as an old tree-stump that had stood there for centuries. All Indians seem to have learned this wonderful way of walking unseen,—making themselves invisible like certain spiders I have been observing here, which, in case of alarm, caused, for example, by a bird alighting on the bush their webs are spread upon, immediately bounce themselves up and down on their elastic threads so rapidly that only a blur is visible. The wild Indian power of escaping observation, even where there is little or no cover to hide in, was probably slowly acquired in hard hunting and fighting lessons while trying to approach game, take enemies by surprise, or get safely away when compelled to retreat. And this experience transmitted through many generations seems at length to have become what is vaguely called instinct.

How smooth and changeless seems the surface of the mountains about us! Scarce a track is to be found beyond the range of the sheep except on small open spots on the sides of the streams, or where the forest carpets are thin or wanting. On the smoothest of these open strips and patches deer tracks may be seen, and the great suggestive footprints of bears, which, with those of the many small animals, are scarce enough to answer as a kind of light ornamental stitching or embroidery. Along the main ridges and larger branches of the river Indian trails may be traced, but they are not nearly as distinct as one would expect to find them. How many centuries Indians have roamed these woods nobody knows, probably a great many, extending far beyond the time that Columbus touched our shores, and it seems strange that heavier marks have not been made. Indians walk softly and hurt the landscape hardly more than the birds and squirrels, and their brush and bark huts last hardly longer than those of wood rats, while their more enduring monuments, excepting those wrought on the forests by the fires they made to improve their hunting grounds, vanish in a few centuries.

How different are most of those of the white man, especially on the lower gold region—roads blasted in the solid rock, wild streams dammed and tamed and turned out of their channels and led along the sides of cañons and valleys to work in mines like slaves. Crossing from ridge to ridge, high in the air, on long straddling trestles as if flowing on stilts, or down and up across valleys and hills, imprisoned in iron pipes to strike and wash away hills and miles of the skin of the mountain's face, riddling, stripping every gold gully and flat. These are the white man's marks made in a few feverish years, to say nothing of mills, fields, villages, scattered hundreds of miles along the flank of the Range. Long will it be ere these marks are effaced, though Nature is doing what she can, replanting, gardening, sweeping away old dams and flumes, leveling gravel and boulder piles, patiently trying to heal every raw scar. The main gold storm is over. Calm enough are the gray old miners scratching a bare living in waste diggings here and there. Thundering underground blasting is still going on to feed the pounding quartz mills, but their influence on the landscape is light as compared with that of the pick-and-shovel storms waged a few years ago. Fortunately for Sierra scenery the gold-bearing slates are mostly restricted to the foothills. The region about our camp is still wild, and higher lies the snow about as trackless as the sky.

Only a few hills and domes of cloudland were built yesterday and none at all to-day. The light is peculiarly white and thin, though pleasantly warm. The serenity of this mountain weather in the spring, just when Nature's pulses are beating highest, is one of its greatest charms. There is only a moderate breeze from the summits of the Range at night, and a slight breathing from the sea and the lowland hills and plains during the day, or stillness so complete no leaf stirs. The trees hereabouts have but little wind history to tell.

Sheep, like people, are ungovernable when hungry. Excepting my guarded lily gardens, almost every leaf that these hoofed locusts can reach within a radius of a mile or two from camp has been devoured. Even the bushes are stripped bare, and in spite of dogs and shepherds the sheep scatter to all points of the compass and vanish in dust. I fear some are lost, for one of the sixteen black ones is missing.

June 17. Counted the wool bundles this morning as they bounced through the narrow corral gate. About three hundred are missing, and as the shepherd could not go to seek them, I had to go. I tied a crust of bread to my belt, and with Carlo set out for the upper slopes of the Pilot Peak Ridge, and had a good day, notwithstanding the care of seeking the silly runaways. I went out for wool, and did not come back shorn. A peculiar light circled around the horizon, white and thin like that often seen over the auroral corona, blending into the blue of the upper sky. The only clouds were a few faint flossy pencilings like combed silk. I pushed direct to the boundary of the usual range of the flock, and around it until I found the outgoing trail of the wanderers. It led far up the ridge into an open place surrounded by a hedge-like growth of ceanothus chaparral. Carlo knew what I was about, and eagerly followed the scent until we came up to them, huddled in a timid, silent bunch. They had evidently been here all night and all the forenoon, afraid to go out to feed. Having escaped restraint, they were, like some people we know of, afraid of their freedom, did not know what to do with it, and seemed glad to get back into the old familiar bondage.

June 18. Another inspiring morning, nothing better in any world can be conceived. No description of Heaven that I have ever heard or read of seems half so fine. At noon the clouds occupied about .05 of the sky, white filmy touches drawn delicately on the azure.

The high ridges and hilltops beyond the woolly locusts are now gay with monardella, clarkia, coreopsis, and tall tufted grasses, some of them tall enough to wave like pines. The lupines, of which there are many ill-defined species, are now mostly out of flower, and many of the compositæ are beginning to fade, their radiant corollas vanishing in fluffy pappus like stars in mist.

We had another visitor from Brown's Flat to-day, an old Indian woman with a basket on her back. Like our first caller from the village, she got fairly into camp and was standing in plain view when discovered. How long she had been quietly looking on, I cannot say.

Even the dogs failed to notice her stealthy approach. She was on her way, I suppose, to some wild garden, probably for lupine and starchy saxifrage leaves and rootstocks. Her dress was calico rags, far from clean. In every way she seemed sadly unlike Nature's neat well-dressed animals, though living like them on the bounty of the wilderness. Strange that mankind alone is dirty. Had she been clad in fur, or cloth woven of grass or shreddy bark, like the juniper and libocedrus mats, she might then have seemed a rightful part of the wilderness; like a good wolf at least, or bear. But from no point of view that I have found are such debased fellow beings a whit more natural than the glaring tailored tourists we saw that frightened the birds and squirrels.

June 19. Pure sunshine all day. How beautiful a rock is made by leaf shadows! Those of the live oak are particularly clear and distinct, and beyond all art in grace and delicacy, now still as if painted on stone, now gliding softly as if afraid of noise, now dancing, waltzing in swift, merry swirls, or jumping on and off sunny rocks in quick dashes like wave embroidery on seashore cliffs. How true and substantial is this shadow beauty, and with what sublime extravagance is beauty thus multiplied! The big orange lilies are now arrayed in all their glory of leaf and flower. Noble plants, in perfect health, Nature's darlings.

June 20. Some of the silly sheep got caught fast in a tangle of chaparral this morning, like flies in a spider's web, and had to be helped out. Carlo found them and tried to drive them from the trap by the easiest way. How far above sheep are intelligent dogs! No friend and helper can be more affectionate and constant than Carlo. The noble St. Bernard is an honor to his race.

The air is distinctly fragrant with balsam and resin and mint,—every breath of it a gift we may well thank God for. Who could ever guess that so rough a wilderness should yet be so fine, so full of good things. One seems to be in a majestic domed pavilion in which a grand play is being acted with scenery and music and incense,—all the furniture and action so interesting we are in no danger of being called on to endure one dull moment. God himself seems to be always doing his best here, working like a man in a glow of enthusiasm.

June 21. Sauntered along the river-bank to my lily gardens. The perfection of beauty in these lilies of the wilderness is a never-ending source of admiration and wonder. Their rhizomes are set in black mould accumulated in hollows of the metamorphic slates beside the pools, where they are well watered without being subjected to flood action. Every leaf in the level whorls around the tall polished stalks is as finely finished as the petals, and the light and heat required are measured for them and tempered in passing through the branches of over-leaning trees. However strong the winds from the noon rainstorms, they are securely sheltered. Beautiful hypnum carpets bordered with ferns are spread beneath them, violets too, and a few daisies. Everything around them sweet and fresh like themselves.

Cloudland to-day is only a solitary white mountain; but it is so enriched with sunshine and shade, the tones of color on its big domed head and bossy outbulging ridges, and in the hollows and ravines between them, are ineffably fine.

June 22. Unusually cloudy. Besides the periodical shower-bearing cumuli there is a thin, diffused, fog-like cloud overhead. About .75 in all.

June 23. Oh, these vast, calm, measureless mountain days, inciting at once to work and rest! Days in whose light everything seems equally divine, opening a thousand windows to show us God. Nevermore, however weary, should one faint by the way who gains the blessings of one mountain day; whatever his fate, long life, short life, stormy or calm, he is rich forever.

June 24. Our regular allowance of clouds and thunder. Shepherd Billy is in a peck of trouble about the sheep; he declares that they are possessed with more of the evil one than any other flock from the beginning of the invention of mutton and wool to the last batch of it. No matter how many are missing, he will not, he says, go a step to seek them, because, as he reasons, while getting back one wanderer he would probably lose ten. Therefore runaway hunting must be Carlo's and mine. Billy's little dog Jack is also giving trouble by leaving camp every night to visit his neighbors up the mountain at Brown's Flat. He is a common-looking cur of no particular breed, but tremendously enterprising in love and war. He has cut all the ropes and leather straps he has been tied with, until his master in desperation, after climbing the brushy mountain again and again to drag him back, fastened him with a pole attached to his collar under his chin at one end, and to a stout sapling at the other. But the pole gave good leverage, and by constant twisting during the night, the fastening at the sapling end was chafed off, and he set out on his usual journey, dragging the pole through the brush, and reached the Indian settlement in safety. His master followed, and making no allowance, gave him a beating, and swore in bad terms that next evening he would "fix that infatuated pup" by anchoring him unmercifully to the heavy cast-iron lid of our Dutch oven, weighing about as much as the dog. It was linked directly to his collar close up under the chin, so that the poor fellow seemed unable to stir. He stood quite discouraged until after dark, unable to look about him, or even to lie down unless he stretched himself out with his front feet across the lid, and his head close down between his paws. Before morning, however, Jack was heard far up the height howling Excelsior, cast-iron anchor to the contrary notwithstanding. He must have walked, or rather climbed, erect on his hind legs, clasping the heavy lid like a shield against his breast, a formidable iron-clad condition in which to meet his rivals. Next night, dog, pot-lid, and all, were tied up in an old bean-sack, and thus at last angry Billy gained the victory. Just before leaving home, Jack was bitten in the lower jaw by a rattlesnake, and for a week or so his head and neck were swollen to more than double the normal size; nevertheless he ran about as brisk and lively as ever, and is now completely recovered. The only treatment he got was fresh milk—a gallon or two at a time forcibly poured down his sore, poisoned throat.

June 25. Though only a sheep camp, this grand mountain hollow is home, sweet home, every day growing sweeter, and I shall be sorry to leave it. The lily gardens are safe as yet from the trampling flock. Poor, dusty, raggedy, famishing creatures, I heartily pity them. Many a mile they must go every day to gather their fifteen or twenty tons of chaparral and grass.

June 26. Nuttall's flowering dogwood makes a fine show when in bloom. The whole tree is then snowy white. The involucres are six to eight inches wide. Along the streams it is a good-sized tree thirty to fifty feet high, with a broad head when not crowded by companions. Its showy involucres attract a crowd of moths, butterflies, and other winged people about it for their own and, I suppose, the tree's advantage. It likes plenty of cool water, and is a great drinker like the alder, willow, and cottonwood, and flourishes best on stream banks, though it often wanders far from streams in damp shady glens beneath the pines, where it is much smaller. When the leaves ripen in the fall, they become more beautiful than the flowers, displaying charming tones of red, purple, and lavender. Another species grows in abundance as a chaparral shrub on the shady sides of the hills, probably *Cornus sessilis.* The leaves are eaten by the sheep.—Heard a few lightning strokes in the distance, with rumbling, mumbling reverberations.

June 27. The beaked hazel (*Corylus rostrata,* var. *Californica*) is common on cool slopes up toward the summit of the Pilot Peak Ridge. There is something peculiarly attractive in the hazel, like the oaks and heaths of the cool countries of our forefathers, and through them our love for these plants has, I suppose, been transmitted. This species is four or five feet high, leaves soft and hairy, grateful to the touch, and the delicious nuts are eagerly gathered by Indians and squirrels. The sky as usual adorned with white noon clouds.

June 28. Warm, mellow summer. The glowing sunbeams make every nerve tingle. The new needles of the pines and firs are nearly full grown and shine gloriously. Lizards are glinting about on the hot rocks; some that live near the camp are more than half tame. They seem attentive to every movement on our part, as if curious to simply look on without suspicion of harm, turning their heads to look back, and making a variety of pretty gestures. Gentle, guileless creatures with beautiful eyes, I shall be sorry to leave them when we leave camp.

June 29. I have been making the acquaintance of a very interesting little bird that flits about the falls and rapids of the main branches of the river. It is not a water-bird in structure, though it gets its living in the water, and never leaves the streams. It is not web-footed, yet it dives fearlessly into deep swirling rapids, evidently to feed at the bottom, using its wings to swim with under water just as ducks and loons do. Sometimes it wades about in shallow places, thrusting its head under from time to time in a jerking, nodding, frisky way that is sure to attract attention. It is about the size of a robin, has short crisp wings serviceable for flying either in water or air, and a tail of moderate size slanted upward, giving it, with its nodding, bobbing manners, a wrennish look. Its color is plain bluish ash, with a tinge of brown on the head and shoulders. It flies from fall to fall, rapid to rapid, with a solid whir of wing-beats like those of a quail, follows the windings of the stream, and usually alights on some rock jutting up out of the current, or on some stranded snag, or rarely on the dry limb of an overhanging tree, perching like regular tree birds when it suits its convenience. It has the oddest, daintiest mincing manners imaginable; and the little fellow can sing too, a sweet, thrushy, fluty song, rather low, not the least boisterous, and much less keen and accentuated than from its vigorous briskness one would be led to look for. What a romantic life this little bird leads on the most beautiful portions of the streams, in a genial climate with shade and cool water and spray to temper the summer heat. No wonder it is a fine singer, considering the stream songs it hears day and night. Every breath the little poet draws is part of a song, for all the air about the rapids and falls is beaten into music, and its first lessons must begin before it is born by the thrilling and quivering of the eggs in unison with the tones of the falls. I have not yet found its nest, but it must be near the streams, for it never leaves them.

June 30. Half cloudy, half sunny, clouds lustrous white. The tall pines crowded along the top of the Pilot Peak Ridge look like six-inch miniatures exquisitely outlined on the satiny sky. Average cloudiness for the day about .25. No rain. And so this memorable month ends, a stream of beauty unmeasured, no more to be sectioned off by almanac arithmetic than sun-radiance or the currents of seas and rivers—a peaceful, joyful stream of beauty. Every morning, arising from the death of sleep, the happy plants and all our fellow animal creatures great and small, and even the rocks, seemed to be shouting, "Awake, awake, rejoice, rejoice, come love us and join in our song. Come! Come!" Looking back through the stillness and romantic enchanting beauty and peace of the camp grove, this June seems the greatest of all the months of my life, the most truly, divinely free, boundless like eternity, immortal. Everything in it seems equally divine—one smooth, pure, wild glow of Heaven's love, never to be blotted or blurred by anything past or to come.

July 1. Summer is ripe. Flocks of seeds are already out of their cups and pods seeking their predestined places. Some will strike root and grow up beside their parents, others flying on the wings of the wind far from them, among strangers. Most of the young birds are full feathered and out of their nests, though still looked after by both father and mother, protected and fed and to some extent educated. How beautiful the home life of birds! No wonder we all love them.

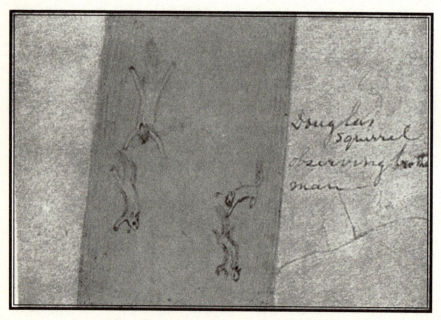

Douglas Squirrel Observing Brother Man

I like to watch the squirrels. There are two species here, the large California gray and the Douglas. The latter is the brightest of all the squirrels I have ever seen, a hot spark of life, making every tree tingle with his prickly toes, a condensed nugget of fresh mountain vigor and valor, as free from disease as a sunbeam. One cannot think of such an animal ever being weary or sick. He seems to think the mountains belong to him, and at first tried to drive away the whole flock of sheep as well as the shepherd and dogs. How he scolds, and what faces he makes, all eyes, teeth, and whiskers! If not so comically small, he would indeed be a dreadful fellow. I should like to know more about his bringing up, his life in the home knot-hole, as well as in the tree-tops, throughout all seasons. Strange that I have not yet found a nest full of young ones. The Douglas is nearly allied to the red squirrel of the Atlantic slope, and may have been distributed to this side of the continent by way of the great unbroken forests of the north.

The California gray is one of the most beautiful, and, next to the Douglas, the most interesting of our hairy neighbors. Compared with the Douglas he is twice as large, but far less lively and influential as a worker in the woods and he manages to make his way through leaves and branches with less stir than his small brother. I have never heard him bark at anything except our dogs. When in search of food he glides silently from branch to branch, examining last year's cones, to see whether some few seeds may not be left between the scales, or gleans fallen ones among the leaves on the ground, since none of the present season's crop is yet available. His tail floats now behind him, now above him, level or gracefully curled like a wisp of cirrus cloud, every hair in its place, clean and shining and radiant as thistle-down in spite of rough, gummy work. His whole body seems about as unsubstantial as his tail. The little Douglas is fiery, peppery, full of brag and fight and show, with movements so quick and keen they almost sting the onlooker, and the harlequin gyrating show he makes of himself turns one giddy to see. The gray is shy, and oftentimes stealthy in his movements, as if half expecting an enemy in every tree and bush, and back of every log, wishing only to be let alone apparently, and manifesting no desire to be seen or admired or feared. The Indians hunt this species for food, a good cause for caution, not to mention other enemies—hawks, snakes, wild cats. In woods where food is abundant they wear paths through sheltering thickets and over prostrate trees to some favorite pool where in hot and dry weather they drink at nearly the same hour every day. These pools are said to be narrowly watched, especially by the boys, who lie in ambush with bow and arrow, and kill without noise. But, in spite of enemies, squirrels are happy fellows, forest favorites, types of tireless life. Of all Nature's wild beasts, they seem to me the wildest. May we come to know each other better. The chaparral-covered hill-slope to the south of the camp, besides furnishing nesting-places for countless merry birds, is the home and hiding-place of the curious wood rat (*Neotoma*), a handsome, interesting animal, always attracting attention wherever seen. It is more like a squirrel than a rat, is much larger, has delicate, thick, soft fur of a bluish slate color, white on the belly; ears large, thin, and translucent; eyes soft, full, and liquid; claws slender, sharp as needles; and as his limbs are strong, he can climb about as well as a squirrel. No rat or squirrel has so innocent a look, is so easily approached, or expresses such confidence in one's good intentions. He seems too fine for the thorny thickets he inhabits, and his hut also is as unlike himself as may be, though softly furnished inside. No other animal inhabitant of these mountains builds houses so large and striking in appearance. The traveler coming suddenly upon a group of them for the first time will not be likely to forget them. They are built of all kinds of sticks, old rotten pieces picked up anywhere, and green prickly twigs bitten from the nearest bushes, the whole mixed with miscellaneous odds and ends of everything movable, such as bits of cloddy earth, stones, bones, deerhorn, etc., piled up in a conical mass as if it were got ready for burning. Some of these curious cabins are six feet high and as wide at the base, and a dozen or more of them are occasionally grouped together, less perhaps for the sake of society than for advantages of food and shelter. Coming through the dense shaggy thickets of some lonely hillside, the solitary explorer happening into one of these strange villages is startled at the sight, and may fancy himself in an Indian settlement, and begin to wonder what kind of reception he is likely to get. But no savage face will he see, perhaps not a single inhabitant, or at most

July 3. Warm. Breeze just enough to sift through the woods and waft fragrance from their thousand fountains. The pine and fir cones are growing well, resin and balsam dripping from every tree, and seeds are ripening fast, promising a fine harvest. The squirrels will have bread. They eat all kinds of nuts long before they are ripe, and yet never seem to suffer in stomach.

two or three seated on top of their wigwams, looking at
with the mildest of wild eyes, and allowing a near app
centre of the rough spiky hut a soft nest is made of th
of bark chewed to tow, and lined with feathers and
various seeds, such as willow and milkweed. The delica
its prickly, thick-walled home suggests a tender flowe
involucre. Some of the nests are built in trees thirty
from the ground, and even in garrets, as if seeking the
protection of man, like swallows and linnets, though
the wildest solitude. Among housekeepers Neotoma
tation of a thief, because he carries away everything
to his queer hut,—knives, forks, combs, nails, tin c
etc.,—merely, however, to strengthen his fortificatio
food at home, as far as I have learned, is nearly th
of the squirrels,—nuts, berries, seeds, and sometim
tender shoots of the various species of ceanothus.

July 2. Warm, sunny day, thrilling plant and an
alike, making sap and blood flow fast, and making
the crystal mountains throb and swirl and dance in
star-dust. No dullness anywhere visible or thinkabl
no death. Everything kept in joyful rhythmic mot
of Nature's big heart.

Pearl cumuli over the higher mountains—cloud
lining, but all silver. The brightest, crispest, rockie
most varied in features and keenest in outline I ev
of year in any country. The daily building and u
snowy cloud-ranges—the highest Sierra—is a pr
and I gaze at the stupendous white domes, mil
fresh admiration. But in the midst of these sky ar
a change of diet is pulling us down. We have b
few days, and begin to miss it more than seem
have plenty of meat and sugar and tea. Strange v
poor in so rich a wilderness. The Indians put us
squirrels,—starchy roots and seeds and bark in
failure of the meal sack disturbs our bodily ba
our best enjoyments.

A Bread Famine

❧

July 4. The air beyond the flock range, full of the essences of the woods, is growing sweeter and more fragrant from day to day, like ripening fruit.

Mr. Delaney is expected to arrive soon from the lowlands with a new stock of provisions, and as the flock is to be moved to fresh pastures we shall all be well fed. In the mean time our stock of beans as well as flour has failed—everything but mutton, sugar, and tea. The shepherd is somewhat demoralized, and seems to care but little what becomes of his flock. He says that since the boss has failed to feed him he is not rightly bound to feed the sheep, and swears that no decent white man can climb these steep mountains on mutton alone. "It's not fittin' grub for a white man really white. For dogs and coyotes and Indians it's different. Good grub, good sheep. That's what I say." Such was Billy's Fourth of July oration.

July 5. The clouds of noon on the high Sierra seem yet more marvelously, indescribably beautiful from day to day as one becomes more wakeful to see them. The smoke of the gunpowder burned yesterday on the lowlands, and the eloquence of the orators has probably settled or been blown away by this time. Here every day is a holiday, a jubilee ever sounding with serene enthusiasm, without wear or waste or cloying weariness. Everything rejoicing. Not a single cell or crystal unvisited or forgotten.

July 6. Mr. Delaney has not arrived, and the bread famine is sore. We must eat mutton a while longer, though it seems hard to get accustomed to it. I have heard of Texas pioneers living without bread or anything made from the cereals for months without suffering, using the breast-meat of wild turkeys for bread. Of this kind they had plenty in the good old days when life, though considered less safe, was fussed over the less. The trappers and fur traders of early days in the Rocky Mountain regions lived on bison and beaver meat for months. Salmon-eaters, too, there are among both Indians and whites who seem to suffer little or not at all from the want of bread. Just at this moment mutton seems the least desirable of food, though of good quality. We pick out the leanest bits, and down they go against heavy disgust, causing nausea and an effort to reject the offensive stuff. Tea makes matters worse, if possible. The stomach begins to assert itself as an independent creature with a will of its own. We should boil lupine leaves, clover, starchy petioles, and saxifrage rootstocks like the Indians. We try to ignore our gastric troubles, rise and gaze about us, turn our eyes to the mountains, and climb doggedly up through brush and rocks into the heart of the scenery. A stifled calm comes on, and the day's duties and even enjoyments are languidly got through with. We chew a few leaves of ceanothus by way of luncheon, and smell or chew the spicy monardella for the dull headache and stomach-ache that now lightens, now comes muffling down upon us and into us like fog. At night more mutton, flesh to flesh, down with it, not too much, and there are the stars shining through the cedar plumes and branches above our beds.

July 7. Rather weak and sickish this morning, and all about a piece of bread. Can scarce command attention to my best studies, as if one couldn't take a few days' saunter in the Godful woods without maintaining a base on a wheat-field and gristmill. Like caged parrots we want a cracker, any of the hundred kinds—the remainder biscuit of a voyage around the world would answer well enough, nor would the wholesomeness of saleratus biscuit be questioned.

Bread without flesh is a good diet, as on many botanical excursions I have proved. Tea also may easily be ignored. Just bread and water and delightful toil is all I need,—not unreasonably much, yet one ought to be trained and tempered to enjoy life in these brave wilds in full independence of any particular kind of nourishment. That this may be accomplished is manifest, as far as bodily welfare is concerned, in the lives of people of other climes. The Eskimo, for example, gets a living far north of the wheat line, from oily seals and whales. Meat, berries, bitter weeds, and blubber, or only the last, for months at a time; and yet these people all around the frozen shores of our continent are said to be hearty, jolly, stout, and brave.

We hear, too, of fish-eaters, carnivorous as spiders, yet well enough as far as stomachs are concerned, while we are so ridiculously helpless, making wry faces over our fare, looking sheepish in digestive distress amid rumbling, grumbling sounds that might well pass for smothered baas. We have a large supply of sugar, and this evening it occurred to me that these belligerent stomachs might possibly, like complaining children, be coaxed with candy. Accordingly the frying-pan was cleansed, and a lot of sugar cooked in it to a sort of wax, but this stuff only made matters worse.

Man seems to be the only animal whose food soils him, making necessary much washing and shield-like bibs and napkins. Moles living in the earth and eating slimy worms are yet as clean as seals or fishes, whose lives are one perpetual wash. And, as we have seen, the squirrels in these resiny woods keep themselves clean in some mysterious way; not a hair is sticky, though they handle the gummy cones, and glide about apparently without care. The birds, too, are clean, though they seem to make a good deal of fuss washing and cleaning their feathers. Certain flies and ants I see are in a fix, entangled and sealed up in the sugar-wax we threw away, like some of their ancestors in amber. Our stomachs, like tired muscles, are sore with long squirming. Once I was very hungry in the Bonaventure graveyard near Savannah, Georgia, having fasted for several days; then the empty stomach seemed to chafe in much the same way as now, and a somewhat similar tenderness and aching was produced, hard to bear, though the pain was not acute. We dream of bread, a sure sign we need it. Like the Indians, we ought to know how to get the starch out of fern and saxifrage stalks, lily bulbs, pine bark, etc. Our education has been sadly neglected for many generations. Wild rice would be good. I noticed a leersia in wet meadow edges, but the seeds are small. Acorns are not ripe, nor pine nuts, nor filberts. The inner bark of pine or spruce might be tried. Drank tea until half intoxicated. Man seems to crave a stimulant when anything extraordinary is going on, and this is the only one I use. Billy chews great quantities of tobacco, which I suppose helps to stupefy and moderate his misery. We look and listen for the Don every hour. How beautiful upon the mountains his big feet would be!

In the warm, hospitable Sierra, shepherds and mountain men in general, as far as I have seen, are easily satisfied as to food supplies and bedding. Most of them are heartily content to "rough it," ignoring Nature's fineness as bothersome or unmanly. The shepherd's bed is often only the bare ground and a pair of blankets, with a stone, a piece of wood, or a pack-saddle for a pillow. In choosing the spot, he shows less care than the dogs, for they usually deliberate before making up their minds in so important an affair, going from place to place, scraping away loose sticks and pebbles, and trying for comfort by making many changes, while the shepherd casts himself down anywhere, seemingly the least skilled of all rest seekers. His food, too, even when he has all he wants, is usually far from delicate, either in kind or cooking. Beans, bread of any sort, bacon, mutton, dried peaches, and sometimes potatoes and onions, make up his bill-of-fare, the two latter articles being regarded as luxuries on account of their weight as compared with the nourishment they contain; a half-sack or so of each may be put into the pack in setting out from the home ranch and in a few days they are done. Beans are the main standby, portable, wholesome, and capable of going far, besides being easily cooked, although curiously enough a great deal of mystery is supposed to lie about the bean-pot. No two cooks quite agree on the methods of making beans do their best, and, after petting and coaxing and nursing the savory mess,—well oiled and mellowed with bacon boiled into the heart of it,—the proud cook will ask, after dishing out a quart or two for trial, "Well, how do you like *my* beans?" as if by no possibility could they be like any other beans cooked in the same way, but must needs possess some special virtue of which he alone is master. Molasses, sugar, or pepper may be used to give desired flavors; or the first water may be poured off and a spoonful or two of ashes or soda added to dissolve or soften the skins more fully, according to various tastes and notions. But, like casks of wine, no two potfuls are exactly alike to every palate. Some are supposed to be spoiled by the moon, by some unlucky day, by the beans having been grown on soil not suitable; or the whole year may be to blame as not favorable for beans.

Coffee, too, has its marvels in the camp kitchen, but not so many, and not so inscrutable as those that beset the bean-pot. A low, complacent grunt follows a mouthful drawn in with a gurgle, and the remark cast forth aimlessly, "That's good coffee." Then another gurgling sip and repetition of the judgment, "Yes, sir, that *is* good coffee." As to tea, there are but two kinds, weak and strong, the stronger the better. The only remark heard is, "That tea's weak," otherwise it is good enough and not worth mentioning. If it has been boiled an hour or two or smoked on a pitchy fire, no matter,— who cares for a little tannin or creosote? they make the black beverage all the stronger and more attractive to tobacco-tanned palates.

Sheep-camp bread, like most California camp bread, is baked in Dutch ovens, some of it in the form of yeast powder biscuit, an unwholesome sticky compound leading straight to dyspepsia. The greater part, however, is fermented with sour dough, a handful from each batch being saved and put away in the mouth of the flour sack to inoculate the next. The oven is simply a cast-iron pot, about five inches deep and from twelve to eighteen inches wide. After the batch has been mixed and kneaded in a tin pan the oven is slightly heated and rubbed with a piece of tallow or pork rind. The dough is then placed in it, pressed out against the sides, and left to rise. When ready for baking a shovelful of coals is spread out by the side of the fire and the oven set upon them, while another shovelful is placed on top of the lid, which is raised from time to time to see that the requisite amount of heat is being kept up. With care good bread may be made in this way, though it is liable to be burned or to be sour, or raised too much, and the weight of the oven is a serious objection.

At last Don Delaney comes doon the lang glen—hunger vanishes, we turn our eyes to the mountains, and to-morrow we go climbing toward cloudland.

Never while anything is left of me shall this first camp be forgotten. It has fairly grown into me, not merely as memory pictures, but as part and parcel of mind and body alike. The deep hopperlike hollow, with its majestic trees through which all the wonderful nights the stars poured their beauty. The flowery wildness of the high steep slope toward Brown's Flat, and its bloom-fragrance descending at the close of the still days. The embowered river-reaches with their multitude of voices making melody, the stately flow and rush and glad exulting onsweeping currents caressing the dipping sedge-leaves and bushes and mossy stones, swirling in pools, dividing against little flowery islands, breaking gray and white here and there, ever rejoicing, yet with deep solemn undertones recalling the ocean—the brave little bird ever beside them, singing with sweet human tones among the waltzing foam-bells, and like a blessed evangel explaining God's love. And the Pilot Peak Ridge, its long withdrawing slopes gracefully modeled and braided, reaching from climate to climate, feathered with trees that are the kings of their race, their ranks nobly marshaled to view, spire above spire, crown above crown, waving their long, leafy arms, tossing their cones like ringing bells—blessed sun-fed mountaineers rejoicing in their strength, every tree tuneful, a harp for the winds and the sun. The hazel and buckthorn pastures of the deer, the sun-beaten brows purple and yellow with mint and golden-rods, carpeted with chamæbatia, humming with bees. And the dawns and sunrises and sundowns of these mountain days,—the rose light creeping higher among the stars, changing to daffodil yellow, the level beams bursting forth, streaming across the ridges, touching pine after pine, awakening and warming all the mighty host to do gladly their shining day's work. The great sun-gold noons, the alabaster cloud-mountains, the landscape beaming with consciousness like the face of a god. The sunsets, when the trees stood hushed awaiting their good-night blessings. Divine, enduring, unwastable wealth.

To The High Mountains

July 8. Now away we go toward the topmost mountains. Many still, small voices, as well as the noon thunder, are calling, "Come higher." Farewell, blessed dell, woods, gardens, streams, birds, squirrels, lizards, and a thousand others. Farewell. Farewell.

Up through the woods the hoofed locusts streamed beneath a cloud of brown dust. Scarcely were they driven a hundred yards from the old corral ere they seemed to know that at last they were going to new pastures, and rushed wildly ahead, crowding through gaps in the brush, jumping, tumbling like exulting hurrahing flood-waters escaping through a broken dam. A man on each flank kept shouting advice to the leaders, who in their famishing condition were behaving like Gadarene swine; two other drivers were busy with stragglers, helping them out of brush tangles; the Indian, calm, alert, silently watched for wanderers likely to be overlooked; the two dogs ran here and there, at a loss to know what was best to be done, while the Don, soon far in the rear, was trying to keep in sight of his troublesome wealth.

Divide between the Tuolumne and the Merced below Hazel Green

As soon as the boundary of the old eaten-out range was passed the hungry horde suddenly became calm, like a mountain stream in a meadow. Thenceforward they were allowed to eat their way as slowly as they wished, care being taken only to keep them headed toward the summit of the Merced and Tuolumne divide. Soon the two thousand flattened paunches were bulged out with sweet-pea vines and grass, and the gaunt, desperate creatures, more like wolves than sheep, became bland and governable, while the howling drivers changed to gentle shepherds, and sauntered in peace.

Toward sundown we reached Hazel Green, a charming spot on the summit of the dividing ridge between the basins of the Merced and Tuolumne, where there is a small brook flowing through hazel and dogwood thickets beneath magnificent silver firs and pines. Here, we are camped for the night, our big fire, heaped high with rosiny logs and branches, is blazing like a sunrise, gladly giving back the light slowly sifted from the sunbeams of centuries of summers; and in the glow of that old sunlight how impressively surrounding objects are brought forward in relief against the outer darkness! Grasses, larkspurs, columbines, lilies, hazel bushes, and the great trees form a circle around the fire like thoughtful spectators, gazing and listening with human-like enthusiasm. The night breeze is cool, for all day we have been climbing into the upper sky, the home of the cloud mountains we so long have admired. How sweet and keen the air! Every breath a blessing. Here the sugar pine reaches its fullest development in size and beauty and number of individuals, filling every swell and hollow and down-plunging ravine almost to the exclusion of other species. A few yellow pines are still to be found as companions, and in the coolest places silver firs; but noble as these are, the sugar pine is king, and spreads long protecting arms above them while they rock and wave in sign of recognition.

We have now reached a height of six thousand feet. In the forenoon we passed along a flat part of the dividing ridge that is planted with manzanita (*Arctostaphylos*), some specimens the largest I have seen. I measured one, the bole of which is four feet in diameter and only eighteen inches high from the ground, where it dissolves into many wide-spreading branches forming a broad round head about ten or twelve feet high, covered with clusters of small narrow-throated pink bells. The leaves are pale green, glandular, and set on edge by a twist of the petiole. The branches seem naked; for the chocolate-colored bark is very smooth and thin, and is shed off in flakes that curl when dry. The wood is red, close-grained, hard, and heavy. I wonder how old these curious tree-bushes are, probably as old as the great pines. Indians and bears and birds and fat grubs feast on the berries, which look like small apples, often rosy on one side, green on the other. The Indians are said to make a kind of beer or cider out of them. There are many species. This one, *Arctostaphylos pungens*, is common hereabouts. No need have they to fear the wind, so low they are and steadfastly rooted. Even the fires that sweep the woods seldom destroy them utterly, for they rise again from the root, and some of the dry ridges they grow on are seldom touched by fire. I must try to know them better.

I miss my river songs to-night. Here Hazel Creek at its topmost springs has a voice like a bird. The wind-tones in the great trees overhead are strangely impressive, all the more because not a leaf stirs below them. But it grows late, and I must to bed. The camp is silent; everybody asleep. It seems extravagant to spend hours so precious in sleep. "He giveth his beloved sleep." Pity the poor beloved needs it, weak, weary, forspent; oh, the pity of it, to sleep in the midst of eternal, beautiful motion instead of gazing forever, like the stars.

July 9. Exhilarated with the mountain air, I feel like shouting this morning with excess of wild animal joy. The Indian lay down away from the fire last night, without blankets, having nothing on, by way of clothing, but a pair of blue overalls and a calico shirt wet with sweat. The night air is chilly at this elevation, and we gave him some horse-blankets, but he didn't seem to care for them. A fine thing to be independent of clothing where it is so hard to carry. When food is scarce, he can live on whatever comes in his way—a few berries, roots, bird eggs, grasshoppers, black ants, fat wasp or bumblebee larvæ, without feeling that he is doing anything worth mention, so I have been told.

A Silver Fir, or Red Fir

(Abies magnifica)

Our course to-day was along the broad top of the main ridge to a hollow beyond Crane Flat. It is scarce at all rocky, and is covered with the noblest pines and spruces I have yet seen. Sugar pines from six to eight feet in diameter are not uncommon, with a height of two hundred feet or even more. The silver firs (*Abies concolor* and *A. magnifica*) are exceedingly beautiful, especially the *magnifica*, which becomes more abundant the higher we go. It is of great size, one of the most notable in every way of the giant conifers of the Sierra. I saw specimens that measured seven feet in diameter and over two hundred feet in height, while the average size for what might be called full-grown mature trees can hardly be less than one hundred and eighty or two hundred feet high and five or six feet in diameter; and with these noble dimensions there is a symmetry and perfection of finish not to be seen in any other tree, hereabout at least. The branches are whorled in fives mostly, and stand out from the tall, straight, exquisitely tapered bole in level collars, each branch regularly pinnated like the fronds of ferns, and densely clad with leaves all around the branchlets, thus giving them a singularly rich and sumptuous appearance. The extreme top of the tree is a thick blunt shoot pointing straight to the zenith like an admonishing finger. The cones stand erect like casks on the upper branches. They are about six inches long, three in diameter, blunt, velvety, and cylindrical in form, and very rich and precious looking. The seeds are about three quarters of an inch long, dark reddish brown with brilliant iridescent purple wings, and when ripe, the cone falls to pieces, and the seeds thus set free at a height of one hundred and fifty or two hundred feet have a good send off and may fly considerable distances in a good breeze; and it is when a good breeze is blowing that most of them are shaken free to fly.

The other species, *Abies concolor*, attains nearly as great a height and thickness as the *magnifica*, but the branches do not form such regular whorls, nor are they so exactly pinnated or richly leaf-clad. Instead of growing all around the branchlets, the leaves are mostly arranged in two flat horizontal rows. The cones and seeds are like those of the *magnifica* in form but less than half as large. The bark of the *magnifica* is reddish purple and closely furrowed, that of the *concolor* gray and widely furrowed. A noble pair.

At Crane Flat we climbed a thousand feet or more in a distance of about two miles, the forest growing more dense and the silvery *magnifica* fir forming a still greater portion of the whole. Crane Flat is a meadow with a wide sandy border lying on the top of the divide. It is often visited by blue cranes to rest and feed on their long journeys, hence the name. It is about half a mile long, draining into the Merced, sedgy in the middle, with a margin bright with lilies, columbines, lark-spurs, lupines, castilleia, then an outer zone of dry, gently sloping ground starred with a multitude of small flowers,—eunanus, mimulus, gilia, with rosettes of spraguea, and tufts of several species of eriogonum and the brilliant zauschneria. The noble forest wall about it is made up of the two silver firs and the yellow and sugar pines, which here seem to reach their highest pitch of beauty and grandeur; for the elevation, six thousand feet or a little more, is not too great for the sugar and yellow pines or too low for the *magnifica* fir, while the *concolor* seems to find this elevation the best possible. About a mile from the north end of the flat there is a grove of *Sequoia gigantea*, the king of all the conifers. Furthermore, the Douglas spruce (*Pseudotsuga Douglasii*) and *Libocedrus decurrens*, and a few two-leaved pines, occur here and there, forming a small part of the forest. Three pines, two silver firs, one Douglas spruce, one sequoia,—all of them, except the two-leaved pine, colossal trees,—are found here together, an assemblage of conifers unrivaled on the globe.

We passed a number of charming garden-like meadows lying on top of the divide or hanging like ribbons down its sides, imbedded in the glorious forest. Some are taken up chiefly with the tall white-flowered *Veratrum Californicum*, with boat-shaped leaves about a foot long, eight or ten inches wide, and veined like those of cypripedium,—a robust, hearty, liliaceous plant, fond of water and determined to be seen. Columbine and larkspur grow on the dryer edges of the meadows, with a tall handsome lupine standing waist-deep in long grasses and sedges. Castilleias, too, of several species make a bright show with beds of violets at their feet. But the glory of these forest meadows is a lily (*L. parvum*). The tallest are from seven to eight feet high with magnificent racemes of ten to twenty or more small orange-colored flowers; they stand out free in open ground, with just enough grass and other companion plants about them to fringe their feet, and show them off to best advantage. This is a grand addition to my lily acquaintances,—a true mountaineer, reaching prime vigor and beauty at a height of seven thousand feet or thereabouts. It varies, I find, very much in size even in the same meadow, not only with the soil, but with age. I saw a specimen that had only one flower, and another within a stone's throw had twenty-five. And to think that the sheep should be allowed in these lily meadows! after how many centuries of Nature's care planting and watering them, tucking the bulbs in snugly below winter frost, shading the tender shoots with clouds drawn above them like curtains, pouring refreshing rain, making them perfect in beauty, and keeping them safe by a thousand miracles; yet, strange to say, allowing the trampling of devastating sheep. One might reasonably look for a wall of fire to fence such gardens. So extravagant is Nature with her choicest treasures, spending plant beauty as she spends sunshine, pouring it forth into land and sea, garden and desert. And so the beauty of lilies falls on angels and men, bears and squirrels, wolves and sheep, birds and bees, but as far as I have seen, man alone, and the animals he tames, destroy these gardens. Awkward, lumbering bears, the Don tells me, love to wallow in them in hot weather, and deer with their sharp feet cross them again and again, sauntering and feeding, yet never a lily have I seen spoiled by them. Rather, like gardeners, they seem to cultivate them, pressing and dibbling as required. Anyhow not a leaf or petal seems misplaced.

The trees round about them seem as perfect in beauty and form as the lilies, their boughs whorled like lily leaves in exact order. This evening, as usual, the glow of our camp-fire is working enchantment on everything within reach of its rays. Lying beneath the firs, it is glorious to see them dipping their spires in the starry sky, the sky like one vast lily meadow in bloom! How can I close my eyes on so precious a night?

July 10. A Douglas squirrel, peppery, pungent autocrat of the woods, is barking overhead this morning, and the small forest birds, so seldom seen when one travels noisily, are out on sunny branches along the edge of the meadow getting warm, taking a sun bath and dew bath—a fine sight. How charming the sprightly confident looks and ways of these little feathered people of the trees! They seem sure of dainty, wholesome breakfasts, and where are so many breakfasts to come from? How helpless should we find ourselves should we try to set a table for them of such buds, seeds, insects, etc., as would keep them in the pure wild health they enjoy! Not a headache or any other ache amongst them, I guess. As for the irrepressible Douglas squirrels, one never thinks of their breakfasts or the possibility of hunger, sickness or death; rather they seem like stars above chance or change, even though we may see them at times busy gathering burrs, working hard for a living.

On through the forest ever higher we go, a cloud of dust dimming the way, thousands of feet trampling leaves and flowers, but in this mighty wilderness they seem but a feeble band, and a thousand gardens will escape their blighting touch. They cannot hurt the trees, though some of the seedlings suffer, and should the woolly locusts be greatly multiplied, as on account of dollar value they are likely to be, then the forests, too, may in time be destroyed. Only the sky will then be safe, though hid from view by dust and smoke, incense of a bad sacrifice. Poor, helpless, hungry sheep, in great part misbegotten, without good right to be, semi-manufactured, made less by God than man, born out of time and place, yet their voices are strangely human and call out one's pity.

Our way is still along the Merced and Tuolumne divide, the streams on our right going to swell the songful Yosemite River, those on our left to the songful Tuolumne, slipping through sunny carex and lily meadows, and breaking into song down a thousand ravines almost as soon as they are born. A more tuneful set of streams surely nowhere exists, or more sparkling crystal pure, now gliding with tinkling whisper, now with merry dimpling rush, in and out through sunshine and shade, shimmering in pools, uniting their currents, bouncing, dancing from form to form over cliffs and inclines, ever more beautiful the farther they go until they pour into the main glacial rivers.

All day I have been gazing in growing admiration at the noble groups of the magnificent silver fir which more and more is taking the ground to itself. The woods above Crane Flat still continue comparatively open, letting in the sunshine on the brown needle-strewn ground. Not only are the individual trees admirable in symmetry and superb in foliage and port, but half a dozen or more often form temple groves in which the trees are so nicely graded in size and position as to seem one. Here, indeed, is the tree-lover's paradise. The dullest eye in the world must surely be quickened by such trees as these.

Fortunately the sheep need little attention, as they are driven slowly and allowed to nip and nibble as they like. Since leaving Hazel Green we have been following the Yosemite trail; visitors to the famous valley coming by way of Coulterville and Chinese Camp pass this way—the two trails uniting at Crane Flat—and enter the valley on the north side. Another trail enters on the south side by way of Mariposa. The tourists we saw were in parties of from three or four to fifteen or twenty, mounted on mules or small mustang if weathered out of the solid as boulders of disintegration; they mostly occur singly, and are lying on a clean pavement on which the sunshine falls in a glare that contrasts with the shimmer of light and shade we have been accustomed to in the leafy woods.

And, strange to say, these boulders lying so still and deserted, with no moving force near them, no boulder carrier anywhere in sight, were nevertheless brought from a distance, as difference in color and composition shows, quarried and carried and laid down here each in its place; nor have they stirred, most of them, through calm and storm since first they arrived. They look lonely here, strangers in a strange land,—huge blocks, angular mountain chips, the largest twenty or thirty feet in diameter, the chips that Nature has made in modeling her landscapes, fashioning the forms of her mountains and valleys. And with what tool were they quarried and carried? On the pavement we find its marks. The most resisting unweathered portion of the surface is scored and striated in a rigidly parallel way, indicating that the region has been overswept by a glacier from the northeastward, grinding down the general mass of the mountains, scoring and polishing, producing a strange, raw, wiped appearance, and dropping whatever boulders it chanced to be carrying at the time it was melted at the close of the Glacial Period. A fine discovery this. As for the forests we have been passing through, they are probably growing on deposits of soil most of which has been laid down by this same ice agent in the form of moraines of different sorts, now in great part disintegrated and outspread by post-glacial weathering.

Out of the grassy meadow and down over this ice-planed granite runs the glad young Tamarack Creek, rejoicing, exulting, chanting, dancing in white, glowing, irised falls and cascades on its way to the Merced Cañon, a few miles below Yosemite, falling more than three thousand feet in a distance of about two miles.

All the Merced streams are wonderful singers, and Yosemite is the centre where the main tributaries meet. From a point about half a mile from our camp we can see into the lower end of the famous valley, with its wonderful cliffs and groves, a grand page of mountain manuscript that I would gladly give my life to be able to read.

ponies. A strange show they made, winding single file throu
solemn woods in gaudy attire, scaring the wild creatures, a
might fancy that even the great pines would be disturbed an
aghast. But what may we say of ourselves and the flock?

We are now camped at Tamarack Flat, within four or fi
of the lower end of Yosemite. Here is another fine meadov
somed in the woods, with a deep, clear stream gliding throu
banks rounded and beveled with a thatch of dipping sedges.
is named after the two-leaved pine (*Pinus contorta*, var. *M*
common here, especially around the cool margin of the
On rocky ground it is a rough, thickset tree, about fort
feet high and one to three feet in diameter, bark thin an
branches rather naked, tassels, leaves, and cones small. Bu
rich soil it grows close and slender, and reaches a height a
nearly a hundred feet. Specimens only six inches in diam
ground are often fifty or sixty feet in height, as slender
in outline as arrows, like the true tamarack (larch) of tl
States; hence the name, though it is a pine.

July 11. The Don has gone ahead on one of the pa
to spy out the land to the north of Yosemite in search
point for a central camp. Much higher than this we canr
for the upper pastures, said to be better than any here
still buried in heavy winter snow. Glad I am that camp is
in the Yosemite region, for many a glorious ramble I'll
the top of the walls, and then what landscapes I shall fir
new mountains and cañons, forests and gardens, lakes
and falls.

We are now about seven thousand feet above the
nights are so cool we have to pile coats and extra clo
of our blankets. Tamarack Creek is icy cold, delicious
champagne water. It is flowing bank-full in the meadc
speed, but only a few hundred yards below our camp
bare gray granite strewn with boulders, large spaces
a single tree or only a small one here and there ancho
seams and cracks. The boulders, many of them very
in piles or scattered like rubbish among loose cruml

How vast it seems, how short human life when we happen to think of it, and how little we may learn, however hard we try! Yet why bewail our poor inevitable ignorance? Some of the external beauty is always in sight, enough to keep every fibre of us tingling, and this we are able to gloriously enjoy though the methods of its creation may lie beyond our ken. Sing on, brave Tamarack Creek, fresh from your snowy fountains, plash and swirl and dance to your fate in the sea; bathing, cheering every living thing along your way.

Have greatly enjoyed all this huge day, sauntering and seeing, steeping in the mountain influences, sketching, noting, pressing flowers, drinking ozone and Tamarack water. Found the white fragrant Washington lily, the finest of all the Sierra lilies. Its bulbs are buried in shaggy chaparral tangles, I suppose for safety from pawing bears; and its magnificent panicles sway and rock over the top of the rough snow-pressed bushes, while big, bold, blunt-nosed bees drone and mumble in its polleny bells. A lovely flower, worth going hungry and footsore endless miles to see. The whole world seems richer now that I have found this plant in so noble a landscape.

A log house serves to mark a claim to the Tamarack meadow, which may become valuable as a station in case travel to Yosemite should greatly increase. Belated parties occasionally stop here. A white man with an Indian woman is holding possession of the place.

Sauntered up the meadow about sundown, out of sight of camp and sheep and all human mark, into the deep peace of the solemn old woods, everything glowing with Heaven's unquenchable enthusiasm.

July 12. The Don has returned, and again we go on pilgrimage. "Looking over the Yosemite Creek country," he said, "from the tops of the hills you see nothing but rocks and patches of trees; but when you go down into the rocky desert you find no end of small grassy banks and meadows, and so the country is not half so lean as it looks. There we'll go and stay until the snow is melted from the upper country."

I was glad to hear that the high snow made a stay in the Yosemite region necessary, for I am anxious to see as much of it as possible. What fine times I shall have sketching, studying plants and rocks, and scrambling about the brink of the great valley alone, out of sight and sound of camp!

We saw another party of Yosemite tourists to-day. Somehow most of these travelers seem to care but little for the glorious objects about them, though enough to spend time and money and endure long rides to see the famous valley. And when they are fairly within the mighty walls of the temple and hear the psalms of the falls, they will forget themselves and become devout. Blessed, indeed, should be every pilgrim in these holy mountains!

We moved slowly eastward along the Mono Trail, and early in the afternoon unpacked and camped on the bank of Cascade Creek. The Mono Trail crosses the range by the Bloody Cañon Pass to gold mines near the north end of Mono Lake. These mines were reported to be rich when first discovered, and a grand rush took place, making a trail necessary. A few small bridges were built over streams where fording was not practicable on account of the softness of the bottom, sections of fallen trees cut out, and lanes made through thickets wide enough to allow the passage of bulky packs; but over the greater part of the way scarce a stone or shovelful of earth has been moved.

The woods we passed through are composed almost wholly of *Abies magnifica*, the companion species, *concolor*, being mostly left behind on account of altitude, while the increasing elevation seems grateful to the charming *magnifica*. No words can do anything like justice to this noble tree. At one place many had fallen during some heavy wind-storm, owing to the loose sandy character of the soil, which offered no secure anchorage. The soil is mostly decomposed and disintegrated moraine material.

The sheep are lying down on a bare rocky spot such as they like, chewing the cud in grassy peace. Cooking is going on, appetites growing keener every day. No lowlander can appreciate the mountain appetite, and the facility with which heavy food called "grub" is disposed of. Eating, walking, resting, seem alike delightful, and one feels inclined to shout lustily on rising in the morning like a crowing cock. Sleep and digestion as clear as the air. Fine spicy plush boughs for bedding we shall have to-night, and a glorious lullaby from this cascading creek. Never was stream more fittingly named, for as far as I have traced it above and below our camp it is one continuous bouncing, dancing, white bloom of cascades. And at the very last unwearied it finishes its wild course in a grand leap of three hundred feet or more to the bottom of the main Yosemite cañon near the fall of Tamarack Creek, a few miles below the foot of the valley. These falls almost rival some of the far-famed Yosemite falls. Never shall I forget these glad cascade songs, the low booming, the roaring, the keen, silvery clashing of the cool water rushing exulting from form to form beneath irised spray; or in the deep still night seen white in the darkness, and its multitude of voices sounding still more impressively sublime. Here I find the little water ouzel as much at home as any linnet in a leafy grove, seeming to take the greater delight the more boisterous the stream. The dizzy precipices, the swift dashing energy displayed, and the thunder tones of the sheer falls are awe inspiring, but there is nothing awful about this little bird. Its song is sweet and low, and all its gestures, as it flits about amid the loud uproar, bespeak strength and peace and joy. Contemplating these darlings of Nature coming forth from spray-sprinkled nests on the brink of savage streams, Samson's riddle comes to mind, "Out of the strong cometh forth sweetness." A yet finer bloom is this little bird than the foam-bells in eddying pools. Gentle bird, a precious message you bring me. We may miss the meaning of the torrent, but thy sweet voice, only love is in it.

July 13. Our course all day has been eastward over the rim of Yosemite Creek basin and down about halfway to the bottom, where we have encamped on a sheet of glacier-polished granite, a firm foundation for beds. Saw the tracks of a very large bear on the trail, and the Don talked of bears in general. I said I should like to see the maker of these immense tracks as he marched along, and follow him for days, without disturbing him, to learn something of the life of this master beast of the wilderness. Lambs, the Don told me, born in the lowland, that never saw or heard a bear, snort and run in terror when they catch the scent, showing how fully they have inherited a knowledge of their enemy. Hogs, mules, horses, and cattle are afraid of bears, and are seized with ungovernable terror when they approach, particularly hogs and mules. Hogs are frequently driven to pastures in the foothills of the Coast Range and Sierra where acorns are abundant, and are herded in droves of hundreds like sheep. When a bear comes to the range they promptly leave it, emigrating in a body, usually in the night time, the keepers being powerless to prevent; they thus show more sense than sheep, that simply scatter in the rocks and brush and await their fate. Mules flee like the wind with or without riders when they see a bear, and, if picketed, sometimes break their necks in trying to break their ropes, though I have not heard of bears killing mules or horses. Of hogs they are said to be particularly fond, bolting small ones, bones and all, without choice of parts. In particular, Mr. Delaney assured me that all kinds of bears in the Sierra are very shy, and that hunters found far greater difficulty in getting within gunshot of them than of deer or indeed any other animal in the Sierra, and if I was anxious to see much of them I should have to wait and watch with endless Indian patience and pay no attention to anything else.

Night is coming on, the gray rock waves are growing dim in the twilight. How raw and young this region appears! Had the ice sheet that swept over it vanished but yesterday, its traces on the more resisting portions about our camp could hardly be more distinct than they now are. The horses and sheep and all of us, indeed, slipped on the smoothest places.

July 14. How deathlike is sleep in this mountain air, and quick the awakening into newness of life! A calm dawn, yellow and purple, then floods of sun-gold, making every thing tingle and glow.

In an hour or two we came to Yosemite Creek, the stream that makes the greatest of all the Yosemite falls. It is about forty feet wide at the Mono Trail crossing, and now about four feet in average depth, flowing about three miles an hour. The distance to the verge of the Yosemite wall, where it makes its tremendous plunge, is only about two miles from here. Calm, beautiful, and nearly silent, it glides with stately gestures, a dense growth of the slender two-leaved pine along its banks, and a fringe of willow, purple spirea, sedges, daisies, lilies, and columbines. Some of the sedges and willow boughs dip into the current, and just outside of the close ranks of trees there is a sunny flat of washed gravelly sand which seems to have been deposited by some ancient flood. It is covered with millions of erethrea, eriogonum, and oxytheca, with more flowers than leaves, forming an even growth, slightly dimpled and ruffled here and there by rosettes of *Spraguea umbellata*. Back of this flowery strip there is a wavy upsloping plain of solid granite, so smoothly ice-polished in many places that it glistens in the sun like glass. In shallow hollows there are patches of trees, mostly the rough form of the two-leaved pine, rather scrawny looking where there is little or no soil. Also a few junipers (*Juniperus occidentalis*), short and stout, with bright cinnamon-colored bark and gray foliage, standing alone mostly, on the sun-beaten pavement, safe from fire, clinging by slight joints,—a sturdy storm-enduring mountaineer of a tree, living on sunshine and snow, maintaining tough health on this diet for perhaps more than a thousand years.

Up towards the head of the basin I see groups of domes rising above the wavelike ridges, and some picturesque castellated masses, and dark strips and patches of silver fir, indicating deposits of fertile soil. Would that I could command the time to study them! What rich excursions one could make in this well-defined basin! Its glacial inscriptions and sculptures, how marvelous they seem, how noble the studies they offer! I tremble with excitement in the dawn of these glorious mountain sublimities, but I can only gaze and wonder, and, like a child, gather here and there a lily, half hoping I may be able to study and learn in years to come.

The drivers and dogs had a lively, laborious time getting the sheep across the creek, the second large stream thus far that they have been compelled to cross without a bridge; the first being the North Fork of the Merced near Bower Cave. Men and dogs, shouting and barking, drove the timid, water-fearing creatures in a close crowd against the bank, but not one of the flock would launch away. While thus jammed, the Don and the shepherd rushed through the frightened crowd to stampede those in front, but this would only cause a break backward, and away they would scamper through the stream-bank trees and scatter over the rocky pavement. Then with the aid of the dogs the runaways would again be gathered and made to face the stream, and again the compacted mass would break away, amid wild shouting and barking that might well have disturbed the stream itself and marred the music of its falls, to which visitors no doubt from all quarters of the globe were listening. "Hold them there! Now hold them there!" shouted the Don; "the front ranks will soon tire of the pressure, and be glad to take to the water, then all will jump in and cross in a hurry." But they did nothing of the kind; they only avoided the pressure by breaking back in scores and hundreds, leaving the beauty of the banks sadly trampled.

If only one could be got to cross over, all would make haste to follow; but that one could not be found. A lamb was caught, carried across, and tied to a bush on the opposite bank, where it cried piteously for its mother. But though greatly concerned, the mother only called it back. That play on maternal affection failed, and we began to fear that we should be forced to make a long roundabout drive and cross the wide-spread tributaries of the creek in succession. This would require several days, but it had its advantages, for I was eager to see the sources of so famous a stream. Don Quixote, however, determined that they must ford just here, and immediately began a sort of siege by cutting down slender pines on the bank and building a corral barely large enough to hold the flock when well pressed together. And as the stream would form one side of the corral he believed that they could easily be forced into the water.

In a few hours the inclosure was completed, and the silly animals were driven in and rammed hard against the brink of the ford. Then the Don, forcing a way through the compacted mass, pitched a few of the terrified unfortunates into the stream by main strength; but instead of crossing over, they swam about close to the bank, making desperate attempts to get back into the flock. Then a dozen or more were shoved off, and the Don, tall like a crane and a good natural wader, jumped in after them, seized a struggling wether, and dragged it to the opposite shore. But no sooner did he let it go than it jumped into the stream and swam back to its frightened companions in the corral, thus manifesting sheep-nature as unchangeable as gravitation. Pan with his pipes would have had no better luck, I fear. We were now pretty well baffled. The silly creatures would suffer any sort of death rather than cross that stream. Calling a council, the dripping Don declared that starvation was now the only likely scheme to try, and that we might as well camp here in comfort and let the besieged flock grow hungry and cool, and come to their senses, if they had any. In a few minutes after being thus let alone, an adventurer in the foremost rank plunged in and swam bravely to the farther shore. Then suddenly all rushed in pell-mell together, trampling one another under water, while we vainly tried to hold them back. The Don jumped into the thickest of the gasping, gurgling, drowning mass, and shoved them right and left as if each sheep was a piece of floating timber. The current also served to drift them apart; a long bent column was soon formed, and in a few minutes all were over and began baaing and feeding as if nothing out of the common had happened. That none were drowned seems wonderful. I fully expected that hundreds would gain the romantic fate of being swept into Yosemite over the highest waterfall in the world.

As the day was far spent, we camped a little way back from the ford, and let the dripping flock scatter and feed until sundown. The wool is dry now, and calm, cud-chewing peace has fallen on all the comfortable band, leaving no trace of the watery battle. I have seen fish driven out of the water with less ado than was made in driving these animals into it. Sheep brain must surely be poor stuff. Compare today's exhibition with the performances of deer swimming quietly across broad and rapid rivers, and from island to island in seas and lakes; or with dogs, or even with the squirrels that, as the story goes, cross the Mississippi River on selected chips, with tails for sails comfortably trimmed to the breeze. A sheep can hardly be called an animal; an entire flock is required to make one foolish individual.

The Yosemite

∽

July 15. Followed the Mono Trail up the eastern rim of the basin nearly to its summit, then turned off southward to a small shallow valley that extends to the edge of the Yosemite, which we reached about noon, and encamped. After luncheon I made haste to high ground, and from the top of the ridge on the west side of Indian Cañon gained the noblest view of the summit peaks I have ever yet enjoyed. Nearly all the upper basin of the Merced was displayed, with its sublime domes and cañons, dark upsweeping forests, and glorious array of white peaks deep in the sky, every feature glowing, radiating beauty that pours into our flesh and bones like heat rays from fire. Sunshine over all; no breath of wind to stir the brooding calm. Never before had I seen so glorious a landscape, so boundless an affluence of sublime mountain beauty. The most extravagant description I might give of this view to any one who has not seen similar landscapes with his own eyes would not so much as hint its grandeur and the spiritual glow that covered it. I shouted and gesticulated in a wild burst of ecstasy, much to the astonishment of St. Bernard Carlo, who came running up to me, manifesting in his intelligent eyes a puzzled concern that was very ludicrous, which had the effect of bringing me to my senses. A brown bear, too, it would seem, had been a spectator of the show I had made of myself, for I had gone but a few yards when I started one from a thicket of brush. He evidently considered me dangerous, for he ran away very fast, tumbling over the tops of the tangled manzanita bushes in his haste. Carlo drew back, with his ears depressed as if afraid, and kept looking me in the face, as if expecting me to pursue and shoot, for he had seen many a bear battle in his day.

Following the ridge, which made a gradual descent to the south, I came at length to the brow of that massive cliff that stands between Indian Cañon and Yosemite Falls, and here the far-famed valley came suddenly into view throughout almost its whole extent. The noble walls—sculptured into endless variety of domes and gables, spires and battlements and plain mural precipices—all a-tremble with the thunder tones of the falling water. The level bottom seemed to be dressed like a garden—sunny meadows here and there, and groves of pine and oak; the river of Mercy sweeping in majesty through the midst of them and flashing back the sunbeams. The great Tissiack, or Half-Dome, rising at the upper end of the valley to a height of nearly a mile, is nobly proportioned and life-like, the most impressive of all the rocks, holding the eye in devout admiration, calling it back again and again from falls or meadows, or even the mountains beyond,—marvelous cliffs, marvelous in sheer dizzy depth and sculpture, types of endurance. Thousands of years have they stood in the sky exposed to rain, snow, frost, earthquake and avalanche, yet they still wear the bloom of youth.

I rambled along the valley rim to the westward; most of it is rounded off on the very brink, so that it is not easy to find places where one may look clear down the face of the wall to the bottom. When such places were found, and I had cautiously set my feet and drawn my body erect, I could not help fearing a little that the rock might split off and let me down, and what a down!—more than three thousand feet. Still my limbs did not tremble, nor did I feel the least uncertainty as to the reliance to be placed on them. My only fear was that a flake of the granite, which in some places showed joints more or less open and running parallel with the face of the cliff, might give way. After withdrawing from such places, excited with the view I had got, I would say to myself, "Now don't go out on the verge again." But in the face of Yosemite scenery cautious remonstrance is vain; under its spell one's body seems to go where it likes with a will over which we seem to have scarce any control.

After a mile or so of this memorable cliff work I approached Yosemite Creek, admiring its easy, graceful, confident gestures as it comes bravely forward in its narrow channel, singing the last of its mountain songs on its way to its fate—a few rods more over the shining granite, then down half a mile in showy foam to another world, to be lost in the Merced, where climate, vegetation, inhabitants, all are different. Emerging from its last gorge, it glides in wide lace-like rapids down a smooth incline into a pool where it seems to rest and compose its gray, agitated waters before taking the grand plunge, then slowly slipping over the lip of the pool basin, it descends another glossy slope with rapidly accelerated speed to the brink of the tremendous cliff, and with sublime, fateful confidence springs out free in the air.

I took off my shoes and stockings and worked my way cautiously down alongside the rushing flood, keeping my feet and hands pressed firmly on the polished rock. The booming, roaring water, rushing past close to my head, was very exciting. I had expected that the sloping apron would terminate with the perpendicular wall of the valley, and that from the foot of it, where it is less steeply inclined, I should be able to lean far enough out to see the forms and behavior of the fall all the way down to the bottom. But I found that there was yet another small brow over which I could not see, and which appeared to be too steep for mortal feet. Scanning it keenly, I discovered a narrow shelf about three inches wide on the very brink, just wide enough for a rest for one's heels. But there seemed to be no way of reaching it over so steep a brow. At length, after careful scrutiny of the surface, I found an irregular edge of a flake of the rock some distance back from the margin of the torrent. If I was to get down to the brink at all that rough edge, which might offer slight finger-holds, was the only way. But the slope beside it looked dangerously smooth and steep, and the swift roaring flood beneath, overhead, and beside me was very nerve-trying. I therefore concluded not to venture farther, but did nevertheless. Tufts of artemisia were growing in clefts of the rock near by, and I filled my mouth with the bitter leaves, hoping they might help to prevent giddiness. Then, with a caution not known in ordinary circumstances, I crept down safely to the little ledge, got my heels well planted on it, then shuffled in a horizontal direction twenty or thirty feet until close to the outplunging current, which, by the time it had descended thus far, was already white. Here I obtained a perfectly free view down into the heart of the snowy, chanting throng of comet-like streamers, into which the body of the fall soon separates.

While perched on that narrow niche I was not distinctly conscious of danger. The tremendous grandeur of the fall in form and sound and motion, acting at close range, smothered the sense of fear, and in such places one's body takes keen care for safety on its own account. How long I remained down there, or how I returned, I can hardly tell. Anyhow I had a glorious time, and got back to camp about dark, enjoying triumphant exhilaration soon followed by dull weariness. Hereafter I'll try to keep from such extravagant, nerve-straining places. Yet such a day is well worth venturing for. My first view of the High Sierra, first view looking down into Yosemite, the death song of Yosemite Creek, and its flight over the vast cliff, each one of these is of itself enough for a great life-long landscape fortune—a most memorable day of days—enjoyment enough to kill if that were possible.

July 16. My enjoyments yesterday afternoon, especially at the head of the fall, were too great for good sleep. Kept starting up last night in a nervous tremor, half awake, fancying that the foundation of the mountain we were camped on had given way and was falling into Yosemite Valley. In vain I roused myself to make a new beginning for sound sleep. The nerve strain had been too great, and again and again I dreamed I was rushing through the air above a glorious avalanche of water and rocks. One time, springing to my feet, I said, "This time it is real—all must die, and where could mountaineer find a more glorious death!"

Left camp soon after sunrise for an all-day ramble eastward. Crossed the head of Indian Basin, forested with *Abies magnifica*, underbrush mostly *Ceanothus cordulatus* and manzanita, a mixture not easily trampled over or penetrated, for the ceanothus is thorny and grows in dense snow-pressed masses, and the manzanita has exceedingly crooked, stubborn branches. From the head of the cañon continued on past North Dome into the basin of Dome or Porcupine Creek. Here are many fine meadows imbedded in the woods, gay with *Lilium parvum* and its companions; the elevation, about eight thousand feet, seems to be best suited for it—saw specimens that were a foot or two higher than my head. Had more magnificent views of the upper mountains, and of the great South Dome, said to be the grandest rock in the world. Well it may be, since it is of such noble dimensions and sculpture. A wonderfully impressive monument, its lines exquisite in fineness, and though sublime in size, is finished like the finest work of art, and seems to be alive.

July 17. A new camp was made to-day in a magnificent silver fir grove at the head of a small stream that flows into Yosemite by way of Indian Cañon. Here we intend to stay several weeks,—a fine location from which to make excursions about the great valley and its fountains. Glorious days I'll have sketching, pressing plants, studying the wonderful topography and the wild animals, our happy fellow mortals and neighbors. But the vast mountains in the distance, shall I ever know them, shall I be allowed to enter into their midst and dwell with them.

The North and South Domes

We were pelted about noon by a short, heavy rainstorm, sublime thunder reverberating among the mountains and cañons,—some strokes near, crashing, ringing in the tense crisp air with startling keenness, while the distant peaks loomed gloriously through the cloud fringes and sheets of rain. Now the storm is past, and the fresh washed air is full of the essences of the flower gardens and groves. Winter storms in Yosemite must be glorious. May I see them!

Have got my bed made in our new camp,—plushy, sumptuous, and deliciously fragrant, most of it *magnifica* fir plumes, of course, with a variety of sweet flowers in the pillow. Hope to sleep to-night without tottering nerve-dreams. Watched a deer eating ceanothus leaves and twigs.

July 18. Slept pretty well; the valley walls did not seem to fall, though I still fancied myself at the brink, alongside the white, plunging flood, especially when half asleep. Strange the danger of that adventure should be more troublesome now that I am in the bosom of the peaceful woods, a mile or more from the fall, than it was while I was on the brink of it.

Bears seem to be common here, judging by their tracks. About noon we had another rainstorm with keen startling thunder, the metallic, ringing, clashing, clanging notes gradually fading into low bass rolling and muttering in the distance. For a few minutes the rain came in a grand torrent like a waterfall, then hail; some of the hail-stones an inch in diameter, hard, icy, and irregular in form, like those oftentimes seen in Wisconsin. Carlo watched them with intelligent astonishment as they came pelting and thrashing through the quivering branches of the trees. The cloud scenery sublime. Afternoon calm, sunful, and clear, with delicious freshness and fragrance from the firs and flowers and steaming ground.

July 19. Watching the daybreak and sunrise. The pale rose and purple sky changing softly to daffodil yellow and white, sunbeams pouring through the passes between the peaks and over the Yosemite domes, making their edges burn; the silver firs in the middle ground catching the glow on their spiry tops, and our camp grove fills and thrills with the glorious light. Everything awakening alert and joyful; the birds begin to stir and innumerable insect people. Deer quietly withdraw into leafy hiding-places in the chaparral; the dew vanishes, flowers spread their petals, every pulse beats high, every life cell rejoices, the very rocks seem to thrill with life. The whole landscape glows like a human face in a glory of enthusiasm, and the blue sky, pale around the horizon, bends peacefully down over all like one vast flower.

About noon, as usual, big bossy cumuli began to grow above the forest, and the rainstorm pouring from them is the most imposing

I have yet seen. The silvery zigzag lightning lances are longer than usual, and the thunder gloriously impressive, keen, crashing, intensely concentrated, speaking with such tremendous energy it would seem that an entire mountain is being shattered at every stroke, but probably only a few trees are being shattered, many of which I have seen on my walks hereabouts strewing the ground. At last the clear ringing strokes are succeeded by deep low tones that grow gradually fainter as they roll afar into the recesses of the echoing mountains, where they seem to be welcomed home. Then another and another peal, or rather crashing, splintering stroke, follows in quick succession, perchance splitting some giant pine or fir from top to bottom into long rails and slivers, and scattering them to all points of the compass. Now comes the rain, with corresponding extravagant grandeur, covering the ground high and low with a sheet of flowing water, a transparent film fitted like a skin upon the rugged anatomy of the landscape, making the rocks glitter and glow, gathering in the ravines, flooding the streams, and making them shout and boom in reply to the thunder.

How interesting to trace the history of a single raindrop! It is not long, geologically speaking, as we have seen, since the first raindrops fell on the newborn leafless Sierra landscapes. How different the lot of these falling now! Happy the showers that fall on so fair a wilderness,—scarce a single drop can fail to find a beautiful spot,—on the tops of the peaks, on the shining glacier pavements, on the great smooth domes, on forests and gardens and brushy moraines, plashing, glinting, pattering, laving. Some go to the high snowy fountains to swell their well-saved stores; some into the lakes, washing the mountain windows, patting their smooth glassy levels, making dimples and bubbles and spray; some into the waterfalls and cascades, as if eager to join in their dance and song and beat their foam yet finer; good luck and good work for the happy mountain raindrops, each one of them a high waterfall in itself, descending from the cliffs and hollows of the clouds to the cliffs and hollows of the rocks, out of the sky-thunder into the thunder of the falling rivers. Some, falling on meadows and bogs, creep silently out of sight to the grass roots, hiding softly as in a nest, slipping, oozing hither, thither, seeking and finding their appointed work. Some, descending through the spires of the woods, sift spray through the shining needles, whispering peace and good cheer to each one of them. Some drops with happy aim glint on the sides of crystals,—quartz, hornblende, garnet, zircon, tourmaline, feldspar,—patter on grains of gold and heavy way-worn nuggets; some, with blunt plap-plap and low bass drumming, fall on the broad leaves of veratrum, saxifrage, cypripedium. Some happy drops fall straight into the cups of flowers, kissing the lips of lilies. How far they have to go, how many cups to fill, great and small, cells too small to be seen, cups holding half a drop as well as lake basins between the hills, each replenished with equal care, every drop in all the blessed throng a silvery newborn star with lake and river, garden and grove, valley and mountain, all that the landscape holds reflected in its crystal depths, God's messenger, angel of love sent on its way with majesty and pomp and display of power that make man's greatest shows ridiculous.

Now the storm is over, the sky is clear, the last rolling thunder-wave is spent on the peaks, and where are the raindrops now—what has become of all the shining throng? In winged vapor rising some are already hastening back to the sky, some have gone into the plants, creeping through invisible doors into the round rooms of cells, some are locked in crystals of ice, some in rock crystals, some in porous moraines to keep their small springs flowing, some have gone journeying on in the rivers to join the larger raindrop of the ocean. From form to form, beauty to beauty, ever changing, never resting, all are speeding on with love's enthusiasm, singing with the stars the eternal song of creation.

July 20. Fine calm morning; air tense and clear; not the slightest breeze astir; everything shining, the rocks with wet crystals, the plants with dew, each receiving its portion of irised dewdrops and sunshine like living creatures getting their breakfast, their dew manna coming down from the starry sky like swarms of smaller stars. How wondrous fine are the particles in showers of dew, thousands required for a single drop, growing in the dark as silently as the grass! What pains are taken to keep this wilderness in health,—showers of snow, showers of rain, showers of dew, floods of light, floods of invisible vapor, clouds, winds, all sorts of weather, inter-action of plant on plant, animal on animal, etc., beyond thought! How fine Nature's methods! How deeply with beauty is beauty overlaid! the ground covered with crystals, the crystals with mosses and lichens and low-spreading grasses and flowers, these with larger plants leaf over leaf with ever-changing color and form, the broad palms of the firs outspread over these, the azure dome over all like a bell-flower, and star above star.

Yonder stands the South Dome, its crown high above our camp, though its base is four thousand feet below us; a most noble rock, it seems full of thought, clothed with living light, no sense of dead stone about it, all spiritualized, neither heavy looking nor light, steadfast in serene strength like a god.

Our shepherd is a queer character and hard to place in this wil-derness. His bed is a hollow made in red dry-rot punky dust beside a log which forms a portion of the south wall of the corral. Here he lies with his wonderful everlasting clothing on, wrapped in a red blanket, breathing not only the dust of the decayed wood but also that of the corral, as if determined to take ammoniacal snuff all night after chewing tobacco all day. Following the sheep he car-ries a heavy six-shooter swung from his belt on one side and his luncheon on the other. The ancient cloth in which the meat, fresh from the frying-pan, is tied serves as a filter through which the clear fat and gravy juices drip down on his right hip and leg in clustering stalactites. This oleaginous formation is soon broken up, however, and diffused and rubbed evenly into his scanty apparel, by sitting down, rolling over, crossing his legs while resting on logs, etc., mak-ing shirt and trousers water-tight and shiny. His trousers, in particu-lar, have become so adhesive with the mixed fat and resin that pine needles, thin flakes and fibres of bark, hair, mica scales and minute grains of quartz, hornblende, etc., feathers, seed wings, moth and butterfly wings, legs and antennæ of innumerable insects, or even whole insects such as the small beetles, moths and mosquitoes, with flower petals, pollen dust and indeed bits of all plants, animals, and minerals of the region adhere to them and are safely imbedded, so that though far from being a naturalist he collects fragmentary specimens of everything and becomes richer than he knows. His specimens are kept passably fresh, too, by the purity of the air and the resiny bituminous beds into which they are pressed. Man is a microcosm, at least our shepherd is, or rather his trousers. These precious overalls are never taken off, and nobody knows how old they are, though one may guess by their thickness and concentric structure. Instead of wearing thin they wear thick, and in their strat-ification have no small geological significance.

Besides herding the sheep, Billy is the butcher, while I have agreed to wash the few iron and tin utensils and make the bread. Then, these small duties done, by the time the sun is fairly above the mountain-tops I am beyond the flock, free to rove and revel in the wilderness all the big immortal days.

Sketching on the North Dome. It commands views of nearly all the valley besides a few of the high mountains. I would fain draw everything in sight—rock, tree, and leaf. But little can I do beyond mere outlines,—marks with meanings like words, readable only to myself,—yet I sharpen my pencils and work on as if oth-ers might possibly be benefited. Whether these picture-sheets are to vanish like fallen leaves or go to friends like letters, matters not much; for little can they tell to those who have not themselves seen similar wildness, and like a language have learned it. No pain here, no dull empty hours, no fear of the past, no fear of the future. These blessed mountains are so compactly filled with God's beauty, no petty personal hope or experience has room to be. Drinking this champagne water is pure pleasure, so is breathing the living air, and every movement of limbs is pleasure, while the whole body seems to feel beauty when exposed to it as it feels the camp-fire or sun-shine, entering not by the eyes alone, but equally through all one's flesh like radiant heat, making a passionate ecstatic pleasure-glow not explainable. One's body then seems homogeneous throughout, sound as a crystal.

Perched like a fly on this Yosemite dome, I gaze and sketch and bask, oftentimes settling down into dumb admiration without defi-nite hope of ever learning much, yet with the longing, unresting effort that lies at the door of hope, humbly prostrate before the vast

display of God's power, and eager to offer self-denial and renuncia-
tion with eternal toil to learn any lesson in the divine manuscript.

It is easier to feel than to realize, or in any way explain, Yosemite
grandeur. The magnitudes of the rocks and trees and streams are
so delicately harmonized they are mostly hidden. Sheer precipices
three thousand feet high are fringed with tall trees growing close
like grass on the brow of a lowland hill, and extending along the feet
of these precipices a ribbon of meadow a mile wide and seven or
eight long, that seems like a strip a farmer might mow in less than a
day. Waterfalls, five hundred to one or two thousand feet high, are
so subordinated to the mighty cliffs over which they pour that they
seem like wisps of smoke, gentle as floating clouds, though their
voices fill the valley and make the rocks tremble. The mountains, too,
along the eastern sky, and the domes in front of them, and the succession of smooth rounded waves between, swelling higher, higher,
with dark woods in their hollows, serene in massive exuberant bulk
and beauty, tend yet more to hide the grandeur of the Yosemite
temple and make it appear as a subdued subordinate feature of the
vast harmonious landscape. Thus every attempt to appreciate any
one feature is beaten down by the overwhelming influence of all
the others. And, as if this were not enough, lo! in the sky arises
another mountain range with topography as rugged and substan-
tial-looking as the one beneath it—snowy peaks and domes and
shadowy Yosemite valleys—another version of the snowy Sierra, a
new creation heralded by a thunder-storm. How fiercely, devoutly
wild is Nature in the midst of her beauty-loving tenderness!—paint-
ing lilies, watering them, caressing them with gentle hand, going
from flower to flower like a gardener while building rock mountains and cloud mountains full of lightning and rain. Gladly we run
for shelter beneath an overhanging cliff and examine the reassuring
ferns and mosses, gentle love tokens growing in cracks and chinks.
Daisies, too, and ivesias, confiding wild children of light, too small
to fear. To these one's heart goes home, and the voices of the storm
become gentle. Now the sun breaks forth and fragrant steam arises.
The birds are out singing on the edges of the groves. The west is
flaming in gold and purple, ready for the ceremony of the sunset,

and back I go to camp with my notes and pictures, the best of them printed in my mind as dreams. A fruitful day, without measured beginning or ending. A terrestrial eternity. A gift of good God.

Wrote to my mother and a few friends, mountain hints to each. They seem as near as if within voice-reach or touch. The deeper the solitude the less the sense of loneliness, and the nearer our friends. Now bread and tea, fir bed and good-night to Carlo, a look at the sky lilies, and death sleep until the dawn of another Sierra to-morrow.

July 21. Sketching on the Dome—no rain; clouds at noon about quarter filled the sky, casting shadows with fine effect on the white mountains at the heads of the streams, and a soothing cover over the gardens during the warm hours.

Saw a common house-fly and a grasshopper and a brown bear. The fly and grasshopper paid me a merry visit on the top of the Dome, and I paid a visit to the bear in the middle of a small garden meadow between the Dome and the camp where he was standing alert among the flowers as if willing to be seen to advantage. I had not gone more than half a mile from camp this morning, when Carlo, who was trotting on a few yards ahead of me, came to a sudden, cautious standstill. Down went tail and ears, and forward went his knowing nose, while he seemed to be saying, "Ha, what's this? A bear, I guess." Then a cautious advance of a few steps, setting his feet down softly like a hunting cat, and questioning the air as to the scent he had caught until all doubt vanished. Then he came back to me, looked me in the face, and with his speaking eyes reported a bear near by; then led on softly, careful, like an experienced hunter, not to make the slightest noise; and frequently looking back as if whispering, "Yes, it's a bear; come and I'll show you." Presently we came to where the sunbeams were streaming through between the purple shafts of the firs, which showed that we were nearing an open spot, and here Carlo came behind me, evidently sure that the bear was very near. So I crept to a low ridge of moraine boulders on the edge of a narrow garden meadow, and in this meadow I felt pretty sure the bear must be. I was anxious to get a good look at the sturdy mountaineer without alarming him; so drawing myself up noiselessly back of one of the largest of the trees I peered past its bulging buttresses, exposing only a part of my head, and there stood neighbor Bruin within a stone's throw, his hips covered by tall grass and flowers, and his front feet on the trunk of a fir that had fallen out into the meadow, which raised his head so high that he seemed to be standing erect. He had not yet seen me, but was looking and listening attentively, showing that in some way he was aware of our approach. I watched his gestures and tried to make the most of my opportunity to learn what I could about him, fearing he would catch sight of me and run away. For I had been told that this sort of bear, the cinnamon, always ran from his bad brother man, never showing fight unless wounded or in defense of young. He made a telling picture standing alert in the sunny forest garden. How well he played his part, harmonizing in bulk and color and shaggy hair with the trunks of the trees and lush vegetation, as natural a feature as any other in the landscape. After examining at leisure, noting the sharp muzzle thrust inquiringly forward, the long shaggy hair on his broad chest, the stiff, erect ears nearly buried in hair, and the slow, heavy way he moved his head, I thought I should like to see his gait in running, so I made a sudden rush at him, shouting and swinging my hat to frighten him, expecting to see him make haste to get away. But to my dismay he did not run or show any sign of running. On the contrary, he stood his ground ready to fight and defend himself, lowered his head, thrust it forward, and looked sharply and fiercely at me. Then I suddenly began to fear that upon me would fall the work of running; but I was afraid to run, and therefore, like the bear, held my ground. We stood staring at each other in solemn silence within a dozen yards or thereabouts, while I fervently hoped that the power of the human eye over wild beasts would prove as great as it is said to be. How long our awfully strenuous interview lasted, I don't know; but at length in the slow fullness of time he pulled his huge paws down off the log, and with magnificent deliberation turned and walked leisurely up the meadow, stopping frequently to look back over his shoulder to see whether I was pursuing him, then moving on again, evidently neither fearing me very much nor trusting me. He was probably about five hundred pounds in weight, a broad, rusty bundle of ungovernable wildness, a happy fellow whose lines have fallen in pleasant places. The flowery glade in which I saw him so well, framed like a picture, is one of the best of all I have yet discovered, a conservatory of Nature's precious plant people. Tall lilies were swinging their bells over that bear's back, with geraniums, larkspurs, columbines, and daisies brushing against his sides. A place for angels, one would say, instead of bears.

In the great cañons Bruin reigns supreme. Happy fellow, whom no famine can reach while one of his thousand kinds of food is spared him. His bread is sure at all seasons, ranged on the mountain shelves like stores in a pantry. From one to the other, up or down he climbs, tasting and enjoying each in turn in different climates, as if he had journeyed thousands of miles to other countries north or south to enjoy their varied productions. I should like to know my hairy brothers better—though after this particular Yosemite bear, my very neighbor, had sauntered out of sight this morning, I reluctantly went back to camp for the Don's rifle to shoot him, if necessary, in defense of the flock. Fortunately I couldn't find him, and after tracking him a mile or two towards Mount Hoffman I bade him Godspeed and gladly returned to my work on the Yosemite Dome.

The house-fly also seemed at home and buzzed about me as I sat sketching, and enjoying my bear interview now it was over. I wonder what draws house-flies so far up the mountains, heavy gross feeders as they are, sensitive to cold, and fond of domestic ease. How have they been distributed from continent to continent, across seas and deserts and mountain chains, usually so influential in determining boundaries of species both of plants and animals. Beetles and butterflies are sometimes restricted to small areas. Each mountain in a range, and even the different zones of a mountain, may have its own peculiar species. But the house-fly seems to be everywhere. I wonder if any island in mid-ocean is flyless. The bluebottle is abundant in these Yosemite woods, ever ready with his marvelous store of eggs to make all dead flesh fly. Bumblebees are here, and are well fed on boundless stores of nectar and pollen. The honeybee, though abundant in the foothills, has not yet got so high. It is only a few years since the first swarm was brought to California.

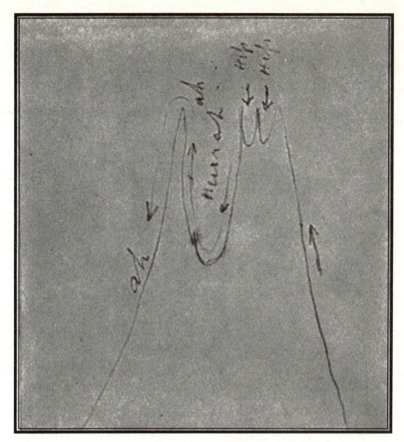

Track of singing dancing grasshopper in the air

Over North Dome

Aqueer fellow and a jolly fellow is the grasshopper. Up the mountains he comes on excursions, how high I don't know, but at least as far and high as Yosemite tourists. I was much interested with the hearty enjoyment of the one that danced and sang for me on the Dome this afternoon. He seemed brimful of glad, hilarious energy, manifested by springing into the air to a height of twenty or thirty feet, then diving and springing up again and making a sharp musical rattle just as the lowest point in the descent was reached. Up and down a dozen times or so he danced and sang, then alighted to rest, then up and at it again. The curves he described in the air in diving and rattling resembled those made by cords hanging loosely and attached at the same height at the ends, the loops nearly covering each other. Braver, heartier, keener, care-free enjoyment of life I have never seen or heard in any creature, great or small. The life of this comic redlegs, the mountain's merriest child, seems to be made up of pure, condensed gayety. The Douglas squirrel is the only living creature that I can compare him with in exuberant, rollicking, irrepressible jollity. Wonderful that these sublime mountains are so loudly cheered and brightened by a creature so queer. Nature in him seems to be snapping her fingers in the face of all earthly dejection and melancholy with a boyish hip-hip-hurrah. How the sound is made I do not understand. When he was on the ground he made not the slightest noise, nor when he was simply flying from place to place, but only when diving in curves, the motion seeming to be required for the sound; for the more vigorous the diving the more energetic the corresponding outbursts of jolly rattling. I tried to observe him closely while he was resting in the intervals of his performances; but he would not allow a near approach, always getting his jumping legs ready to spring for immediate flight, and keeping his eyes on me. A fine sermon the little fellow danced for me on the Dome, a likely place to look for sermons in stones, but not for grasshopper sermons. A large and imposing pulpit for so small a preacher. No danger of weakness in the knees of the world while Nature can spring such a rattle as this. Even the bear did not express for me the mountain's wild health and strength and happiness so tellingly as did this comical little hopper. No cloud of care in his day, no winter of discontent in sight. To him every day is a holiday; and when at length his sun sets, I fancy he will cuddle down on the forest floor and die like the leaves and flowers, and like them leave no unsightly remains calling for burial.

Sundown, and I must to camp. Good-night, friends three,— brown bear, rugged boulder of energy in groves and gardens fair as Eden; restless, fussy fly with gauzy wings stirring the air around all the world; and grasshopper, crisp, electric spark of joy enlivening the massy sublimity of the mountains like the laugh of a child. Thank you, thank you all three for your quickening company. Heaven guide every wing and leg. Good-night friends three, good-night.

July 22. A fine specimen of the black-tailed deer went bounding past camp this morning. A buck with wide spread of antlers, showing admirable vigor and grace. Wonderful the beauty, strength, and graceful movements of animals in wildernesses, cared for by Nature only, when our experience with domestic animals would lead us to fear that all the so-called neglected wild beasts would degenerate. Yet the upshot of Nature's method of breeding and teaching seems to lead to excellence of every sort. Deer, like all wild animals, are as clean as plants. The beauties of their gestures and attitudes, alert or in repose, surprise yet more than their bounding exuberant strength. Every movement and posture is graceful, the very poetry of manners and motion. Mother Nature is too often spoken of as in reality no mother at all. Yet how wisely, sternly, tenderly she loves and looks after her children in all sorts of weather and wildernesses. The more I see of deer the more I admire them as mountaineers. They make their way into the heart of the roughest solitudes with smooth reserve of strength, through dense belts of brush and forest encumbered with fallen trees and boulder piles, across cañons, roaring streams, and snow-fields, ever showing forth beauty and courage. Over nearly all the continent the deer find homes. In the Florida savannas and hummocks, in the Canada woods, in the far north, roaming over mossy tundras, swimming lakes and rivers and arms of the sea from island to island washed with waves, or climbing rocky mountains, everywhere healthy and able, adding beauty to every landscape,—a truly admirable creature and great credit to Nature.

Have been sketching a silver fir that stands on a granite ridge a few hundred yards to the eastward of camp—a fine tree with a particular snow-storm story to tell. It is about one hundred feet high, growing on bare rock, thrusting its roots into a weathered joint less than an inch wide, and bulging out to form a base to bear its weight. The storm came from the north while it was young and broke it down nearly to the ground, as is shown by the old, dead, weather-beaten top leaning out from the living trunk built up from a new shoot below the break. The annual rings of the trunk that have overgrown the dead sapling tell the year of the storm. Wonderful that a side branch forming a portion of one of the level collars that encircle the trunk of this species (*Abies magnifica*) should bend upward, grow erect, and take the place of the lost axis to form a new tree. Many others, pines as well as firs, bear testimony to the crushing severity of this particular storm. Trees, some of them fifty to seventy-five feet high, were bent to the ground and buried like grass, whole groves vanishing as if the forest had been cleared away, leaving not a branch or needle visible until the spring thaw. Then the more elastic undamaged saplings rose again, aided by the wind, some reaching a nearly erect attitude, others remaining more or less bent, while those with broken backs endeavored to specialize a side branch below the break and make a leader of it to form a new axis of development. It is as if a man, whose back was broken or nearly so and who was compelled to go bent, should find a branch backbone sprouting straight up from below the break and should gradually develop new arms and shoulders and head, while the old damaged portion of his body died.

Grand white cloud mountains and domes created about noon as usual, ridges and ranges of endless variety, as if Nature dearly loved this sort of work, doing it again and again nearly every day with infinite industry, and producing beauty that never palls. A few zig-zags of lightning, five minutes' shower, then a gradual wilting and clearing

July 23. Another midday cloudland, displaying power and beauty that one never wearies in beholding, but hopelessly unsketchable and untellable. What can poor mortals say about clouds? While a description of their huge glowing domes and ridges, shadowy gulfs and cañons, and feather-edged ravines is being tried, they vanish, leaving no visible ruins. Nevertheless, these fleeting sky mountains are as substantial and significant as the more lasting upheavals of granite beneath them. Both alike are built up and die, and in God's calendar difference of duration is nothing. We can only dream about them in wondering, worshiping admiration, happier than we dare tell even to friends who see farthest in sympathy, glad to know that not a crystal or vapor particle of them, hard or soft, is lost; that they sink and vanish only to rise again and again in higher and higher beauty. As to our own work, duty, influence, etc., concerning which so much fussy pother is made, it will not fail of its due effect, though, like a lichen on a stone, we keep silent.

July 24. Clouds at noon occupying about half the sky gave half an hour of heavy rain to wash one of the cleanest landscapes in the world. How well it is washed! The sea is hardly less dusty than the ice-burnished pavements and ridges, domes and cañons, and summit peaks plashed with snow like waves with foam. How fresh the woods are and calm after the last films of clouds have been wiped from the sky! A few minutes ago every tree was excited, bowing to the roaring storm, waving, swirling, tossing their branches in glorious enthusiasm like worship. But though to the outer ear these trees are now silent, their songs never cease. Every hidden cell is throbbing with music and life, every fibre thrilling like harp strings, while incense is ever flowing from the balsam bells and leaves. No wonder the hills and groves were God's first temples, and the more they are cut down and hewn into cathedrals and churches, the farther off and dimmer seems the Lord himself. The same may be said of stone temples. Yonder, to the eastward of our camp grove, stands one of Nature's cathedrals, hewn from the living rock, almost conventional in form, about two thousand feet high, nobly adorned with spires and pinnacles, thrilling under floods of sunshine as if alive like a grove-temple, and well named "Cathedral Peak." Even Shepherd Billy turns at times to this wonderful mountain building, though apparently deaf to all stone sermons. Snow that refused to melt in fire would hardly be more wonderful than unchanging dullness in the rays of God's beauty. I have been trying to get him to walk to the brink of Yosemite for a view, offering to watch the sheep for a day, while he should enjoy what tourists come from all

over the world to see. But though within a mile of the famous valley, he will not go to it even out of mere curiosity. "What," says he,
"is Yosemite but a cañon—a lot of rocks—a hole in the ground—a
place dangerous about falling into—a d——d good place to keep
away from." "But think of the waterfalls, Billy—just think of that
big stream we crossed the other day, falling half a mile through the
air—think of that, and the sound it makes. You can hear it now like
the roar of the sea." Thus I pressed Yosemite upon him like a missionary offering the gospel, but he would have none of it. "I should
be afraid to look over so high a wall," he said. "It would make my
head swim. There is nothing worth seeing anywhere, only rocks, and
I see plenty of them here. Tourists that spend their money to see
rocks and falls are fools, that's all. You can't humbug me. I've been
in this country too long for that." Such souls, I suppose, are asleep,
or smothered and befogged beneath mean pleasures and cares.

July 25. Another cloudland. Some clouds have an over-ripe decaying look, watery and bedraggled and drawn out into wind-torn
shreds and patches, giving the sky a littered appearance; not so these
Sierra summer midday clouds. All are beautiful with smooth defi-
nite outlines and curves like those of glacier-polished domes. They
begin to grow about eleven o'clock, and seem so wonderfully near
and clear from this high camp one is tempted to try to climb them
and trace the streams that pour like cataracts from their shadowy
fountains. The rain to which they give birth is often very heavy, a
sort of waterfall as imposing as if pouring from rock mountains.
Never in all my travels have I found anything more truly novel and
interesting than these midday mountains of the sky, their fine tones
of color, majestic visible growth, and ever-changing scenery and
general effects, though mostly as well let alone as far as description
goes. I oftentimes think of Shelley's cloud poem, "I sift the snow
on the mountains below."

A Strange Experience

❦

August 2. Clouds and showers, about the same as yesterday. Sketching all day on the North Dome until four or five o'clock in the afternoon, when, as I was busily employed thinking only of the glorious Yosemite landscape, trying to draw every tree and every line and feature of the rocks, I was suddenly, and without warning, possessed with the notion that my friend, Professor J. D. Butler, of the State University of Wisconsin, was below me in the valley, and I jumped up full of the idea of meeting him, with almost as much startling excitement as if he had suddenly touched me to make me look up. Leaving my work without the slightest deliberation, I ran down the western slope of the Dome and along the brink of the valley wall, looking for a way to the bottom, until I came to a side cañon, which, judging by its apparently continuous growth of trees and bushes, I thought might afford a practical way into the valley, and immediately began to make the descent, late as it was, as if drawn irresistibly. But after a little, common sense stopped me and explained that it would be long after dark ere I could possibly reach the hotel, that the visitors would be asleep, that nobody would know me, that I had no money in my pockets, and moreover was without a coat. I therefore compelled myself to stop, and finally succeeded in reasoning myself out of the notion of seeking my friend in the dark, whose presence I only felt in a strange, telepathic way. I succeeded in dragging myself back through the woods to camp, never for a moment wavering, however, in my determination to go down to him next morning. This I think is the most unexplainable notion that ever struck me. Had some one whispered in my ear while I sat on the Dome, where I had spent so many days, that Professor Butler was in the valley, I could not have been more surprised and startled. When I was leaving the university, he said, "Now, John, I want to hold you in sight and watch your career. Promise to write me at least once a year." I received a letter from him in July, at our first camp in the Hollow, written in May, in which he said that he might possibly visit California some time this summer, and therefore hoped to meet me. But inasmuch as he named no meeting-place, and gave no directions as to the course he would probably follow, and as I should be in the wilderness all summer, I had not the slightest hope of seeing him, and all thought of the matter had vanished from my mind until this afternoon, when he seemed to be wafted bodily almost against my face. Well, to-morrow I shall see; for, reasonable or unreasonable, I feel I must go.

August 3. Had a wonderful day. Found Professor Butler as the compass-needle finds the pole. So last evening's telepathy, transcendental revelation, or whatever else it may be called, was true; for, strange to say, he had just entered the valley by way of the Coulterville Trail and was coming up the valley past El Capitan when his presence struck me. Had he then looked toward the North Dome with a good glass when it first came in sight, he might have seen me jump up from my work and run toward him. This seems the one well-defined marvel of my life of the kind called supernatural; for, absorbed in glad Nature, spirit-rappings, second sight, ghost stories, etc., have never interested me since boyhood, seeming comparatively useless and infinitely less wonderful than Nature's open, harmonious, songful, sunny, everyday beauty.

This morning, when I thought of having to appear among tourists at a hotel, I was troubled because I had no suitable clothes, and at best am desperately bashful and shy. I was determined to go, however, to see my old friend after two years among strangers; got on a clean pair of overalls, a cashmere shirt, and a sort of jacket,—the best my camp wardrobe afforded,—tied my notebook on my belt, and strode away on my strange journey, followed by Carlo. I made my way though the gap discovered last evening, which proved to be Indian Cañon. There was no trail in it, and the rocks and brush were so rough that Carlo frequently called me back to help him down precipitous places. Emerging from the cañon shadows, I found a man making hay on one of the meadows, and asked him whether Professor Butler was in the valley. "I don't know," he replied; "but you can easily find out at the hotel. There are but few visitors in the valley just now. A small party came in yesterday afternoon, and I heard some one called Professor Butler, or Butterfield, or some name like that."

The Vernal Falls, Yosemite National Park

In front of the gloomy hotel I found a tourist party adjusting their fishing tackle. They all stared at me in silent wonderment, as if I had been seen dropping down through the trees from the clouds, mostly, I suppose, on account of my strange garb. Inquiring for the office, I was told it was locked, and that the landlord was away, but I might find the landlady, Mrs. Hutchings, in the parlor. I entered in a sad state of embarrassment, and after I had waited in the big, empty room and knocked at several doors the landlady at length appeared, and in reply to my question said she rather thought Professor Butler *was* in the valley, but to make sure, she would bring the register from the office. Among the names of the last arrivals I soon discovered the Professor's familiar handwriting, at the sight of which bashfulness vanished; and having learned that his party had gone up the valley,—probably to the Vernal and Nevada Falls,—I pushed on in glad pursuit, my heart now sure of its prey. In less than an hour

I reached the head of the Nevada Cañon at the Vernal Fall, and just outside of the spray discovered a distinguished-looking gentleman, who, like everybody else I have seen to-day, regarded me curiously as I approached. When I made bold to inquire if he knew where Professor Butler was, he seemed yet more curious to know what could possibly have happened that required a messenger for the Professor, and instead of answering my question he asked with military sharpness, "Who wants him?" "I want him," I replied with equal sharpness. "Why? Do *you* know him?" "Yes," I said. "Do *you* know him?" Astonished that any one in the mountains could possibly know Professor Butler and find him as soon as he had reached the valley, he came down to meet the strange mountaineer on equal terms, and courteously replied, "Yes, I know Professor Butler very well. I am General Alvord, and we were fellow students in Rutland, Vermont, long ago, when we were both young." "But where is he now?" I persisted, cutting short his story. "He has gone beyond the falls with a companion, to try to climb that big rock, the top of which you see from here." His guide now volunteered the information that it was the Liberty Cap Professor Butler and his companion had gone to climb, and that if I waited at the head of the fall I should be sure to find them on their way down. I therefore climbed the ladders alongside the Vernal Fall, and was pushing forward, determined to go to the top of Liberty Cap rock in my hurry, rather than wait, if I should not meet my friend sooner. So heart-hungry at times may one be to see a friend in the flesh, however happily full and care-free one's life may be. I had gone but a short distance, however, above the brow of the Vernal Fall when I caught sight of him in the brush and rocks, half erect, groping his way, his sleeves rolled up, vest open, hat in his hand, evidently very hot and tired. When he saw me coming he sat down on a boulder to wipe the perspiration from his brow and neck, and taking me for one of the valley guides, he inquired the way to the fall ladders. I pointed out the path marked with little piles of stones, on seeing which he called his companion, saying that the way was found; but he did not yet recognize me. Then I stood directly in front of him, looked him in the face, and held out my hand. He thought I was offering to assist him in rising. "Never mind," he said. Then I said, "Professor Butler, don't you know me?" "I think not," he replied; but catching my eye, sudden recognition followed, and astonishment that I should have found him just when he was lost in the brush and did not know that I was within hundreds of miles of him. "John Muir, John Muir, where have you come from?" Then I told him the story of my feeling his presence when he entered the valley last evening, when he was four or five miles distant, as I sat sketching on the North Dome. This, of course, only made him wonder the more. Below the foot of the Vernal Fall the guide was waiting with his saddle-horse, and I walked along the trail, chatting all the way back to the hotel, talking of school days, friends in Madison, of the students, how each had prospered, etc., ever and anon gazing at the stupendous rocks about us, now growing indistinct in the gloaming, and again quoting from the poets—a rare ramble.

It was late ere we reached the hotel, and General Alvord was waiting the Professor's arrival for dinner. When I was introduced he seemed yet more astonished than the Professor at my descent from cloudland and going straight to my friend without knowing in any ordinary way that he was even in California. They had come on direct from the East, had not yet visited any of their friends in the state, and considered themselves undiscoverable. As we sat at dinner, the General leaned back in his chair, and looking down the table, thus introduced me to the dozen guests or so, including the staring fisherman mentioned above: "This man, you know, came down out of these huge, trackless mountains, you know, to find his friend Professor Butler here, the very day he arrived; and how did he know he was here? He just felt him, he says. This is the queerest case of Scotch farsightedness I ever heard of," etc., etc. While my friend quoted Shakespeare: "More things in heaven and earth, Horatio, than are dreamt of in your philosophy," "As the sun, ere he has risen, sometimes paints his image in the firmament, e'en so the shadows of events precede the events, and in to-day already walks to-morrow."

Had a long conversation, after dinner, over Madison days. The Professor wants me to promise to go with him, sometime, on a camping trip in the Hawaiian Islands, while I tried to get him to go back with me to camp in the high Sierra. But he says, "Not now." He must not leave the General; and I was surprised to learn they are to leave the valley to-morrow or next day. I'm glad I'm not great enough to be missed in the busy world.

August 4. It seemed strange to sleep in a paltry hotel chamber after the spacious magnificence and luxury of the starry sky and silver fir grove. Bade farewell to my friend and the General. The old soldier was very kind, and an interesting talker. He told me long stories of the Florida Seminole war, in which he took part, and invited me to visit him in Omaha. Calling Carlo, I scrambled home through the Indian Cañon gate, rejoicing, pitying the poor Professor and General, bound by clocks, almanacs, orders, duties, etc., and compelled to dwell with lowland care and dust and din, where Nature is covered and her voice smothered, while the poor, insignificant wanderer enjoys the freedom and glory of God's wilderness.

Apart from the human interest of my visit to-day, I greatly enjoyed Yosemite, which I had visited only once before, having spent eight days last spring in rambling amid its rocks and waters. Wherever we go in the mountains, or indeed in any of God's wild fields, we find more than we seek. Descending four thousand feet in a few hours, we enter a new world—climate, plants, sounds, inhabitants, and scenery all new or changed. Near camp the goldcup oak forms sheets of chaparral, on top of which we may make our beds. Going down the Indian Cañon we observe this little bush changing by regular gradations to a large bush, to a small tree, and then larger, until on the rocky taluses near the bottom of the valley we find it developed into a broad, wide-spreading, gnarled, picturesque tree from four to eight feet in diameter, and forty or fifty feet high. Innumerable are the forms of water displayed. Every gliding reach, cascade, and fall has characters of its own. Had a good view of the Vernal and Nevada, two of the main falls of the valley, less than a mile apart, and offering striking differences in voice, form, color, etc. The Vernal, four hundred feet high and about seventy-five or eighty feet wide, drops smoothly over a round-lipped precipice and forms a superb apron of embroidery, green and white, slightly folded and fluted, maintaining this form nearly to the bottom, where it is suddenly veiled in quick-flying billows of spray and mist, in which the afternoon sunbeams play with ravishing beauty of rainbow colors.

The Nevada is white from its first appearance as it leaps out into the freedom of the air. At the head it presents a twisted appearance, by an overfolding of the current from striking on the side of its channel just before the first free out-bounding leap is made. About two thirds of the way down, the hurrying throng of comet-shaped masses glance on an inclined part of the face of the precipice and are beaten into yet whiter foam, greatly expanded, and sent bounding outward, making an indescribably glorious show, especially when the afternoon sunshine is pouring into it. In this fall—one of the most wonderful in the world—the water does not seem to be under the dominion of ordinary laws, but rather as if it were a living creature, full of the strength of the mountains and their huge, wild joy.

From beneath heavy throbbing blasts of spray the broken river is seen emerging in ragged boulder-chafed strips. These are speedily gathered into a roaring torrent, showing that the young river is still gloriously alive. On it goes, shouting, roaring, exulting in its strength, passes through a gorge with sublime display of energy, then suddenly expands on a gently inclined pavement, down which it rushes in thin sheets and folds of lace-work into a quiet pool,—"Emerald Pool," as it is called,—a stopping-place, a period separating two grand sentences. Resting here long enough to part with its foam-bells and gray mixtures of air, it glides quietly to the verge of the Vernal precipice in a broad sheet and makes its new display in the Vernal Fall; then more rapids and rock tossings down the cañon, shaded by live oak, Douglas spruce, fir, maple, and dogwood. It receives the Illilouette tributary, and makes a long sweep out into the level, sun-filled valley to join the other streams which, like itself, have danced and sung their way down from snowy heights to form the main Merced—the river of Mercy. But of this there is no end, and life, when one thinks of it, is so short. Never mind, one day in the midst of these divine glories is well worth living and toiling and starving for.

Before parting with Professor Butler he gave me a book, and I gave him one of my pencil sketches for his little son Henry, who is a favorite of mine. He used to make many visits to my room when I was a student. Never shall I forget his patriotic speeches for the Union, mounted on a tall stool, when he was only six years old.

It seems strange that visitors to Yosemite should be so little influenced by its novel grandeur, as if their eyes were bandaged and their ears stopped. Most of those I saw yesterday were looking down as if wholly unconscious of anything going on about them, while the sublime rocks were trembling with the tones of the mighty chanting congregation of waters gathered from all the mountains round about, making music that might draw angels out of heaven. Yet respectable-looking, even wise-looking people were fixing bits of worms on bent pieces of wire to catch trout. Sport they called it. Should church-goers try to pass the time fishing in baptismal fonts while dull sermons were being preached, the so-called sport might not be so bad; but to play in the Yosemite temple, seeking pleasure in the pain of fishes struggling for their lives, while God himself is preaching his sublimest water and stone sermons!

The Happy Isles, Yosemite National Park

Now I'm back at the camp-fire, and cannot help thinking about my recognition of my friend's presence in the valley while he was four or five miles away, and while I had no means of knowing that he was not thousands of miles away. It seems supernatural, but only because it is not understood. Anyhow, it seems silly to make so much of it, while the natural and common is more truly marvelous and mysterious than the so-called supernatural. Indeed most of the miracles we hear of are infinitely less wonderful than the commonest of natural phenomena, when fairly seen. Perhaps the invisible rays that struck me while I sat at work on the Dome are something like those which attract and repel people at first sight, concerning which so much nonsense has been written. The worst apparent effect of these mysterious odd things is blindness to all that is divinely common. Hawthorne, I fancy, could weave one of his weird romances out of this little telepathic episode, the one strange marvel of my life, probably replacing my good old Professor by an attractive woman.

August 5. We were awakened this morning before daybreak by the furious barking of Carlo and Jack and the sound of stampeding sheep. Billy fled from his punk bed to the fire, and refused to stir into the darkness to try to gather the scattered flock, or ascertain the nature of the disturbance. It was a bear attack, as we afterward learned, and I suppose little was gained by attempting to do anything before daylight. Nevertheless, being anxious to know what was up, Carlo and I groped our way through the woods, guided by the rustling sound made by fragments of the flock, not fearing the bear, for I knew that the runaways would go from their enemy as far as possible and Carlo's nose was also to be depended upon. About half a mile east of the corral we overtook twenty or thirty of the flock and succeeded in driving them back; then turning to the westward, we traced another band of fugitives and got them back to the flock. After daybreak I discovered the remains of a sheep carcass, still warm, showing that Bruin must have been enjoying his early mutton breakfast while I was seeking the runaways. He had eaten about half of it. Six dead sheep lay in the corral, evidently smothered by the crowding and piling up of the flock against the side of the corral wall when the bear entered. Making a wide circuit of the camp, Carlo and I discovered a third band of fugitives and drove them back to camp. We also discovered another dead sheep half eaten, showing there had been two of the shaggy freebooters at this early breakfast. They were easily traced. They had each caught a sheep, jumped over the corral fence with them, carrying them as a cat carries a mouse, laid them at the foot of fir trees a hundred yards or so back from the corral, and eaten their fill. After breakfast I set out to seek more of the lost, and found seventy-five at a considerable distance from camp. In the afternoon I succeeded, with Carlo's help, in getting them back to the flock. I don't know whether all are together again or not. I shall make a big fire this evening and keep watch.

When I asked Billy why he made his bed against the corral in rotten wood, when so many better places offered, he replied that he "wished to be as near the sheep as possible in case bears should attack them." Now that the bears have come, he has moved his bed to the far side of the camp, and seems afraid that he may be mistaken for a sheep.

This has been mostly a sheep day, and of course studies have been interrupted. Nevertheless, the walk through the gloom of the woods before the dawn was worth while, and I have learned something about these noble bears. Their tracks are very telling, and so are their breakfasts. Scarce a trace of clouds to-day, and of course our ordinary midday thunder is wanting.

August 6. Enjoyed the grand illumination of the camp grove, last night, from the fire we made to frighten the bears—compensation for loss of sleep and sheep. The noble pillars of verdure, vividly aglow, seemed to shoot into the sky like the flames that lighted them. Nevertheless, one of the bears paid us another visit, as if more attracted than repelled by the fire, climbed into the corral, killed a sheep and made off with it without being seen, while still another was lost by trampling and suffocation against the side of the corral. Now that our mutton has been tasted, I suppose it will be difficult to put a stop to the ravages of these freebooters.

The Don arrived to-day from the lowlands with provisions and a letter. On learning the losses he had sustained, he determined to move the flock at once to the Upper Tuolumne region, saying that the bears would be sure to visit the camp every night as long as we stayed, and that no fire or noise we might make would avail to frighten them. No clouds save a few thin, lustrous touches on the eastern horizon. Thunder heard in the distance.

The Mono Trail

∾

August 7. Early this morning bade good-bye to the bears and blessed silver fir camp, and moved slowly eastward along the Mono Trail. At sundown camped for the night on one of the many small flowery meadows so greatly enjoyed on my excursion to Lake Tenaya. The dusty, noisy flock seems outrageously foreign and out of place in these nature gardens, more so than bears among sheep. The harm they do goes to the heart, but glorious hope lifts above all the dust and din and bids me look forward to a good time coming, when money enough will be earned to enable me to go walking where I like in pure wildness, with what I can carry on my back, and when the bread-sack is empty, run down to the nearest point on the bread-line for more. Nor will these run-downs be blanks, for, whether up or down, every step and jump on these blessed mountains is full of fine lessons.

One of the tributary fountains of the Tuolumne Canon waters

August 8. Camp at the west end of Lake Tenaya. Arriving early, I took a walk on the glacier-polished pavements along the north shore, and climbed the magnificent mountain rock at the east end of the lake, now shining in the late afternoon light. Almost every yard of its surface shows the scoring and polishing action of a great glacier that enveloped it and swept heavily over its summit, though it is about two thousand feet high above the lake and ten thousand above sea-level. This majestic, ancient ice-flood came from the eastward, as the scoring and crushing of the surface shows. Even below the waters of the lake the rock in some places is still grooved and polished; the lapping of the waves and their disintegrating action have not as yet obliterated even the superficial marks of glaciation. In climbing the steepest polished places I had to take off shoes and stockings. A fine region this for study of glacial action in mountain-making. I found many charming plants: arctic daisies, phlox, white spiræa, bryanthus, and rock-ferns,—pellæa, cheilanthes, allosorus,—fringing weathered seams all the way up to the summit; and sturdy junipers, grand old gray and brown monuments, stood bravely erect on fissured spots here and there, telling storm and avalanche stories of hundreds of winters. The view of the lake from the top is, I think, the best of all. There is another rock, more striking in form than this, standing isolated at the head of the lake, but it is not more than half as high. It is a knob or knot of burnished granite, perhaps about a thousand feet high, apparently as flawless and strong in structure as a wave-worn pebble, and probably owes its existence to the superior resistance it offered to the action of the overflowing ice-flood.

Made sketch of the lake, and sauntered back to camp, my iron-shod shoes clanking on the pavements disturbing the chipmunks and birds. After dark went out to the shore,—not a breath of air astir, the lake a perfect mirror reflecting the sky and mountains with their stars and trees and wonderful sculpture, all their grandeur refined and doubled,—a marvelously impressive picture, that seemed to belong more to heaven than earth.

August 9. I went ahead of the flock, and crossed over the divide between the Merced and Tuolumne Basins. The gap between the east end of the Hoffman spur and the mass of mountain rocks about Cathedral Peak, though roughened by ridges and waving folds, seems to be one of the channels of a broad ancient glacier that came from the mountains on the summit of the range. In crossing this divide the ice-river made an ascent of about five hundred feet from the Tuolumne meadows. This entire region must have been overswept by ice.

From the top of the divide, and also from the big Tuolumne Meadows, the wonderful mountain called Cathedral Peak is in sight. From every point of view it shows marked individuality. It is a majestic temple of one stone, hewn from the living rock, and adorned with spires and pinnacles in regular cathedral style. The dwarf pines on the roof look like mosses. I hope some time to climb to it to say my prayers and hear the stone sermons.

The big Tuolumne Meadows are flowery lawns, lying along the south fork of the Tuolumne River at a height of about eighty-five hundred to nine thousand feet above the sea, partially separated by forests and bars of glaciated granite. Here the mountains seem to have been cleared away or set back, so that wide-open views may be had in every direction. The upper end of the series lies at the base of Mount Lyell, the lower below the east end of the Hoffman Range, so the length must be about ten or twelve miles. They vary in width from a quarter of a mile to perhaps three quarters, and a good many branch meadows put out along the banks of the tributary streams. This is the most spacious and delightful high pleasure-ground I have yet seen. The air is keen and bracing, yet warm during the day; and though lying high in the sky, the surrounding mountains are so much higher, one feels protected as if in a grand hall. Mounts Dana and Gibbs, massive red mountains, perhaps thirteen thousand feet high or more, bound the view on the east, the Cathedral and Unicorn Peaks, with many nameless peaks, on the south, the Hoffman Range on the west, and a number of peaks unnamed, as far as I know, on the north. One of these last is much like the Cathedral. The grass of the meadows is mostly fine and silky, with exceedingly slender leaves, making a close sod, above which the panicles of minute purple flowers seem to float in airy, misty lightness, while the sod is enriched with at least three species of gentian and as many or more of orthocarpus, potentilla, ivesia, solidago, pentstemon, with their gay colors,—purple, blue, yellow, and red,—all of which I may know better ere long. A central camp will probably be made in this region, from which I hope to make long excursions into the surrounding mountains.

On the return trip I met the flock about three miles east of Lake Tenaya. Here we camped for the night near a small lake lying on top of the divide in a clump of the two-leaved pine. We are now about nine thousand feet above the sea. Small lakes abound in all sorts of situations,—on ridges, along mountain sides, and in piles of moraine boulders, most of them mere pools. Only in those cañons of the larger streams at the foot of declivities, where the down thrust of the glaciers was heaviest, do we find lakes of considerable size and depth. How grateful a task it would be to trace them all and study them! How pure their waters are, clear as crystal in polished stone basins! None of them, so far as I have seen, have fishes, I suppose on account of falls making them inaccessible. Yet one would think their eggs might get into these lakes by some chance or other; on ducks' feet, for example, or in their mouths, or in their crops, as some plant seeds are distributed. Nature has so many ways of doing such things. How did the frogs, found in all the bogs and pools and lakes, however high, manage to get up these mountains? Surely not by jumping. Such excursions through miles of dry brush and boulders would be very hard on frogs. Perhaps their stringy gelatinous spawn is occasionally entangled or glued on the feet of water birds. Anyhow, they are here and in hearty health and voice. I like their cheery tronk and crink. They take the place of songbirds at a pinch.

August 10. Another of those charming exhilarating days that make the blood dance and excite nerve currents that render one unweariable and well-nigh immortal. Had another view of the broad ice-ploughed divide, and gazed again and again at the Sierra temple and the great red mountains east of the meadows.

We are camped near the Soda Springs on the north side of the river. A hard time we had getting the sheep across. They were driven into a horseshoe bend and fairly crowded off the bank. They seemed willing to suffer death rather than risk getting wet, though they swim well enough when they have to. Why sheep should be so unreasonably afraid of water, I don't know, but they do fear it as soon as they are born and perhaps before. I once saw a lamb only a few hours old approach a shallow stream about two feet wide and an inch deep, after it had walked only about a hundred yards on its life journey. All the flock to which it belonged had crossed this inch-deep stream, and as the mother and her lamb were the last to cross, I had a good opportunity to observe them. As soon as the flock was out of the way, the anxious mother crossed over and called the youngster. It walked cautiously to the brink, gazed at the water, bleated piteously, and refused to venture. The patient mother went back to it again and again to encourage it, but long without avail. Like the pilgrim on Jordan's stormy bank it feared to launch away. At length, gathering its trembling inexperienced legs for the mighty effort, throwing up its head as if it knew all about drowning, and was anxious to keep its nose above water, it made the tremendous leap, and landed in the middle of the inch-deep stream. It seemed astonished to find that, instead of sinking over head and ears, only its toes were wet, gazed at the shining water a few seconds, and then sprang to the shore safe and dry through the dreadful adventure. All kinds of wild sheep are mountain animals, and their descendants' dread of water is not easily accounted for.

August 11. Fine shining weather, with a ten minutes' noon thunderstorm and rain. Rambling all day getting acquainted with the region north of the river. Found a small lake and many charming glacier meadows embosomed in an extensive forest of the two-leaved pine. The forest is growing on broad, almost continuous deposits of moraine material, is remarkably even in its growth, and the trees are much closer together than in any of the fir or pine woods farther down the range. The evenness of the growth would seem to indicate that the trees are all of the same age or nearly so. This regularity has probably been in great part the result of fire. I saw several large patches and strips of dead bleached spars, the ground beneath them covered with a young even growth. Fire can run in these woods, not only because the thin bark of the trees is dripping with resin, but because the growth is close, and the comparatively rich soil produces good crops of tall broad-leaved grasses on which fire can travel, even when the weather is calm. Besides these fire-killed patches there are a good many fallen uprooted trees here and there, some with the bark and needles still on, as if they had lately been blown down in some thunderstorm blast. Saw a large black-tailed deer, a buck with antlers like the upturned roots of a fallen pine.

After a long ramble through the dense encumbered woods I emerged upon a smooth meadow full of sunshine like a lake of light, about a mile and a half long, a quarter to half a mile wide, and bounded by tall arrowy pines. The sod, like that of all the glacier meadows hereabouts, is made of silky agrostis and calamagrostis chiefly; their panicles of purple flowers and purple stems, exceedingly light and airy, seem to float above the green plush of leaves like a thin misty cloud, while the sod is brightened by several species of gentian, potentilla, ivesia, orthocarpus, and their corresponding bees and butterflies. All the glacier meadows are beautiful, but few are so perfect as this one. Compared with it the most carefully leveled, licked, snipped artificial lawns of pleasure-grounds are coarse things. I should like to live here always. It is so calm and withdrawn while open to the universe in full communion with everything good. To the north of this glorious meadow I discovered the camp of some Indian hunters. Their fire was still burning, but they had not yet returned from the chase.

From meadow to meadow, every one beautiful beyond telling, and from lake to lake through groves and belts of arrowy trees, I held my way northward toward Mount Conness, finding telling beauty everywhere, while the encompassing mountains were calling "Come." Hope I may climb them all.

August 12. The sky-scenery has changed but little so far with the change in elevation. Clouds about .05. Glorious pearly cumuli tinted with purple of ineffable fineness of tone. Moved camp to the side of the glacier meadow mentioned above. To let sheep trample so divinely fine a place seems barbarous. Fortunately they prefer the succulent broad-leaved triticum and other woodland grasses to the silky species of the meadows, and therefore seldom bite them or set foot on them.

Glacier Meadow, on the headwaters of the Tuolumne 9500 feet above the sea

The shepherd and the Don cannot agree about methods of herd-ing. Billy sets his dog Jack on the sheep far too often, so the Don thinks; and after some dispute to-day, in which the shepherd loudly claimed the right to dog the sheep as often as he pleased, he started for the plains. Now I suppose the care of the sheep will fall on me, though Mr. Delaney promises to do the herding himself for a while, then return to the lowlands and bring another shepherd, so as to leave me free to rove as I like.

Had another rich ramble. Pushed northward beyond the forests to the head of the general basin, where traces of glacial action are strikingly clear and interesting. The recesses among the peaks look like quarries, so raw and fresh are the moraine chips and boulders that strew the ground in Nature's glacial workshops.

Soon after my return to camp we received a visit from an Indian, probably one of the hunters whose camp I had discovered. He came from Mono, he said, with others of his tribe, to hunt deer. One that he had killed a short distance from here he was carrying on his back, its legs tied together in an ornamental bunch on his forehead. Throwing down his burden, he gazed stolidly for a few minutes in silent Indian fashion, then cut off eight or ten pounds of venison for us, and begged a "lill" (little) of everything he saw or could think of—flour, bread, sugar, tobacco, whiskey, needles, etc. We gave a fair price for the meat in flour and sugar and added a few needles. A strangely dirty and irregular life these dark-eyed, dark-haired, half-happy savages lead in this clean wilderness,—starvation and abundance, deathlike calm, indolence, and admirable, indefatigable action succeeding each other in stormy rhythm like winter and summer. Two things they have that civilized toilers might well envy them—pure air and pure water. These go far to cover and cure the grossness of their lives. Their food is mostly good berries, pine nuts, clover, lily bulbs, wild sheep, antelope, deer, grouse, sage hens, and the larvæ of ants, wasps, bees, and other insects.

August 13. Day all sunshine, dawn and evening purple, noon gold, no clouds, air motionless. Mr. Delaney arrived with two shepherds, one of them an Indian. On his way up from the plains he left some provisions at the Portuguese camp on Porcupine Creek near our old Yosemite camp, and I set out this morning with one of the pack animals to fetch them. Arrived at the Porcupine camp at noon, and might have returned to the Tuolumne late in the evening, but concluded to stay over night with the Portuguese shepherds at their pressing invitation. They had sad stories to tell of losses from the Yosemite bears, and were so discouraged they seemed on the point of leaving the mountains; for the bears came every night and helped themselves to one or several of the flock in spite of all their efforts to keep them off.

I spent the afternoon in a grand ramble along the Yosemite walls. From the highest of the rocks called the Three Brothers, I enjoyed a magnificent view comprehending all the upper half of the floor of the valley and nearly all the rocks of the walls on both sides and at the head, with snowy peaks in the background. Saw also the Vernal and Nevada Falls, a truly glorious picture,—rocky strength and permanence combined with beauty of plants frail and fine and evanescent; water descending in thunder, and the same water gliding through meadows and groves in gentlest beauty. This standpoint is about eight thousand feet above the sea, or four thousand feet above the floor of the valley, and every tree, though looking small and feathery, stands in admirable clearness, and the shadows they cast are as distinct in outline as if seen at a distance of a few yards. They appeared even more so. No words will ever describe the exquisite beauty and charm of this mountain park—Nature's landscape garden at once tenderly beautiful and sublime. No wonder it draws nature-lovers from all over the world.

Glacial action even on this lofty summit is plainly displayed. Not only has all the lovely valley now smiling in sunshine been filled to the brim with ice, but it has been deeply overflowed.

I visited our old Yosemite camp-ground on the head of Indian Creek, and found it fairly patted and smoothed down with bear-tracks. The bears had eaten all the sheep that were smothered in the corral, and some of the grand animals must have died, for Mr. Delaney, before leaving camp, put a large quantity of poison in the carcasses. All sheep-men carry strychnine to kill coyotes, bears, and panthers, though neither coyotes nor panthers are at all numerous in the upper mountains. The little dog-like wolves are far more numerous in the foothill region and on the plains, where they find a better supply of food,—saw only one panther-track above eight thousand feet.

The Three Brothers, Yosemite National Park

On my return after sunset to the Portuguese camp I found the shepherds greatly excited over the behavior of the bears that have learned to like mutton. "They are getting worse and worse," they lamented. Not willing to wait decently until after dark for their suppers, they come and kill and eat their fill in broad daylight. The evening before my arrival, when the two shepherds were leisurely driving the flock toward camp half an hour before sunset, a hungry bear came out of the chaparral within a few yards of them and shuffled deliberately toward the flock. "Portuguese Joe," who always carried a gun loaded with buckshot, fired excitedly, threw down his gun, fled to the nearest suitable tree, and climbed to a safe height without waiting to see the effect of his shot. His companion also ran, but said that he saw the bear rise on its hind legs and throw out its arms as if feeling for somebody, and then go into the brush as if wounded.

At another of their camps in this neighborhood, a bear with two cubs attacked the flock before sunset, just as they were approaching the corral. Joe promptly climbed a tree out of danger, while Antone, rebuking his companion for cowardice in abandoning his charge, said that he was not going to let bears "eat up his sheeps" in daylight, and rushed towards the bears, shouting and setting his dog on them. The frightened cubs climbed a tree, but the mother ran to meet the shepherd and seemed anxious to fight. Antone stood astonished for a moment, eyeing the oncoming bear, then turned and fled, closely pursued. Unable to reach a suitable tree for climbing, he ran to the camp and scrambled up to the roof of the little cabin; the bear followed, but did not climb to the roof,—only stood glaring up at him for a few minutes, threatening him and holding him in mortal terror, then went to her cubs, called them down, went to the flock, caught a sheep for supper, and vanished in the brush. As soon as the bear left the cabin, the trembling Antone begged Joe to show him a good safe tree, up which he climbed like a sailor climbing a mast, and remained as long as he could hold on, the tree being almost branchless. After these disastrous experiences the two shepherds chopped and gathered large piles of dry wood and made a ring of fire around the corral every night, while one with a gun kept watch from a comfortable stage built on a neighboring pine that commanded a view of the corral. This evening the show made by the circle of fire was very fine, bringing out the surrounding trees in most impressive relief, and making the thousands of sheep eyes glow like a glorious bed of diamonds.

August 14. Up to the time I went to bed last night all was quiet, though we expected the shaggy freebooters every minute. They did not come till near midnight, when a pair walked boldly to the corral between two of the great fires, climbed in, killed two sheep and smothered ten, while the frightened watcher in the tree did not fire a single shot, saying that he was afraid he might kill some of the sheep, for the bears got into the corral before he got a good clear view of them. I told the shepherds they should at once move the flock to another camp. "Oh, no use, no use," they lamented; "where we go, the bears go too. See my poor dead sheeps—soon all dead. No use try another camp. We go down to the plains." And as I afterwards learned, they were driven out of the mountains a month before the usual time. Were bears much more numerous and destructive, the sheep would be kept away altogether.

It seems strange that bears, so fond of all sorts of flesh, running the risks of guns and fires and poison, should never attack men except in defense of their young. How easily and safely a bear could pick us up as we lie asleep! Only wolves and tigers seem to have learned to hunt man for food, and perhaps sharks and crocodiles. Mosquitoes and other insects would, I suppose, devour a helpless man in some parts of the world, and so might lions, leopards, wolves, hyenas, and panthers at times if pressed by hunger,—but under ordinary circumstances, perhaps, only the tiger among land animals may be said to be a man-eater,—unless we add man himself.

Clouds as usual about .05. Another glorious Sierra day, warm, crisp, fragrant, and clear. Many of the flowering plants have gone to seed, but many others are unfolding their petals every day, and the firs and pines are more fragrant than ever. Their seeds are nearly ripe, and will soon be flying in the merriest flocks that ever spread a wing.

On the way back to our Tuolumne camp, I enjoyed the scenery if possible more than when it first came to view. Every feature already seems familiar as if I had lived here always. I never weary gazing at the wonderful Cathedral. It has more individual character than any other rock or mountain I ever saw, excepting perhaps the Yosemite South Dome. The forests, too, seem kindly familiar, and the lakes and meadows and glad singing streams. I should like to dwell with them forever. Here with bread and water I should be content. Even if not allowed to roam and climb, tethered to a stake or tree in some meadow or grove, even then I should be content forever. Bathed in such beauty, watching, the expressions ever varying on the faces of the mountains, watching the stars, which here have a glory that the lowlander never dreams of, watching the circling seasons, listening to the songs of the waters and winds and birds, would be endless pleasure. And what glorious cloudlands I should see, storms and calms,—a new heaven and a new earth every day, aye and new inhabitants. And how many visitors I should have. I feel sure I should not have one dull moment. And why should this appear extravagant? It is only common sense, a sign of health, genuine, natural, all-awake health. One would be at an endless Godful play, and what speeches and music and acting and scenery and lights!—sun, moon, stars, auroras. Creation just beginning, the morning stars "still singing together and all the sons of God shouting for joy."

Bloody Cañon And Mono Lake

∞

August 21. Have just returned from a fine wild excursion across the range to Mono Lake, by way of the Mono or Bloody Cañon Pass. Mr. Delaney has been good to me all summer, lending a helping, sympathizing hand at every opportunity, as if my wild notions and rambles and studies were his own. He is one of those remarkable California men who have been overflowed and denuded and remodeled by the excitements of the gold fields, like the Sierra landscapes by grinding ice, bringing the harder bosses and ridges of character into relief,—a tall, lean, big-boned, big-hearted Irishman, educated for a priest in Maynooth College,—lots of good in him, shining out now and then in this mountain light. Recognizing my love of wild places, he told me one evening that I ought to go through Bloody Cañon, for he was sure I should find it wild enough. He had not been there himself, he said, but had heard many of his mining friends speak of it as the wildest of all the Sierra passes. Of course I was glad to go. It lies just to the east of our camp and swoops down from the summit of the range to the edge of the Mono Desert, making a descent of about four thousand feet in a distance of about four miles. It was known and traveled as a pass by wild animals and the Indians long before its discovery by white men in the gold year of 1858, as is shown by old trails which come together at the head of it. The name may have been suggested by the red color of the metamorphic slates in which the cañon abounds, or by the blood stains on the rocks from the unfortunate animals that were compelled to slide and shuffle over the sharp-angled boulders.

Early in the morning I tied my notebook and some bread to my belt, and strode away full of eager hope, feeling that I was going to have a glorious revel. The glacier meadows that lay along my way served to soothe my morning speed, for the sod was full of blue gentians and daisies, kalmia and dwarf vaccinium, calling for recognition as old friends, and I had to stop many times to examine the shining rocks over which the ancient glacier had passed with tremendous pressure, polishing them so well that they reflected the sunlight like glass in some places, while fine striæ, seen clearly through a lens, indicated the direction in which the ice had flowed. On some of the sloping polished pavements abrupt steps occur, showing that occasionally large masses of the rock had given way before the glacial pressure, as well as small particles; moraines, too, some scattered, others regular like long curving embankments and dams, occur here and there, giving the general surface of the region a young, new-made appearance. I watched the gradual dwarfing of the pines as I ascended, and the corresponding dwarfing of nearly all the rest of the vegetation. On the slopes of Mammoth Mountain, to the south of the pass, I saw many gaps in the woods reaching from the upper edge of the timber-line down to the level meadows, where avalanches of snow had descended, sweeping away every tree in their paths as well as the soil they were growing in, leaving the bedrock bare. The trees are nearly all uprooted, but a few that had been extremely well anchored in clefts of the rock were broken off near the ground. It seems strange at first sight that trees that had been allowed to grow for a century or more undisturbed should in their old age be thus swished away at a stroke. Such avalanches can only occur under rare conditions of weather and snowfall. No doubt on some positions of the mountain slopes the inclination and smoothness of the surface is such that avalanches must occur every winter, or even after every heavy snowstorm, and of course no trees or even bushes can grow in their channels. I noticed a few clean-swept slopes of this kind. The uprooted trees that had grown in the pathway of what might be called "century avalanches" were piled in windrows, and tucked snugly against the wall-trees of the gaps, heads downward, excepting a few that were carried out into the open ground of the meadows, where the heads of the avalanches had stopped. Young pines, mostly the two-leaved and the white-barked, are already springing up in these cleared gaps. It would be interesting to ascertain the age of these saplings, for thus we should gain a fair approximation to the year that the great avalanches occurred. Perhaps most or all of them occurred the same winter. How glad I should be if free to pursue such studies!

Near the summit at the head of the pass I found a species of dwarf willow lying perfectly flat on the ground, making a nice, soft, silky gray carpet, not a single stem or branch more than three inches high; but the catkins, which are now nearly ripe, stand erect and make a close, nearly regular gray growth, being larger than all the rest of the plants. Some of these interesting dwarfs have only one catkin—willow bushes reduced to their lowest terms. I found patches of dwarf vaccinium also forming smooth carpets, closely pressed to the ground or against the sides of stones, and covered with round pink flowers in lavish abundance as if they had fallen from the sky like hail. A little higher, almost at the very head of the pass, I found the blue arctic daisy and purple-flowered bryanthus, the mountain's own darlings, gentle mountaineers face to face with the sky, kept safe and warm by a thousand miracles, seeming always the finer and purer the wilder and stormier their homes. The trees, tough and resiny, seem unable to go a step farther; but up and up, far above the tree-line, these tender plants climb, cheerily spreading their gray and pink carpets right up to the very edges of the snow-banks in deep hollows and shadows. Here, too, is the familiar robin, tripping on the flowery lawns, bravely singing the same cheery song I first heard when a boy in Wisconsin newly arrived from old Scotland. In this fine company sauntering enchanted, taking no heed of time, I at length entered the gate of the pass, and the huge rocks began to close around me in all their mysterious impressiveness. Just then I was startled by a lot of queer, hairy, muffled creatures coming shuffling, shambling, wallowing toward me as if they had no bones in their bodies. Had I discovered them while they were yet a good way off, I should have tried to avoid them. What a picture they made contrasted with the others I had just been admiring. When I came up to them, I found that they were only a band of Indians from Mono on their way to Yosemite for a load of acorns. They were wrapped in blankets made of the skins of sage-rabbits. The dirt on some of the faces seemed almost old enough and thick enough to have a geological significance; some were strangely blurred and divided into sections by seams and wrinkles that looked like cleavage joints, and had a worn abraded look as if they had lain exposed to the weather for ages. I tried to pass them without stopping, but they wouldn't let me; forming a dismal circle about me, I was closely besieged while they begged whiskey or tobacco, and it was hard to convince them that I hadn't any. How glad I was to get away from the gray, grim crowd and see them vanish down the trail! Yet it seems sad to feel such desperate repulsion from one's fellow beings, however degraded. To prefer the society of squirrels and woodchucks to that of our own species must surely be unnatural. So with a fresh breeze and a hill or mountain between us I must wish them Godspeed and try to pray and sing with Burns, "It's coming yet, for a' that, that man to man, the warld o'er, shall brothers be for a' that."

How the day passed I hardly know. By the map I have come only about ten or twelve miles, though the sun is already low in the west, showing how long I must have lingered, observing, sketching, taking notes among the glaciated rocks and moraines and Alpine flower-beds.

At sundown the somber crags and peaks were inspired with the ineffable beauty of the alpenglow, and a solemn, awful stillness hushed everything in the landscape. Then I crept into a hollow by the side of a small lake near the head of the cañon, smoothed a sheltered spot, and gathered a few pine tassels for a bed. After the short twilight began to fade I kindled a sunny fire, made a tin cupful of tea, and lay down to watch the stars. Soon the night-wind began to flow from the snowy peaks overhead, at first only a gentle breathing, then gaining strength, in less than an hour rumbled in massive volume something like a boisterous stream in a boulder-choked channel, roaring and moaning down the cañon as if the work it had to do was tremendously important and fateful; and mingled with these storm tones were those of the waterfalls on the north side of the cañon, now sounding distinctly, now smothered by the heavier cataracts of air, making a glorious psalm of savage wildness. My fire squirmed and struggled as if ill at ease, for though in a sheltered nook, detached masses of icy wind often fell like icebergs on top of it, scattering sparks and coals, so that I had to keep well back to avoid being burned. But the big resiny roots and knots of the dwarf pine could neither be beaten out nor blown away, and the flames, now rushing up in long lances, now flattened and twisted on the rocky ground, roared as if trying to tell the storm stories of the trees they belonged to, as the light given out was telling the story of the sunshine they had gathered in centuries of summers.

The stars shone clear in the strip of sky between the huge dark cliffs; and as I lay recalling the lessons of the day, suddenly the full moon looked down over the cañon wall, her face apparently filled with eager concern, which had a startling effect, as if she had left her place in the sky and had come down to gaze on me alone, like a person entering one's bedroom. It was hard to realize that she was in her place in the sky, and was looking abroad on half the globe, land and sea, mountains, plains, lakes, rivers, oceans, ships, cities with their myriads of inhabitants sleeping and waking, sick and well. No, she seemed to be just on the rim of Bloody Cañon and looking only at me. This was indeed getting near to Nature. I remember watching the harvest moon rising above the oak trees in Wisconsin apparently as big as a cart-wheel and not farther than half a mile distant. With these exceptions I might say I never before had seen the moon, and this night she seemed so full of life and so near, the effect was marvelously impressive and made me forget the Indians, the great black rocks above me, and the wild uproar of the winds and waters making their way down the huge jagged gorge. Of course I slept but little and gladly welcomed the dawn over the Mono Desert. By the time I had made a cupful of tea the sunbeams were pouring through the cañon, and I set forth, gazing eagerly at the tremendous walls of red slates savagely hacked and scarred and apparently ready to fall in avalanches great enough to choke the pass and fill up the chain of lakelets. But soon its beauties came to view, and I bounded lightly from rock to rock, admiring the polished bosses shining in the slant sunshine with glorious effect in the general roughness of moraines and avalanche taluses, even toward the head of the cañon near the highest fountains of the ice. Here, too, are most of the lowly plant people seen yesterday on the other side of the divide now opening their beautiful eyes. None could fail to glory in Nature's tender care for them in so wild a place. The little ouzel is flitting from rock to rock along the rapid swirling Cañon Creek, diving for breakfast in icy pools, and merrily singing as if the huge rugged avalanche-swept gorge was the most delightful of all its mountain homes. Besides a high fall on the north wall of the cañon, apparently coming direct from the sky, there are many narrow cascades, bright silvery ribbons zigzagging down the red cliffs, tracing the diagonal cleavage joints of the metamorphic slates, now contracted and out of sight, now leaping from ledge to ledge in filmy sheets through which the sunbeams sift. And on the main Cañon Creek, to which all these are tributary, is a series of small falls, cascades, and rapids extending all the way down to the foot of the cañon, interrupted only by the lakes in which the tossed and beaten waters rest. One of the finest of the cascades is outspread on the face of a precipice, its waters separated into ribbon-like strips, and woven into a diamond-like pattern by tracing the cleavage joints of the rock, while tufts of bryanthus, grass, sedge, saxifrage form beautiful fringes. Who could imagine beauty so fine in so savage a place? Gardens are blooming in all sorts of nooks and hollows,—at the head alpine eriogonums, erigerons, saxifrages, gentians, cowania, bush primula; in the middle region larkspur, columbine, orthocarpus, castilleia, harebell, epilobium, violets, mints, yarrow; near the foot sunflowers, lilies, brier rose, iris, lonicera, clematis.

One of the smallest of the cascades, which I name the Bower Cascade, is in the lower region of the pass, where the vegetation is snowy and luxuriant. Wild rose and dogwood form dense masses overarching the stream, and out of this bower the creek, grown strong with many indashing tributaries, leaps forth into the light, and descends in a fluted curve thick-sown with crisp flashing spray. At the foot of the cañon there is a lake formed in part at least by the damming of the stream by a terminal moraine. The three other lakes in the cañon are in basins eroded from the solid rock, where the pressure of the glacier was greatest, and the most resisting portions of the basin rims are beautifully, tellingly polished. Below Moraine Lake at the foot of the cañon there are several old lake-basins lying between the large lateral moraines which extend out into the desert.

These basins are now completely filled up by the material carried in by the streams, and changed to dry sandy flats covered mostly by grass and artemisia and sun-loving flowers. All these lower lake-basins were evidently formed by terminal moraine dams deposited where the receding glacier had lingered during short periods of less waste, or greater snowfall, or both.

Looking up the cañon from the warm sunny edge of the Mono plain my morning ramble seems a dream, so great is the change in the vegetation and climate. The lilies on the bank of Moraine Lake are higher than my head, and the sunshine is hot enough for palms. Yet the snow round the arctic gardens at the summit of the pass is plainly visible, only about four miles away, and between lie specimen zones of all the principal climates of the globe. In little more than an hour one may swoop down from winter to summer, from an Arctic to a torrid region, through as great changes of climate as one would encounter in traveling from Labrador to Florida.

The Indians I had met near the head of the cañon had camped at the foot of it the night before they made the ascent, and I found their fire still smoking on the side of a small tributary stream near Moraine Lake; and on the edge of what is called the Mono Desert, four or five miles from the lake, I came to a patch of elymus, or wild rye, growing in magnificent waving clumps six or eight feet high, bearing heads six to eight inches long. The crop was ripe, and Indian women were gathering the grain in baskets by bending down large handfuls, beating out the seed, and fanning it in the wind. The grains are about five eighths of an inch long, dark-colored and sweet. I fancy the bread made from it must be as good as wheat bread. A fine squirrelish employment this wild grain gathering seems, and the women were evidently enjoying it, laughing and chattering and looking almost natural, though most Indians I have seen are not a whit more natural in their lives than we civilized whites. Perhaps if I knew them better I should like them better. The worst thing about them is their uncleanliness. Nothing truly wild is unclean. Down on the shore of Mono Lake I saw a number of their flimsy huts on the banks of streams that dash swiftly into that dead sea,—mere brush tents where they lie and eat at their ease. Some of the men were feasting on buffalo berries, lying beneath the tall bushes now red with fruit. The berries are rather insipid, but they must needs be wholesome, since for days and weeks the Indians, it is said, eat nothing else. In the season they in like manner depend chiefly on the fat larvæ of a fly that breeds in the salt water of the lake, or on the big fat corrugated caterpillars of a species of silkworm that feeds on the leaves of the yellow pine. Occasionally a grand rabbit-drive is organized and hundreds are slain with clubs on the lake shore, chased and frightened into a dense crowd by dogs, boys, girls, men and women, and rings of sage brush fire, when of course they are quickly killed. The skins are made into blankets. In the autumn the more enterprising of the hunters bring in a good many deer, and rarely a wild sheep from the high peaks. Antelopes used to be abundant on the desert at the base of the interior mountain-ranges. Sage hens, grouse, and squirrels help to vary their wild diet of worms; pine nuts also from the small inter-esting *Pinus monophylla*, and good bread and good mush are made from acorns and wild rye. Strange to say, they seem to like the lake larvæ best of all. Long windrows are washed up on the shore, which they gather and dry like grain for winter use. It is said that wars, on account of encroachments on each other's worm-grounds, are of common occurrence among the various tribes and families. Each claims a certain marked portion of the shore. The pine nuts are delicious—large quantities are gathered every autumn. The tribes of the west flank of the range trade acorns for worms and pine nuts. The squaws carry immense loads on their backs across the rough passes and down the range, making journeys of about forty or fifty miles each way.

The desert around the lake is surprisingly flowery. In many places among the sage bushes I saw mentzelia, abronia, aster, bigelovia, and gilia, all of which seemed to enjoy the hot sunshine. The abro-nia, in particular, is a delicate, fragrant, and most charming plant.

Opposite the mouth of the cañon a range of volcanic cones extends southward from the lake, rising abruptly out of the des-ert like a chain of mountains. The largest of the cones are about

Mono Lake and volcanic cones, looking South

twenty-five hundred feet high above the lake level, have well-formed craters, and all of them are evidently comparatively recent additions to the landscape. At a distance of a few miles they look like heaps of loose ashes that have never been blest by either rain or snow, but, for a' that and a' that, yellow pines are climbing their gray slopes, trying to clothe them and give beauty for ashes. A country of wonderful contrasts. Hot deserts bounded by snow-laden mountains,—cinders and ashes scattered on glacier-polished pavements,—frost and fire working together in the making of beauty. In the lake are several volcanic islands, which show that the waters were once mingled with fire.

Glad to get back to the green side of the mountains, though I have greatly enjoyed the gray east side and hope to see more of it. Reading these grand mountain manuscripts displayed through every vicissitude of heat and cold, calm and storm, upheaving volcanoes and down-grinding glaciers, we see that everything in Nature called destruction must be creation—a change from beauty to beauty.

Our glacier meadow camp north of the Soda Springs seems more beautiful every day. The grass covers all the ground though the leaves are thread-like in fineness, and in walking on the sod it seems like a plush carpet of marvelous richness and softness, and the purple panicles brushing against one's feet are not felt. This is a typical glacier meadow, occupying the basin of a vanished lake, very definitely bounded by walls of the arrowy two-leaved pines drawn up in a handsome orderly array like soldiers on parade. There are many other meadows of the same kind hereabouts imbedded in the woods. The main big meadows along the river are the same in general and extend with but little interruption for ten or twelve miles, but none I have seen are so finely finished and perfect as this one. It is richer in flowering plants than the prairies of Wisconsin and Illinois were when in all their wild glory. The showy flowers are mostly three species of gentian, a purple and yellow orthocarpus, a golden-rod or two, a small blue pentstemon almost like a gentian, potentilla, ivesia, pedicularis, white violet, kalmia, and bryanthus. There are no coarse weedy plants. Through this flowery lawn flows a stream silently gliding, swirling, slipping as if careful not to make the slightest noise. It is only about three feet wide in most places, widening here and there into pools six or eight feet in diameter with no apparent current, the banks bossily rounded by the down-curving mossy sod, grass panicles over-leaning like miniature pine trees, and rugs of bryanthus spreading here and there over sunken boulders. At the foot of the meadow the stream, rich with the juices of the plants it has refreshed, sings merrily down over shelving rock ledges on its way to the Tuolumne River. The sublime, massive Mount Dana and its companions, green, red, and white, loom impressively above the pines along the eastern horizon; a range or spur of gray rugged granite crags and mountains on the north; the curiously crested and battlemented Mount Hoffman on the west; and the Cathedral Range on the south with its grand Cathedral Peak, Cathedral Spires, Unicorn Peak, and several others, gray and pointed or massively rounded.

Highest Mono volcanic cones (near view)

The Tuolumne Camp

August 22. Clouds none, cool west wind, slight hoarfrost on the meadows. Carlo is missing; have been seeking him all day. In the thick woods between camp and the river, among tall grass and fallen pines, I discovered a baby fawn. At first it seemed inclined to come to me; but when I tried to catch it, and got within a rod or two, it turned and walked softly away, choosing its steps like a cautious, stealthy, hunting cat. Then, as if suddenly called or alarmed, it began to buck and run like a grown deer, jumping high above the fallen trunks, and was soon out of sight. Possibly its mother may have called it, but I did not hear her. I don't think fawns ever leave the home thicket or follow their mothers until they are called or frightened. I am distressed about Carlo. There are several other camps and dogs not many miles from here, and I still hope to find him. He never left me before. Panthers are very rare here, and I don't think any of these cats would dare touch him. He knows bears too well to be caught by them, and as for Indians, they don't want him.

August 23. Cool, bright day, hinting Indian summer. Mr. Delaney has gone to the Smith Ranch, on the Tuolumne below Hetch-Hetchy Valley, thirty-five or forty miles from here, so I'll be alone for a week or more,—not really alone, for Carlo has come back. He was at a camp a few miles to the northwestward. He looked sheepish and ashamed when I asked him where he had been and why he had gone away without leave. He is now trying to get me to caress him and show signs of forgiveness. A wondrous wise dog. A great load is off my mind. I could not have left the mountains without him. He seems very glad to get back to me.

August 24. Another charming day, warm and calm soon after sunrise, clouds only about .01,—faint, silky cirrus wisps, scarcely visible. Slight frost, Indian summerish, the mountains growing softer in outline and dreamy looking, their rough angles melted off, apparently. Sky at evening with fine, dark, subdued purple, almost like the evening purple of the San Joaquin plains in settled weather. The moon is now gazing over the summit of Dana. Glorious exhilarating air. I wonder if in all the world there is another mountain range of equal height blessed with weather so fine, and so openly kind and hospitable and approachable.

August 25. Cool as usual in the morning, quickly changing to the ordinary serene generous warmth and brightness. Toward evening the west wind was cool and sent us to the camp-fire. Of all Nature's flowery carpeted mountain halls none can be finer than this glacier meadow. Bees and butterflies seem as abundant as ever. The birds are still here, showing no sign of leaving for winter quarters though the frost must bring them to mind. For my part I should like to stay here all winter or all my life or even all eternity.

August 26. Frost this morning; all the meadow grass and some of the pine needles sparkling with irised crystals,—flowers of light. Large picturesque clouds, craggy like rocks, are piled on Mount Dana, reddish in color like the mountain itself; the sky for a few degrees around the horizon is pale purple, into which the pines dip their spires with fine effect. Spent the day as usual looking about me, watching the changing lights, the ripening autumn colors of the grass, seeds, late-blooming gentians, asters, goldenrods; parting the meadow grass here and there and looking down into the underworld of mosses and liverworts; watching the busy ants and beetles and other small people at work and play like squirrels and bears in a forest; studying the formation of lakes and meadows, moraines, mountain sculpture; making small beginnings in these directions, charmed by the serene beauty of everything.

The day has been extra cloudy, though bright on the whole, for the clouds were brighter than common. Clouds about .15, which in Switzerland would be considered extra clear. Probably more free sunshine falls on this majestic range than on any other in the world I've ever seen or heard of. It has the brightest weather, brightest glacier-polished rocks, the greatest abundance of irised spray from its glorious waterfalls, the brightest forests of silver firs and silver pines, more star-shine, moonshine, and perhaps more crystal-shine than any other mountain chain, and its countless mirror lakes, having more light poured into them, glow and spangle most. And how glorious the shining after the short summer showers and after frosty nights when the morning sunbeams are pouring through the crystals on the grass and pine needles, and how ineffably spiritually fine is the morning-glow on the mountain- tops and the alpenglow of evening. Well may the Sierra be named, not the Snowy Range, but the Range of Light.

August 27. Clouds only .05,—mostly white and pink cumuli over the Hoffman spur towards evening,—frosty morning. Crystals grow in marvelous beauty and perfection of form these still nights, every one built as carefully as the grandest holiest temple, as if planned to endure forever.

Contemplating the lace-like fabric of streams outspread over the mountains, we are reminded that everything is flowing—going somewhere, animals and so-called lifeless rocks as well as water. Thus the snow flows fast or slow in grand beauty-making glaciers and avalanches; the air in majestic floods carrying minerals, plant leaves, seeds, spores, with streams of music and fragrance; water streams carrying rocks both in solution and in the form of mud particles, sand, pebbles, and boulders. Rocks flow from volcanoes like water from springs, and animals flock together and flow in currents modified by stepping, leaping, gliding, flying, swimming, etc. While the stars go streaming through space pulsed on and on forever like blood globules in Nature's warm heart.

August 28. The dawn a glorious song of color. Sky absolutely cloudless. A fine crop hoarfrost. Warm after ten o'clock. The gentians don't mind the first frost though their petals seem so delicate; they close every night as if going to sleep, and awake fresh as ever in the morning sun-glory. The grass is a shade browner since last week, but there are no nipped wilted plants of any sort as far as I have seen. Butterflies and the grand host of smaller flies are benumbed every night, but they hover and dance in the sunbeams over the meadows before noon with no apparent lack of playful, joyful life. Soon they must all fall like petals in an orchard, dry and wrinkled, not a wing of all the mighty host left to tingle the air. Nevertheless new myriads will arise in the spring, rejoicing, exulting, as if laughing cold death to scorn.

August 29. Clouds about .05, slight frost. Bland serene Indian summer weather. Have been gazing all day at the mountains, watching the changing lights. More and more plainly are they clothed with light as a garment, white tinged with pale purple, palest during the midday hours, richest in the morning and evening. Everything seems consciously peaceful, thoughtful, faithfully waiting God's will.

August 30. This day just like yesterday. A few clouds motionless and apparently with no work to do beyond looking beautiful. Frost enough for crystal building,—glorious fields of ice-diamonds destined to last but a night. How lavish is Nature building, pulling down, creating, destroying, chasing every material particle from form to form, ever changing, ever beautiful.

Mr. Delaney arrived this morning. Felt not a trace of loneliness while he was gone. On the contrary, I never enjoyed grander company. The whole wilderness seems to be alive and familiar, full of humanity. The very stones seem talkative, sympathetic, brotherly. No wonder when we consider that we all have the same Father and Mother.

August 31. Clouds .05. Silky cirrus wisps and fringes so fine they almost escape notice. Frost enough for another crop of crystals on the meadows but none on the forests. The gentians, goldenrods, asters, etc., don't seem to feel it; neither petals nor leaves are touched though they seem so tender. Every day opens and closes like a flower, noiseless, effortless. Divine peace glows on all the majestic landscape like the silent enthusiastic joy that sometimes transfigures a noble human face.

September 1. Clouds .05—motionless, of no particular color—ornaments with no hint of rain or snow in them. Day all calm—another grand throb of Nature's heart, ripening late flowers and seeds for next summer, full of life and the thoughts and plans of life to come, and full of ripe and ready death beautiful as life, telling divine wisdom and goodness and immortality. Have been up Mount Dana, making haste to see as much as I can now that the time of departure is drawing nigh. The views from the summit reach far and wide, eastward over the Mono Lake and Desert; mountains beyond mountains looking strangely barren and gray and bare like heaps of ashes dumped from the sky. The lake, eight or ten miles in diameter, shines like a burnished disk of silver, no trees about its gray, ashy, cindery shores. Looking westward, the glorious forests are seen sweeping over countless ridges and hills, girdling domes and subordinate mountains, fringing in long curving lines the dividing ridges, and filling every hollow where the glaciers have spread soil-beds however rocky or smooth. Looking northward and southward along the axis of the range, you see the glorious array of high mountains, crags and peaks and snow, the fountain-heads of rivers that are flowing west to the sea through the famous Golden Gate, and east to hot salt lakes and deserts to evaporate and hurry back into the sky. Innumerable lakes are shining like eyes beneath heavy rock brows, bare or tree fringed, or imbedded in black forests. Meadow openings in the woods seem as numerous as the lakes or perhaps more so. Far up the moraine-covered slopes and among crumbling rocks I found many delicate hardy plants, some of them still in flower. The best gains of this trip were the lessons of unity and interrelation of all the features of the landscape revealed in general views. The lakes and meadows are located just where the ancient glaciers bore heaviest at the foot of the steepest parts of their channels, and of course their longest diameters are approximately parallel with each other and with the belts of forests growing in long curving lines on the lateral and medial moraines, and in broad outspreading fields on the terminal beds deposited toward the end of the ice period when the glaciers were receding. The domes, ridges, and spurs also show the influence of glacial action in their forms, which approximately seem to be the forms of greatest strength with reference to the stress of oversweeping, past-sweeping, down-grinding ice-streams; survivals of the most resisting masses, or those most favorably situated. How interesting everything is! Every rock, mountain, stream, plant, lake, lawn, forest, garden, bird, beast, insect seems to call and invite us to come and learn something of its history and relationship. But shall the poor ignorant scholar be allowed to try the lessons they offer? It seems too great and good to be true. Soon I'll be going to the lowlands. The bread camp must soon be removed. If I had a few sacks of flour, an axe, and some matches, I would build a cabin of pine logs, pile up plenty of firewood about it and stay all winter to see the grand fertile snow-storms, watch the birds and animals that winter thus high, how they live, how the forests look snow-laden or buried, and how the avalanches look and sound on their way down the mountains. But now I'll have to go, for there is nothing to spare in the way of provisions. I'll surely be back, however, surely I'll be back. No other place has ever so overwhelmingly attracted me as this hospitable, Godful wilderness.

One of the highest Mount Ritter fountains

September 2. A grand, red, rosy, crimson day,—a perfect glory of a day. What it means I don't know. It is the first marked change from tranquil sunshine with purple mornings and evenings and still, white noons. There is nothing like a storm, however. The average cloudiness only about .08, and there is no sighing in the woods to betoken a big weather change. The sky was red in the morning and evening, the color not diffused like the ordinary purple glow, but loaded upon separate well-defined clouds that remained motionless, as if anchored around the jagged mountain-fenced horizon. A deep-red cap, bluffy around its sides, lingered a long time on Mount Dana and Mount Gibbs, drooping so low as to hide most of their bases, but leaving Dana's round summit free, which seemed to float separate and alone over the big crimson cloud. Mammoth Mountain, to the south of Gibbs and Bloody Cañon, striped and spotted with snowbanks and clumps of dwarf pine, was also favored with a glorious crimson cap, in the making of which there was no trace of economy—a huge bossy pile colored with a perfect passion of crimson that seemed important enough to be sent off to burn among the stars in majestic independence. One is constantly reminded of the infinite lavishness and fertility of Nature—inexhaustible abundance amid what seems enormous waste. And yet when we look into any of her operations that lie within reach of our minds, we learn that no particle of her material is wasted or worn out. It is eternally flowing from use to use, beauty to yet higher beauty; and we soon cease to lament waste and death, and rather rejoice and exult in the imperishable, unspendable wealth of the universe, and faithfully watch and wait the reappearance of everything that melts and fades and dies about us, feeling sure that its next appearance will be better and more beautiful than the last.

I watched the growth of these red-lands of the sky as eagerly as if new mountain ranges were being built. Soon the group of snowy peaks in whose recesses lie the highest fountains of the Tuolumne, Merced, and North Fork of the San Joaquin were decorated with majestic colored clouds like those already described, but more complicated, to correspond with the grand fountain-heads of the rivers they overshadowed. The Sierra Cathedral, to the south of camp, was overshadowed like Sinai. Never before noticed so fine a union of rock and cloud in form and color and substance, drawing earth and sky together as one; and so human is it, every feature and tint of color goes to one's heart, and we shout, exulting in wild enthusiasm as if all the divine show were our own. More and more, in a place like this, we feel ourselves part of wild Nature, kin to everything. Spent most of the day high up on the north rim of the valley, commanding views of the clouds in all their red glory spreading their wonderful light over all the basin, while the rocks and trees and small Alpine plants at my feet seemed hushed and thoughtful, as if they also were conscious spectators of the glorious new cloud-world.

Here and there, as I plodded farther and higher, I came to small garden-patches and ferneries just where one would naturally decide that no plant-creature could possibly live. But, as in the region about the head of Mono Pass and the top of Dana, it was in the wildest, highest places that the most beautiful and tender and enthusiastic plant-people were found. Again and again, as I lingered over these charming plants, I said, How came you here? How do you live through the winter? Our roots, they explained, reach far down the joints of the summer-warmed rocks, and beneath our fine snow mantle killing frosts cannot reach us, while we sleep away the dark half of the year dreaming of spring.

Ever since I was allowed entrance into these mountains I have been looking for cassiope, said to be the most beautiful and best loved of the heathworts, but, strange to say, I have not yet found it. On my high mountain walks I keep muttering, "Cassiope, cassiope." This name, as Calvinists say, is driven in upon me, notwithstanding the glorious host of plants that come about me uncalled as soon as I show myself. Cassiope seems the highest name of all the small mountain-heath people, and as if conscious of her worth, keeps out of my way. I must find her soon, if at all this year.

September 4. All the vast sky dome is clear, filled only with mellow Indian summer light. The pine and hemlock and fir cones are nearly ripe and are falling fast from morning to night, cut off and gathered by the busy squirrels. Almost all the plants have matured their seeds, their summer work done; and the summer crop of birds and deer will soon be able to follow their parents to the foothills and plains at the approach of winter, when the snow begins to fly.

September 5. No clouds. Weather cool, calm, bright as if no great thing was yet ready to be done. Have been sketching the North Tuolumne Church. The sunset gloriously colored.

September 6. Still another perfectly cloudless day, purple evening and morning, all the middle hours one mass of pure serene sunshine. Soon after sunrise the air grew warm, and there was no wind. One naturally halted to see what Nature intended to do. There is a suggestion of real Indian summer in the hushed brooding, faintly hazy weather. The yellow atmosphere, though thin, is still plainly of the same general character as that of eastern Indian summer. The peculiar mellowness is perhaps in part caused by myriads of ripe spores adrift in the sky.

Mr. Delaney now keeps up a solemn talk about the need of getting away from these high mountains, telling sad stories of flocks that perished in storms that broke suddenly into the midst of fine innocent weather like this we are now enjoying. "In no case," said he, "will I venture to stay so high and far back in the mountains as we now are later than the middle of this month, no matter how warm and sunny it may be." He would move the flock slowly at first, a few miles a day until the Yosemite Creek basin was reached and crossed, then while lingering in the heavy pine woods should the weather threaten he could hurry down to the foothills, where the snow never falls deep enough to smother a sheep. Of course I am anxious to see as much of the wilderness as possible in the few days left me, and I say again,—May the good time come when I can stay as long as I like with plenty of bread, far and free from trampling flocks, though I may well be thankful for this generous foodful inspiring summer. Anyhow we never know where we must go nor what guides we are to get,—men, storms, guardian angels, or sheep. Perhaps almost everybody in the least natural is guarded more than he is ever aware of. All the wilderness seems to be full of tricks and plans to drive and draw us up into God's Light.

Have been busy planning, and baking bread for at least one more good wild excursion among the high peaks, and surely none, however hopefully aiming at fortune or fame, ever felt so gloriously happily excited by the outlook.

September 7. Left camp at daybreak and made direct for Cathedral Peak, intending to strike eastward and southward from that point among the peaks and ridges at the heads of the Tuolumne, Merced, and San Joaquin Rivers. Down through the pine woods I made my way, across the Tuolumne River and meadows, and up the heavily timbered slope forming the south boundary of the upper Tuolumne basin, along the east side of Cathedral Peak, and up to its topmost spire, which I reached at noon, having loitered by the way to study the fine trees—two-leaved pine, mountain pine, albicaulis pine, silver fir, and the most charming, most graceful of all the evergreens, the mountain hemlock. High, cool, late-flowering meadows also detained me, and lakelets and avalanche tracks and huge quarries of moraine rocks above the forests.

Glacier Meadow strewn with moraine boulders

All the way up from the Big Meadows to the base of the Cathedral the ground is covered with moraine material, the left lateral moraine of the great glacier that must have completely filled this upper Tuolumne basin. Higher there are several small terminal moraines of residual glaciers shoved forward at right angles against the grand simple lateral of the main Tuolumne Glacier. A fine place to study mountain sculpture and soil making. The view from the Cathedral Spires is very fine and telling in every direction. Innumerable peaks, ridges, domes, meadows, lakes, and woods; the forests extending in long curving lines and broad fields wherever the glaciers have left soil for them to grow on, while the sides of the highest mountains show a straggling dwarf growth clinging to rifts in the rocks apparently independent of soil. The dark heath-like growth on the Cathedral roof I found to be dwarf snow-pressed albicaulis pine, about three or four feet high, but very old looking. Many of them are bearing cones, and the noisy Clarke crow is eating the seeds, using his long bill like a woodpecker in digging them out of the cones. A good many flowers are still in bloom about the base of the peak, and even on the roof among the little pines. The body of the Cathedral is nearly square, and the roof slopes are wonderfully regular and symmetrical, the ridge trending northeast and southwest. This direction has apparently been determined by structure joints in the granite. The gable on the northeast end is magnificent in size and simplicity, and at its base there is a big snow-bank protected by the shadow of the building. The front is adorned with many pinnacles and a tall spire of curious workmanship. Here too the joints in the rock are seen to have played an important part in determining their forms and size and general arrangement. The Cathedral is said to be about eleven thousand feet above the sea, but the height of the building itself above the level of the ridge it stands on is about fifteen hundred feet. A mile or so to the westward there is a handsome lake, and the glacier-polished granite about it is shining so brightly it is not easy in some places to trace the line between the rock and water, both shining alike. Of this lake with its silvery basin and bits of meadow and groves I have a fine view from the spires; also of Lake Tenaya, Cloud's Rest and the South Dome of Yosemite, Mount Starr King, Mount Hoffman, the Merced peaks, and the vast multitude of snowy fountain peaks extending far north and south along the axis of the range. No feature, however, of all the noble landscape as seen from here seems more wonderful than the Cathedral itself, a temple displaying Nature's best masonry and sermons in stones. How often I have gazed at it from the tops of hills and ridges, and through openings in the forests on my many short excursions, devoutly wondering, admiring, longing! This I may say is the first time I have been at church in California, led here at last, every door graciously opened for the poor lonely worshiper. In our best times everything turns into religion, all the world seems a church and the mountains altars. And lo, here at last in front of the Cathedral is blessed cassiope, ringing her thousands of sweet-toned bells, the sweetest church music I ever enjoyed. Listening, admiring, until late in the afternoon I compelled myself to hasten away eastward back of rough, sharp, spiry, splintery peaks, all of them granite like the Cathedral, sparkling with crystals—feldspar, quartz, hornblende, mica, tourmaline. Had a rather difficult walk and creep across an immense snow and ice cliff which gradually increased in steepness as I advanced until it was almost impassable. Slipped on a dangerous place, but managed to stop by digging my heels into the thawing surface just on the brink of a yawning ice gulf. Camped beside a little pool and a group of crinkled dwarf pines; and as I sit by the fire trying to write notes the shallow pool seems fathomless with the infinite starry heavens in it, while the onlooking rocks and trees, tiny shrubs and daisies and sedges, brought forward in the fire-glow, seem full of thought as if about to speak aloud and tell all their wild stories. A marvelously impressive meeting in which every one has something worth while to tell. And beyond the fire-beams out in the solemn darkness, how impressive is the music of a choir of rills singing their way down from the snow to the river! And when we call to mind that thousands of these rejoicing rills are assembled in each one of the main streams, we wonder the less that our Sierra rivers are songful all the way to the sea.

About sundown saw a flock of dun grayish sparrows going to roost in crevices of a crag above the big snow-field. Charming little mountaineers! Found a species of sedge in flower within eight or ten feet of a snow-bank. Judging by the looks of the ground, it can hardly have been out in the sunshine much longer than a week, and it is likely to be buried again in fresh snow in a month or so, thus making a winter about ten months long, while spring, summer, and autumn are crowded and hurried into two months. How delightful it is to be alone here! How wild everything is—wild as the sky and as pure! Never shall I forget this big, divine day—the Cathedral and its thousands of cassiope bells, and the landscapes around them, and this camp in the gray crags above the woods, with its stars and streams and snow.

September 8. Day of climbing, scrambling, sliding on the peaks around the highest source of the Tuolumne and Merced. Climbed three of the most commanding of the mountains, whose names I don't know; crossed streams and huge beds of ice and snow more than I could keep count of. Neither could I keep count of the lakes scattered on tablelands and in the cirques of the peaks, and in chains in the cañons, linked together by the streams—a tremendously wild gray wilderness of hacked, shattered crags, ridges, and peaks, a few clouds drifting over and through the midst of them as if looking for work. In general views all the immense round landscape seems raw and lifeless as a quarry, yet the most charming flowers were found rejoicing in countless nooks and garden-like patches everywhere. I must have done three or four days' climbing work in this one. Limbs perfectly tireless until near sundown, when I descended into the main upper Tuolumne valley at the foot of Mount Lyell, the camp still eight or ten miles distant. Going up through the pine woods past the Soda Springs Dome in the dark, where there is much fallen timber, and when all the excitement of seeing things was wanting, I was tired. Arrived at the main camp at nine o'clock, and soon was sleeping sound as death.

Back To The Lowlands

❦

September 9. Weariness rested away and I feel eager and ready for another excursion a month or two long in the same wonderful wilderness. Now, however, I must turn toward the lowlands, praying and hoping Heaven will shove me back again.

The most telling thing learned in these mountain excursions is the influence of cleavage joints on the features sculptured from the general mass of the range. Evidently the denudation has been enormous, while the inevitable outcome is subtle balanced beauty. Comprehended in general views, the features of the wildest land-scape seem to be as harmoniously related as the features of a human face. Indeed, they look human and radiate spiritual beauty, divine thought, however covered and concealed by rock and snow.

Mr. Delaney has hardly had time to ask me how I enjoyed my trip, though he has facilitated and encouraged my plans all summer, and declares I'll be famous some day, a kind guess that seems strange and incredible to a wandering wilderness-lover with never a thought or dream of fame while humbly trying to trace and learn and enjoy Nature's lessons.

The camp stuff is now packed on the horses, and the flock is headed for the home ranch. Away we go, down through the pines, leaving the lovely lawn where we have camped so long. I wonder if I'll ever see it again. The sod is so tough and close it is scarcely at all injured by the sheep. Fortunately they are not fond of silky glacier meadow grass. The day is perfectly clear, not a cloud or the faintest hint of a cloud is visible, and there is no wind. I wonder if in all the world, at a height of nine thousand feet, weather so steadily, faith-fully calm and bright and hospitable may anywhere else be found. We are going away fearing destructive storms, though it is difficult to conceive weather changes so great.

Though the water is now low in the river, the usual difficulty occurred in getting the flock across it. Every sheep seemed to be invincibly determined to die any sort of dry death rather than wet its feet. Carlo has learned the sheep business as perfectly as the best shepherd, and it is interesting to watch his intelligent efforts to push or frighten the silly creatures into the water. They had to be fairly crowded and shoved over the bank; and when at last one crossed because it could not push its way back, the whole flock suddenly plunged in headlong together, as if the river was the only desirable part of the world. Aside from mere money profit one would rather herd wolves than sheep. As soon as they clambered up the opposite bank, they began baaing and feeding as if nothing unusual had happened. We crossed the meadows and drove slowly up the south rim of the valley through the same woods I had passed on my way to Cathedral Peak, and camped for the night by the side of a small pond on top of the big lateral moraine.

September 10. In the morning at daybreak not one of the two thousand sheep was in sight. Examining the tracks, we discovered that they had been scattered, perhaps by a bear. In a few hours all were found and gathered into one flock again. Had fine view of a deer. How graceful and perfect in every way it seemed as compared with the silly, dusty, tousled sheep! From the high ground hereabouts had another grand view to the northward—a heaving, swelling sea of domes and round-backed ridges fringed with pines, and bounded by innumerable sharp-pointed peaks, gray and barren-looking, though so full of beautiful life. Another day of the calm, cloudless kind, purple in the morning and evening. The evening glow has been very marked for the last two or three weeks. Perhaps the "zodiacal light."

September 11. Cloudless. Slight frost. Calm. Fairly started downhill, and now are camped at the west end meadows of Lake Tenaya—a charming place. Lake smooth as glass, mirroring its miles of glacier-polished pavements and bold mountain walls. Find aster still in flower. Here is about the upper limit of the dwarf form of the gold-cup oak,—eight thousand feet above sea-level,—reaching about two thousand feet higher than the California black oak (*Quercus*

Californica). Lovely evening, the lake reflections after dark marvelously impressive.

September 12. Cloudless day, all pure sun-gold. Among the magnificent silver firs once more, within two miles of the brink of Yosemite, at the famous Portuguese bear camp. Chaparral of gold-cup oak, manzanita, and ceanothus abundant hereabouts, wanting about the Tuolumne meadows, although the elevation is but little higher there. The two-leaved pine, though far more abundant about the Tuolumne meadow region, reaches its greatest size on streamsides hereabouts and around meadows that are rather boggy. All the best dry ground is taken by the magnificent silver fir, which here reaches its greatest size and forms a well-defined belt. A glorious tree. Have fine bed of its boughs to-night.

September 13. Camp this evening at Yosemite Creek, close to the stream, on a little sand flat near our old camp-ground. The vegetation is already brown and yellow and dry; the creek almost dry also. The slender form of the two-leaved pine on its banks is, I think, the handsomest I have anywhere seen. It might easily pass at first sight for a distinct species, though surely only a variety (*Murrayana*), due to crowded and rapid growth on good soil. The yellow pine is as variable, or perhaps more so. The form here and a thousand feet higher, on crumbling rocks, is broad branching, with closely furrowed, reddish bark, large cones, and long leaves. It is one of the hardiest of pines, and has wonderful vitality. The tassels of long, stout needles shining silvery in the sun, when the wind is blowing them all in the same direction, is one of the most splendid spectacles these glorious Sierra forests have to show. This variety of *Pinus ponderosa* is regarded as a distinct species, *Pinus Jeffreyi*, by some botanists. The basin of this famous Yosemite stream is extremely rocky,—seems fairly to be paved with domes like a street with big cobblestones. I wonder if I shall ever be allowed to explore it. It draws me so strongly, I would make any sacrifice to try to read its lessons. I thank God for this glimpse of it. The charms of these mountains are beyond all common reason, unexplainable and mysterious as life itself.

September 14. Nearly all day in magnificent fir forest, the top branches laden with superb erect gray cones shining with beads of pure balsam. The squirrels are cutting them off at a great rate. Bump, bump, I hear them falling, soon to be gathered and stored for winter bread. Those that chance to be left by the industrious harvesters drop the scales and bracts when fully ripe, and it is fine to see the purple-winged seeds flying in swirling, merry-looking flocks seeking their fortunes. The bole and dead limbs of nearly every tree in the main forest-belt are ornamented by conspicuous tufts and strips of a yellow lichen.

Camped for the night at Cascade Creek, near the Mono Trail crossing. Manzanita berries now ripe. Cloudiness to-day about .10. The sunset very rich, flaming purple and crimson showing gloriously through the aisles of the woods.

September 15. The weather pure gold, cloudiness about .05, white cirrus flects and pencilings around the horizon. Move two or three miles and camp at Tamarack Flat. Wandering in the woods here back of the pines which bound the meadows, I found very noble specimens of the magnificent silver fir, the tallest about two hundred and forty feet high and five feet in diameter four feet from the ground.

September 16. Crawled slowly four or five miles to-day through the glorious forest to Crane Flat, where we are camped for the night. The forests we so admired in summer seem still more beautiful and sublime in this mellow autumn light. Lovely starry night, the tall, spiring tree-tops relieved in jet black against the sky. I linger by the fire, loath to go to bed.

September 17. Left camp early. Ran over the Tuolumne divide and down a few miles to a grove of sequoias that I had heard of, directed by the Don. They occupy an area of perhaps less than a hundred acres. Some of the trees are noble, colossal old giants, surrounded by magnificent sugar pines and Douglas spruces. The perfect specimens not burned or broken are singularly regular and symmetrical, though not at all conventional, showing infinite variety in general unity and harmony; the noble shafts with rich purplish brown fluted bark, free of limbs for one hundred and fifty feet or so, ornamented here and there with leafy rosettes; main branches of the oldest trees very large, crooked and rugged, zigzagging stiffly outward seemingly lawless, yet unexpectedly stooping just at the right distance from the trunk and dissolving in dense bossy masses of branchlets, thus making a regular though greatly varied outline,—a cylinder of leafy, outbulging spray masses, terminating in a noble dome, that may be recognized while yet far off upheaved against the sky above the dark bed of pines and firs and spruces, the king of all conifers, not only in size but in sublime majesty of behavior and port. I found a black, charred stump about thirty feet in diameter and eighty or ninety feet high—a venerable, impressive old monument of a tree that in its prime may have been the monarch of the grove; seedlings and saplings growing up here and there, thrifty and hopeful, giving no hint of the dying out of the species. Not any unfavorable change of climate, but only fire, threatens the existence of these noblest of God's trees. Sorry I was not able to get a count of the old monument's annual rings.

Camp this evening at Hazel Green, on the broad back of the dividing ridge near our old camp-ground when we were on the way up the mountains in the spring. This ridge has the finest sugar-pine groves and finest manzanita and ceanothus thickets I have yet found on all this wonderful summer journey.

September 18. Made a long descent on the south side of the divide to Brown's Flat, the grand forests now left above us, though the sugar pine still flourishes fairly well, and with the yellow pine, libocedrus, and Douglas spruce, makes forests that would be considered most wonderful in any other part of the world.

The Indians here, with great concern, pointed to an old garden patch on the flat and told us to keep away from it. Perhaps some of their tribe are buried here.

September 19. Camped this evening at Smith's Mill, on the first broad mountain bench or plateau reached in ascending the range, where pines grow large enough for good lumber. Here wheat, apples, peaches, and grapes grow, and we were treated to wine and apples. The wine I didn't like, but Mr. Delaney and the Indian driver and the shepherd seemed to think the stuff divine. Compared to sparkling

Sierra water fresh from the heavens, it seemed a dull, muddy, stupid drink. But the apples, best of fruits, how delicious they were—fit for gods or men.

On the way down from Brown's Flat we stopped at Bower Cave, and I spent an hour in it—one of the most novel and interesting of all Nature's underground mansions. Plenty of sunlight pours into it through the leaves of the four maple trees growing in its mouth, illuminating its clear, calm pool and marble chambers,—a charming place, ravishingly beautiful, but the accessible parts of the walls sadly disfigured with names of vandals.

September 20. The weather still golden and calm, but hot. We are now in the foot-hills, and all the conifers are left behind, except the gray Sabine pine. Camped at the Dutch Boy's Ranch, where there are extensive barley fields now showing nothing save dusty stubble.

September 21. A terribly hot, dusty, sunburned day, and as nothing was to be gained by loitering where the flock could find nothing to eat save thorny twigs and chaparral, we made a long drive, and before sundown reached the home ranch on the yellow San Joaquin plain.

September 22. The sheep were let out of the corral one by one, this morning, and counted, and strange to say, after all their adventurous wanderings in bewildering rocks and brush and streams, scattered by bears, poisoned by azalea, kalmia, alkali, all are accounted for. Of the two thousand and fifty that left the corral in the spring lean and weak, two thousand and twenty-five have returned fat and strong. The losses are: ten killed by bears, one by a rattlesnake, one that had to be killed after it had broken its leg on a boulder slope, and one that ran away in blind terror on being accidentally separated from the flock,—thirteen all told. Of the other twelve doomed never to return, three were sold to ranchmen and nine were made camp mutton.

Here ends my forever memorable first High Sierra excursion. I have crossed the Range of Light, surely the brightest and best of all the Lord has built; and rejoicing in its glory, I gladly, gratefully, hopefully pray I may see it again.

PART THREE

Stickeen

∽

In the summer of 1880 I set out from Fort Wrangel in a canoe to continue the exploration of the icy region of southeastern Alaska, begun in the fall of 1879. After the necessary provisions, blankets, etc., had been collected and stowed away, and my Indian crew were in their places ready to start, while a crowd of their relatives and friends on the wharf were bidding them good-by and good-luck, my companion, the Rev. S.H. Young, for whom we were waiting, at last came aboard, followed by a little black dog, that immediately made himself at home by curling up in a hollow among the baggage. I like dogs, but this one seemed so small and worthless that I objected to his going, and asked the missionary why he was taking him.

"Such a little helpless creature will only be in the way," I said; "you had better pass him up to the Indian boys on the wharf, to be taken home to play with the children. This trip is not likely to be good for toy-dogs. The poor silly thing will be in rain and snow for weeks or months, and will require care like a baby."

But his master assured me that he would be no trouble at all; that he was a perfect wonder of a dog, could endure cold and hunger like a bear, swim like a seal, and was wondrous wise and cunning, etc., making out a list of virtues to show he might be the most interesting member of the party.

Nobody could hope to unravel the lines of his ancestry. In all the wonderfully mixed and varied dog-tribe I never saw any creature very much like him, though in some of his sly, soft, gliding motions and gestures he brought the fox to mind. He was short-legged and bunchy-bodied, and his hair, though smooth, was long and silky and slightly waved, so that when the wind was at his back it ruffled, making him look shaggy. At first sight his only noticeable feature was his fine tail, which was about as airy and shady as a squirrel's, and was carried curling forward almost to his nose. On closer inspection you might notice his thin sensitive ears, and sharp eyes with cunning tan-spots above them. Mr. Young told me that when the little fellow was a pup about the size of a woodrat he was presented to his wife by an Irish prospector at Sitka, and that on his arrival at Fort Wrangel he was adopted with enthusiasm by the Stickeen Indians as a sort of new good-luck totem, was named "Stickeen" for the tribe, and became a universal favorite; petted, protected, and admired wherever he went, and regarded as a mysterious fountain of wisdom.

On our trip he soon proved himself a queer character—odd, concealed, independent, keeping invincibly quiet, and doing many little puzzling things that piqued my curiosity. As we sailed week after week through the long intricate channels and inlets among the innumerable islands and mountains of the coast, he spent most of the dull days in sluggish ease, motionless, and apparently as unobserving as if in deep sleep. But I discovered that somehow he always knew what was going on. When the Indians were about to shoot at ducks or seals, or when anything along the shore was exciting our attention, he would rest his chin on the edge of the canoe and calmly look out like a dreamy-eyed tourist. And when he heard us talking about making a landing, he immediately roused himself to see what sort of a place we were coming to, and made ready to jump overboard and swim ashore as soon as the canoe neared the beach. Then, with a vigorous shake to get rid of the brine in his hair, he ran into the woods to hunt small game. But though always the first out of the canoe, he was always the last to get into it. When we were ready to start he could never be found, and refused to come to our call. We soon found out, however, that though we could not see him at such times, he saw us, and from the cover of the briers and huckleberry bushes in the fringe of the woods was watching the canoe with wary eye. For as soon as we were fairly off he came trotting down the beach, plunged into the surf, and swam after us, knowing well that we would cease rowing and take him in. When the contrary little vagabond came alongside, he was lifted by the neck, held at arm's length a moment to drip, and dropped aboard. We tried to cure him of this trick by compelling him to swim a long way, as if we had a mind to abandon him; but this did no good: the longer the swim the better he seemed to like it.

Though capable of great idleness, he never failed to be ready for all sorts of adventures and excursions. One pitch-dark rainy night we landed about ten o'clock at the mouth of a salmon stream when the water was phosphorescent. The salmon were running, and the myriad fins of the onrushing multitude were churning all the stream into a silvery glow, wonderfully beautiful and impressive in the ebon darkness. To get a good view of the show I set out with one of the Indians and sailed up through the midst of it to the foot of a rapid about half a mile from camp, where the swift current dashing over rocks made the luminous glow most glorious. Happening to look back down the stream, while the Indian was catching a few of the struggling fish, I saw a long spreading fan of light like the tail of a comet, which we thought must be made by some big strange animal that was pursuing us. On it came with its magnificent train, until we imagined we could see the monster's head and eyes; but it was only Stickeen, who, finding I had left the camp, came swimming after me to see what was up.

When we camped early, the best hunter of the crew usually went to the woods for a deer, and Stickeen was sure to be at his heels, provided I had not gone out. For, strange to say, though I never carried a gun, he always followed me, forsaking the hunter and even his master to share my wanderings. The days that were too stormy for sailing I spent in the woods, or on the adjacent mountains, wherever my studies called me; and Stickeen always insisted on going with me, however wild the weather, gliding like a fox through dripping huckleberry bushes and thorny tangles of panax and rubus, scarce stirring their rain-laden leaves; wading and wallowing through snow, swimming icy streams, skipping over logs and rocks and the crevasses of glaciers with the patience and endurance of a determined mountaineer, never tiring or getting discouraged. Once he followed me over a glacier the surface of which was so crusty and rough that it cut his feet until every step was marked with blood; but he trotted on with Indian fortitude until I noticed his red track, and, taking pity on him, made him a set of moccasins out of a handkerchief. However great his troubles he never asked help or made any complaint, as if, like a philosopher, he had learned that without hard work and suffering there could be no pleasure worth having.

Yet none of us was able to make out what Stickeen was really good for. He seemed to meet danger and hardships without anything like reason, insisted on having his own way, never obeyed an order, and the hunter could never set him on anything, or make him fetch the birds he shot. His equanimity was so steady it seemed due to want of feeling; ordinary storms were pleasures to him, and as for mere rain, he flourished in it like a vegetable. No matter what advances you might make, scarce a glance or a tail-wag would you get for your pains. But though he was apparently as cold as a glacier and about as impervious to fun, I tried hard to make his acquaintance, guessing there must be something worth while hidden beneath so much courage, endurance, and love of wild-weathery adventure. No superannuated mastiff or bulldog grown old in office surpassed this fluffy midget in stoic dignity. He sometimes reminded me of a small, squat, unshakable desert cactus. For he never displayed a single trace of the merry, tricksy, elfish fun of the terriers and collies that we all know, nor of their touching affection and devotion. Like children, most small dogs beg to be loved and allowed to love; but Stickeen seemed a very Diogenes, asking only to be let alone: a true child of the wilderness, holding the even tenor of his hidden life with the silence and serenity of nature. His strength of character lay in his eyes. They looked as old as the hills, and as young, and as wild. I never tired of looking into them: it was like looking into a landscape; but they were small and rather deep-set, and had no explaining lines around them to give out particulars. I was accustomed to look into the faces of plants and animals, and I watched the little sphinx more and more keenly as an interesting study. But there is no estimating the wit and wisdom concealed and latent in our lower fellow mortals until made manifest by profound experiences; for it is through suffering that dogs as well as saints are developed and made perfect.

After exploring the Sumdum and Tahkoo fiords and their glaciers, we sailed through Stephen's Passage into Lynn Canal and thence through Icy Strait into Cross Sound, searching for unexplored inlets leading toward the great fountain ice-fields of the Fairweather Range. Here, while the tide was in our favor, we were accompanied by a fleet of icebergs drifting out to the ocean from Glacier Bay. Slowly we paddled around Vancouver's Point, Wimbledon, our frail canoe tossed like a feather on the massive heaving swells coming in past Cape Spenser. For miles the sound is bounded by precipitous mural cliffs, which, lashed with wave-spray and their heads hidden in clouds, looked terribly threatening and stern. Had our canoe been crushed or upset we could have made no landing here, for the cliffs, as high as those of Yosemite, sink sheer into deep water. Eagerly we scanned the wall on the north side for the first sign of an opening fiord or harbor, all of us anxious except Stickeen, who dozed in peace or gazed dreamily at the tremendous precipices when he heard us talking about them. At length we made the joyful discovery of the mouth of the inlet now called "Taylor Bay," and about five o'clock reached the head of it and encamped in a spruce grove near the front of a large glacier.

While camp was being made, Joe the hunter climbed the mountain wall on the east side of the fiord in pursuit of wild goats, while Mr. Young and I went to the glacier. We found that it is separated from the waters of the inlet by a tide-washed moraine, and extends, an abrupt barrier, all the way across from wall to wall of the inlet, a distance of about three miles. But our most interesting discovery was that it had recently advanced, though again slightly receding. A portion of the terminal moraine had been plowed up and shoved forward, uprooting and overwhelming the woods on the east side. Many of the trees were down and buried, or nearly so, others were leaning away from the ice-cliffs, ready to fall, and some stood erect, with the bottom of the ice plow still beneath their roots and its lofty crystal spires towering high above their tops. The spectacle presented by these century-old trees standing close beside a spiry wall of ice, with their branches almost touching it, was most novel and striking. And when I climbed around the front, and a little way up the west side of the glacier, I found that it had swelled and increased in height and width in accordance with its advance, and carried away the outer ranks of trees on its bank.

On our way back to camp after these first observations I planned a far-and-wide excursion for the morrow. I awoke early, called not only by the glacier, which had been on my mind all night, but by a grand flood-storm. The wind was blowing a gale from the north and the rain was flying with the clouds in a wide passionate horizontal flood, as if it were all passing over the country instead of falling on it. The main perennial streams were booming high above their banks, and hundreds of new ones, roaring like the sea, almost covered the lofty gray walls of the inlet with white cascades and falls. I had intended making a cup of coffee and getting something like a breakfast before starting, but when I heard the storm and looked out I made haste to join it; for many of Nature's finest lessons are to be found in her storms, and if careful to keep in right relations with them, we may go safely abroad with them, rejoicing in the grandeur and beauty of their works and ways, and chanting with the old Norsemen, "The blast of the tempest aids our oars, the hurricane is our servant and drives us whither we wish to go." So, omitting breakfast, I put a piece of bread in my pocket and hurried away.

Mr. Young and the Indians were asleep, and so, I hoped, was Stickeen; but I had not gone a dozen rods before he left his bed in the tent and came boring through the blast after me. That a man should welcome storms for their exhilarating music and motion, and go forth to see God making landscapes, is reasonable enough; but what fascination could there be in such tremendous weather for a dog? Surely nothing akin to human enthusiasm for scenery or geology. Anyhow, on he came, breakfastless, through the choking blast. I stopped and did my best to turn him back. "Now don't," I said, shouting to make myself heard in the storm, "now don't, Stickeen. What has got into your queer noddle now? You must be daft. This wild day has nothing for you. There is no game abroad, nothing but weather. Go back to camp and keep warm, get a good breakfast with your master, and be sensible for once. I can't carry you all day or feed you, and this storm will kill you."

But Nature, it seems, was at the bottom of the affair, and she gains her ends with dogs as well as with men, making us do as she likes, shoving and pulling us along her ways, however rough, all but killing us at times in getting her lessons driven hard home. After I had stopped again and again, shouting good warning advice, I saw that he was not to be shaken off; as well might the earth try to shake off the moon. I had once led his master into trouble, when he fell on one of the topmost jags of a mountain and dislocated his arm; now the turn of his humble companion was coming. The pitiful little wanderer just stood there in the wind, drenched and blinking, saying doggedly, "Where thou goest I will go." So at last I told him to come on if he must, and gave him a piece of the bread I had in my pocket; then we struggled on together, and thus began the most memorable of all my wild days.

The level flood, driving hard in our faces, thrashed and washed us wildly until we got into the shelter of a grove on the east side of the glacier near the front, where we stopped awhile for breath and to listen and look out. The exploration of the glacier was my main object, but the wind was too high to allow excursions over its open surface, where one might be dangerously shoved while balancing for a jump on the brink of a crevasse. In the mean time the storm was a fine study. Here the end of the glacier, descending an abrupt swell of resisting rock about five hundred feet high, leans forward and falls in ice cascades. And as the storm came down the glacier from the north, Stickeen and I were beneath the main current of the blast, while favorably located to see and hear it. What a psalm the storm was singing, and how fresh the smell of the washed earth and leaves, and how sweet the still small voices of the storm! Detached wafts and swirls were coming through the woods, with music from the leaves and branches and furrowed boles, and even from the splintered rocks and ice-crags overhead, many of the tones soft and low and flute-like, as if each leaf and tree, crag and spire were a tuned reed. A broad torrent, draining the side of the glacier, now swollen by scores of new streams from the mountains, was rolling boulders along its rocky channel, with thudding, bumping, muffled sounds, rushing towards the bay with tremendous energy, as if in haste to get out of the mountains; the waters above and beneath calling to each other, and all to the ocean, their home.

Looking southward from our shelter, we had this great torrent and the forested mountain wall above it on our left, the spiry ice-crags on our right, and smooth gray gloom ahead. I tried to draw the marvelous scene in my note-book, but the rain blurred the page in spite of all my pains to shelter it, and the sketch was almost worthless. When the wind began to abate, I traced the east side of the glacier. All the trees standing on the edge of the woods were barked and bruised, showing high-ice mark in a very telling way, while tens of thousands of those that had stood for centuries on the bank of the glacier farther out lay crushed and being crushed. In many places I could see down fifty feet or so beneath the margin of the glacier-mill, where trunks from one to two feet in diameter were being ground to pulp against outstanding rock-ribs and bosses of the bank.

About three miles above the front of the glacier I climbed to the surface of it by means of axe-steps made easy for Stickeen. As far as the eye could reach, the level, or nearly level, glacier stretched away indefinitely beneath the gray sky, a seemingly boundless prairie of ice. The rain continued, and grew colder, which I did not mind, but a dim snowy look in the drooping clouds made me hesitate about venturing far from land. No trace of the west shore was visible, and in case the clouds should settle and give snow, or the wind again become violent, I feared getting caught in a tangle of crevasses. Snow-crystals, the flowers of the mountain clouds, are frail, beautiful things, but terrible when flying on storm-winds in darkening, benumbing swarms or when welded together into glaciers full of deadly crevasses. Watching the weather, I sauntered about on the crystal sea. For a mile or two out I found the ice remarkably safe. The marginal crevasses were mostly narrow, while the few wider ones were easily avoided by passing around them, and the clouds began to open here and there.

Thus encouraged, I at last pushed out for the other side; for Nature can make us do anything she likes. At first we made rapid progress, and the sky was not very threatening, while I took bearings occasionally with a pocket compass to enable me to find my way back more surely in case the storm should become blinding; but the structure lines of the glacier were my main guide. Toward the west side we came to a closely crevassed section in which we had to make long, narrow tacks and doublings, tracing the edges of tremendous transverse and longitudinal crevasses, many of which were from twenty to thirty feet wide, and perhaps a thousand feet deep—beautiful and awful. In working a way through them I was severely cautious, but Stickeen came on as unhesitating as the flying clouds. The widest crevasse that I could jump he would leap without so much as halting to take a look at it. The weather was now making quick changes, scattering bits of dazzling brightness through the wintry gloom; at rare intervals, when the sun broke forth wholly free, the glacier was seen from shore to shore with a bright array of encompassing mountains partly revealed, wearing the clouds as garments, while the prairie bloomed and sparkled with irised light from myriads of washed crystals. Then suddenly all the glorious show would be darkened and blotted out.

Stickeen seemed to care for none of these things, bright or dark, nor for the crevasses, wells, moulins, or swift flashing streams into which he might fall. The little adventurer was only about two years old, yet nothing seemed novel to him, nothing daunted him. He showed neither caution nor curiosity, wonder nor fear, but bravely trotted on as if glaciers were playgrounds. His stout, muffled body seemed all one skipping muscle, and it was truly wonderful to see how swiftly and to all appearance heedlessly he flashed across nerve-trying chasms six or eight feet wide. His courage was so unwavering that it seemed to be due to dullness of perception, as if he were only blindly bold; and I kept warning him to be careful. For we had been close companions on so many wilderness trips that I had formed the habit of talking to him as if he were a boy and understood every word.

We gained the west shore in about three hours; the width of the glacier here being about seven miles. Then I pushed northward in order to see as far back as possible into the fountains of the Fairweather Mountains, in case the clouds should rise. The walking was easy along the margin of the forest, which, of course, like that on the other side, had been invaded and crushed by the swollen, overflowing glacier. In an hour or so, after passing a massive headland, we came suddenly on a branch of the glacier, which, in the form of a magnificent ice-cascade two miles wide, was pouring over the rim of the main basin in a westerly direction, its surface broken into wave-shaped blades and shattered blocks, suggesting the wildest updashing, heaving, plunging motion of a great river cataract. Tracing it down three or four miles, I found that it discharged into a lake, filling it with icebergs.

I would gladly have followed the lake outlet to tide-water, but the day was already far spent, and the threatening sky called for haste on the return trip to get off the ice before dark. I decided therefore to go no farther, and, after taking a general view of the wonderful region, turned back, hoping to see it again under more favorable auspices. We made good speed up the cañon of the great ice-torrent, and out on the main glacier until we had left the west shore about two miles behind us. Here we got into a difficult network of crevasses, the gathering clouds began to drop misty fringes, and soon the dreaded snow came flying thick and fast. I now began to feel anxious about finding a way in the blurring storm. Stickeen showed no trace of fear. He was still the same silent, able little hero. I noticed, however, that after the storm-darkness came on he kept close up behind me. The snow urged us to make still greater haste, but at the same time hid our way. I pushed on as best I could, jumping innumerable crevasses, and for every hundred rods or so of direct advance traveling a mile in doubling up and down in the turmoil of chasms and dislocated ice-blocks. After an hour or two of this work we came to a series of longitudinal crevasses of appalling width, and almost straight and regular in trend, like immense furrows. These I traced with firm nerve, excited and strengthened by the danger, making wide jumps, poising cautiously on their dizzy edges after cutting hollows for my feet before making the spring, to avoid possible slipping or any uncertainty on the farther sides, where only one trial is granted—exercise at once frightful and inspiring. Stickeen followed seemingly without effort.

Many a mile we thus traveled, mostly up and down, making but little real headway in crossing, running instead of walking most of the time as the danger of being compelled to spend the night on the glacier became threatening. Stickeen seemed able for anything. Doubtless we could have weathered the storm for one night, dancing on a flat spot to keep from freezing, and I faced the threat without feeling anything like despair; but we were hungry and wet, and the wind from the mountains was still thick with snow and bitterly cold, so of course that night would have seemed a very long one. I could not see far enough through the blurring snow to judge in which general direction the least dangerous route lay, while the few dim, momentary glimpses I caught of mountains through rifts in the flying clouds were far from encouraging either as weather signs or as guides. I had simply to grope my way from crevasse to crevasse, holding a general direction by the ice-structure, which was not to be seen everywhere, and partly by the wind. Again and again I was put to my mettle, but Stickeen followed easily, his nerve apparently growing more unflinching as the danger increased. So it always is with mountaineers when hard beset. Running hard and jumping, holding every minute of the remaining daylight, poor as it was, precious, we doggedly persevered and tried to hope that every difficult crevasse we overcame would prove to be the last of its kind. But on the contrary, as we advanced they became more deadly trying.

At length our way was barred by a very wide and straight crevasse, which I traced rapidly northward a mile or so without finding a crossing or hope of one; then down the glacier about as far, to where it united with another uncrossable crevasse. In all this distance of perhaps two miles there was only one place where I could possibly jump it, but the width of this jump was the utmost I dared attempt, while the danger of slipping on the farther side was so great that I was loath to try it. Furthermore, the side I was on was about a foot higher than the other, and even with this advantage the crevasse seemed dangerously wide. One is liable to underestimate the width of crevasses where the magnitudes in general are great,

I therefore stared at this one mighty keenly, estimating its width and the shape of the edge on the farther side, until I thought that I could jump it if necessary, but that in case I should be compelled to jump back from the lower side I might fail. Now, a cautious mountaineer seldom takes a step on unknown ground which seems at all dangerous that he cannot retrace in case he should be stopped by unseen obstacles ahead. This is the rule of mountaineers who live long, and, though in haste, I compelled myself to sit down and calmly deliberate before I broke it.

Retracing my devious path in imagination as if it were drawn on a chart, I saw that I was recrossing the glacier a mile or two farther up stream than the course pursued in the morning, and that I was now entangled in a section I had not before seen. Should I risk this dangerous jump, or try to regain the woods on the west shore, make a fire, and have only hunger to endure while waiting for a new day? I had already crossed so broad a stretch of dangerous ice that I saw it would be difficult to get back to the woods through the storm, before dark, and the attempt would most likely result in a dismal night-dance on the glacier; while just beyond the present barrier the surface seemed more promising, and the east shore was now perhaps about as near as the west. I was therefore eager to go on. But this wide jump was a dreadful obstacle.

At length, because of the dangers already behind me, I determined to venture against those that might be ahead, jumped and landed well, but with so little to spare that I more than ever dreaded being compelled to take that jump back from the lower side. Stickeen followed, making nothing of it, and we ran eagerly forward, hoping we were leaving all our troubles behind. But within the distance of a few hundred yards we were stopped by the widest crevasse yet encountered. Of course I made haste to explore it, hoping all might yet be remedied by finding a bridge or a way around either end. About three-fourths of a mile upstream I found that it united with the one we had just crossed, as I feared it would. Then, tracing it down, I found it joined the same crevasse at the lower end also, maintaining throughout its whole course a width of forty to fifty feet. Thus to my dismay I discovered that we were on a narrow island about two miles long, with two barely possible ways of escape: one back by the way we came, the other ahead by an almost inaccessible sliver-bridge that crossed the great crevasse from near the middle of it!

After this nerve-trying discovery I ran back to the sliver-bridge and cautiously examined it. Crevasses, caused by strains from variations in the rate of motion of different parts of the glacier and convexities in the channel, are mere cracks when they first open, so narrow as hardly to admit the blade of a pocket-knife, and gradually widen according to the extent of the strain and the depth of the glacier. Now some of these cracks are interrupted, like the cracks in wood, and in opening, the strip of ice between overlapping ends is dragged out, and may maintain a continuous connection between the sides, just as the two sides of a slivered crack in wood that is being split are connected. Some crevasses remain open for months or even years, and by the melting of their sides continue to increase in width long after the opening strain has ceased; while the sliver-bridges, level on top at first and perfectly safe, are at length melted to thin, vertical, knife-edged blades, the upper portion being most exposed to the weather; and since the exposure is greatest in the middle, they at length curve downward like the cables of suspension bridges. This one was evidently very old, for it had been weathered and wasted until it was the most dangerous and inaccessible that ever lay in my way. The width of the crevasse was here about fifty feet, and the sliver crossing diagonally was about seventy feet long; its thin knife-edge near the middle was depressed twenty-five or thirty feet below the level of the glacier, and the upcurving ends were attached to the sides eight or ten feet below the brink. Getting down the nearly vertical wall to the end of the sliver and up the other side were the main difficulties, and they seemed all but insurmountable. Of the many perils encountered in my years of wandering on mountains and glaciers none seemed so plain and stern and merciless as this. And it was presented when we were wet to the skin and hungry, the sky dark with quick driving snow, and the night near. But we were forced to face it. It was a tremendous necessity.

Beginning, not immediately above the sunken end of the bridge, but a little to one side, I cut a deep hollow on the brink for my knees to rest in. Then, leaning over, with my short-handled axe I cut a step sixteen or eighteen inches below, which on account of the sheerness of the wall was necessarily shallow. That step, however, was well made; its floor sloped slightly inward and formed a good hold for my heels. Then, slipping cautiously upon it, and crouching as low as possible, with my left side toward the wall, I steadied myself against the wind with my left hand in a slight notch, while with the right I cut other similar steps and notches in succession, guarding against losing balance by glinting of the axe, or by wind-gusts, for life and death were in every stroke and in the niceness of finish of every foothold.

After the end of the bridge was reached I chipped it down until I had made a level platform six or eight inches wide, and it was a trying thing to poise on this little slippery platform while bending over to get safely astride of the sliver. Crossing was then comparatively easy by chipping off the sharp edge with short, careful strokes, and hitching forward an inch or two at a time, keeping my balance with my knees pressed against the sides. The tremendous abyss on either hand I studiously ignored. To me the edge of that blue sliver was then all the world. But the most trying part of the adventure, after working my way across inch by inch and chipping another small platform, was to rise from the safe position astride and to cut a step-ladder in the nearly vertical face of the wall,—chipping, climbing, holding on with feet and fingers in mere notches. At such times one's whole body is eye, and common skill and fortitude are replaced by power beyond our call or knowledge. Never before had I been so long under deadly strain. How I got up that cliff I never could tell. The thing seemed to have been done by somebody else. I never have held death in contempt, though in the course of my explorations I have oftentimes felt that to meet one's fate on a noble mountain, or in the heart of a glacier, would be blessed as compared with death from disease, or from some shabby lowland accident. But the best death, quick and crystal-pure, set so glaringly open before us, is hard enough to face, even though we feel gratefully sure that we have already had happiness enough for a dozen lives.

But poor Stickeen, the wee, hairy, sleekit beastie, think of him! When I had decided to dare the bridge, and while I was on my knees chipping a hollow on the rounded brow above it, he came behind me, pushed his head past my shoulder, looked down and across, scanned the sliver and its approaches with his mysterious eyes, then looked me in the face with a startled air of surprise and concern, and began to mutter and whine; saying as plainly as if speaking with words, "Surely, you are not going into that awful place." This was the first time I had seen him gaze deliberately into a crevasse, or into my face with an eager, speaking, troubled look. That he should have recognized and appreciated the danger at the first glance showed wonderful sagacity. Never before had the daring midget seemed to know that ice was slippery or that there was any such thing as danger anywhere. His looks and tones of voice when he began to complain and speak his fears were so human that I unconsciously talked to him in sympathy as I would to a frightened boy, and in trying to calm his fears perhaps in some measure moderated my own. "Hush your fears, my boy," I said, "we will get across safe, though it is not going to be easy. No right way is easy in this rough world. We must risk our lives to save them. At the worst we can only slip, and then how grand a grave we will have, and by and by our nice bones will do good in the terminal moraine."

But my sermon was far from reassuring him: he began to cry, and after taking another piercing look at the tremendous gulf, ran away in desperate excitement, seeking some other crossing. By the time he got back, baffled of course, I had made a step or two. I dared not look back, but he made himself heard; and when he saw that I was certainly bent on crossing he cried aloud in despair. The danger was enough to daunt anybody, but it seems wonderful that he should have been able to weigh and appreciate it so justly. No mountaineer could have seen it more quickly or judged it more wisely, discriminating between real and apparent peril.

When I gained the other side, he screamed louder than ever, and after running back and forth in vain search for a way of escape, he would return to the brink of the crevasse above the bridge, moaning and wailing as if in the bitterness of death. Could this be the silent, philosophic Stickeen? I shouted encouragement, telling him the bridge was not so bad as it looked, that I had left it flat and safe for his feet, and he could walk it easily. But he was afraid to try. Strange so small an animal should be capable of such big, wise fears. I called again and again in a reassuring tone to come on and fear nothing; that he could come if he would only try. He would hush for a moment, look down again at the bridge, and shout his unshakable conviction that he could never, never come that way; then lie back in despair, as if howling, "O-o-oh! what a place! No-o-o, I can never go-o-o down there!" His natural composure and courage had vanished utterly in a tumultuous storm of fear. Had the danger been less, his distress would have seemed ridiculous. But in this dismal, merciless abyss lay the shadow of death, and his heartrending cries might well have called Heaven to his help. Perhaps they did. So hidden before, he was now transparent, and one could see the workings of his heart and mind like the movements of a clock out of its case. His voice and gestures, hopes and fears, were so perfectly human that none could mistake them; while he seemed to understand every word of mine. I was troubled at the thought of having to leave him out all night, and of the danger of not finding him in the morning. It seemed impossible to get him to venture. To compel him to try through fear of being abandoned, I started off as if leaving him to his fate, and disappeared back of a hummock; but this did no good; he only lay down and moaned in utter hopeless misery. So, after hiding a few minutes, I went back to the brink of the crevasse and in a severe tone of voice shouted across to him that now I must certainly leave him, I could wait no longer, and that, if he would not come, all I could promise was that I would return to seek him next day. I warned him that if he went back to the woods the wolves would kill him, and finished by urging him once more by words and gestures to come on, come on.

He knew very well what I meant, and at last, with the courage of despair, hushed and breathless, he crouched down on the brink in the hollow I had made for my knees, pressed his body against the ice as if trying to get the advantage of the friction of every hair, gazed into the first step, put his little feet together and slid them slowly, slowly over the edge and down into it, bunching all four in it and almost standing on his head. Then, without lifting his feet, as well as I could see through the snow, he slowly worked them over the edge of the step and down into the next and the next in succession in the same way, and gained the end of the bridge. Then, lifting his feet with the regularity and slowness of the vibrations of a seconds pendulum, as if counting and measuring *one-two-three*, holding himself steady against the gusty wind, and giving separate attention to each little step, he gained the foot of the cliff, while I was on my knees leaning over to give him a lift should he succeed in getting within reach of my arm. Here he halted in dead silence, and it was here I feared he might fail, for dogs are poor climbers. I had no cord. If I had had one, I would have dropped a noose over his head and hauled him up. But while I was thinking whether an available cord might be made out of clothing, he was looking keenly into the series of notched steps and finger-holds I had made, as if counting them, and fixing the position of each one of them in his mind. Then suddenly up he came in a springy rush, hooking his paws into the steps and notches so quickly that I could not see how it was done, and whizzed past my head, safe at last!

And now came a scene! "Well done, well done, little boy! Brave boy!" I cried, trying to catch and caress him; but he would not be caught. Never before or since have I seen anything like so passionate a revulsion from the depths of despair to exultant, triumphant, uncontrollable joy. He flashed and darted hither and thither as if fairly demented, screaming and shouting, swirling round and round in giddy loops and circles like a leaf in a whirlwind, lying down, and rolling over and over, sidewise and heels over head, and pouring forth a tumultuous flood of hysterical cries and sobs and gasping mutterings. When I ran up to him to shake him, fearing he might die of joy, he flashed off two or three hundred yards, his feet in a mist of motion; then, turning suddenly, came back in a wild rush and launched himself at my face, almost knocking me down, all the time screeching and screaming and shouting as if saying, "Saved! saved! saved!" Then away again, dropping suddenly at times with his feet in the air, trembling and fairly sobbing. Such passionate emotion was enough to kill him. Moses' stately song of triumph after escaping the Egyptians and the Red Sea was nothing to it. Who could have guessed the capacity of the dull, enduring little fellow for all that most stirs this mortal frame? Nobody could have helped crying with him!

But there is nothing like work for toning down excessive fear or joy. So I ran ahead, calling him in as gruff a voice as I could command to come on and stop his nonsense, for we had far to go and it would soon be dark. Neither of us feared another trial like this. Heaven would surely count one enough for a lifetime. The ice ahead was gashed by thousands of crevasses, but they were common ones. The joy of deliverance burned in us like fire, and we ran without fatigue, every muscle with immense rebound glorying in its strength. Stickeen flew across everything in his way, and not till dark did he settle into his normal fox-like trot. At last the cloudy mountains came in sight, and we soon felt the solid rock beneath our feet, and were safe. Then came weakness. Danger had vanished, and so had our strength. We tottered down the lateral moraine in the dark, over boulders and tree trunks, through the bushes and devil-club thickets of the grove where we had sheltered ourselves in the morning, and across the level mud-slope of the terminal moraine. We reached camp about ten o'clock, and found a big fire and a big supper. A party of Hoona Indians had visited Mr. Young, bringing a gift of porpoise meat and wild strawberries, and Hunter Joe had brought in a wild goat. But we lay down, too tired to eat much, and soon fell into a troubled sleep. The man who said, "The harder the toil, the sweeter the rest," never was profoundly tired. Stickeen kept springing up and muttering in his sleep, no doubt dreaming that he was still on the brink of the crevasse; and so did I, that night and many others long afterward, when I was overtired.

Thereafter Stickeen was a changed dog. During the rest of the trip, instead of holding aloof, he always lay by my side, tried to keep me constantly in sight, and would hardly accept a morsel of food, however tempting, from any hand but mine. At night, when all was quiet about the camp-fire, he would come to me and rest his head on my knee with a look of devotion as if I were his god. And often as he caught my eye he seemed to be trying to say, "Wasn't that an awful time we had together on the glacier?"

Nothing in after years has dimmed that Alaska storm-day. As I write it all comes rushing and roaring to mind as if I were again in the heart of it. Again I see the gray flying clouds with their rain-floods and snow, the ice-cliffs towering above the shrinking forest, the majestic ice-cascade, the vast glacier outspread before its white mountain fountains, and in the heart of it the tremendous crevasse,—emblem of the valley of the shadow of death,—low clouds trailing over it, the snow falling into it; and on its brink I see little Stickeen, and I hear his cries for help and his shouts of joy. I have known many dogs, and many a story I could tell of their wisdom and devotion; but to none do I owe so much as to Stickeen. At first the least promising and least known of my dog-friends, he suddenly became the best known of them all. Our storm-battle for life brought him to light, and through him as through a window I have ever since been looking with deeper sympathy into all my fellow mortals.

None of Stickeen's friends knows what finally became of him. After my work for the season was done I departed for California, and I never saw the dear little fellow again. In reply to anxious inquiries his master wrote me that in the summer of 1883 he was stolen by a tourist at Fort Wrangel and taken away on a steamer. His fate is wrapped in mystery. Doubtless he has left this world—crossed the last crevasse—and gone to another. But he will not be forgotten. To me Stickeen is immortal.

Theodore Roosevelt and John Muir in Yosemite.